HENRY BOGUET

An Examen of Witches

EDITED AND WITH AN INTRODUCTION BY
MONTAGUE SUMMERS

Drawn from various trials of many of this sect in the district of SAINT OYAN DE JOUX commonly known as SAINT CLAUDE in the county of BURGUNDY *including the procedure necessary to a judge in trials for witchcraft.*

DOVER PUBLICATIONS, INC.
MINEOLA, NEW YORK

Bibliographical Note

This Dover edition, first published in 2009, is an unabridged republication of the John Rodker work, originally published by Richard Clay & Sons, Ltd., Suffolk, Great Britain, in 1929.

Library of Congress Cataloging-in-Publication Data

Boguet, Henry, d. 1619.
[Discours des sorciers. English]
An examen of witches / Henry Boguet ; edited and with an introduction by Montague Summers.
p. cm.
Originally published: Suffolk, Great Britain : R. Clay, 1929.
ISBN-13: 978-0-486-47358-1 (pbk.)
ISBN-10: 0-486-47358-9 (pbk.)
1. Witchcraft—France—Burgundy—Early works to 1800. 2. Trials (Witchcraft)—France—Burgundy—Early works to 1800. 3. Criminal procedure—France—Burgundy—Rarly works to 1800. I. Summers, Montague, 1880–1948. II. Title.

BF1582.B6213 2009
133.4'3094441—dc22

2009023827

Manufactured in the United States by Courier Corporation
47358901
www.doverpublications.com

EDITOR'S PREFACE

Although, as Henry Boguet himself points out in the Preface to his *Discours des Sorciers,* he has freely used the ample assistance of such authorities in the matter of witchcraft as Sprenger and Kramer; the celebrated Jean Bodin; Nicolas Remy of the supreme judicial court of Nancy; Peter Binsfeld, Bishop Suffragan of Trèves; Paul Grilland; Bartolomeo de Spina; Thyraeus; Leonard Vair; his many citations from the *Malleus Maleficarum,* the *Démonomanie,* the *Dæmonolatreia,* Raemond's *L'Antéchrist,* and other encyclopædic manuals, must in no wise be taken as impairing either the interest or the originality of his own most remarkable and memorable work. Indeed it may be said that throughout the whole vast library of demonology, after the great *Malleus Maleficarum,* there is perhaps no treatise more authoritative, and certainly no treatise more revelatory of the human side of trials for witchcraft and of the psychology of those involved in such trials than the *Discours des Sorciers (An Examen of Witches)* of Henry Boguet, "Grand Juge de St. Claude, au Comté de Bourgogne." Boguet's appeal to authority is but to confirm his own long and infinitely patient experience. "I have founded the following *Examen* upon certain trials which I have myself conducted, during the last two years, of several members of this sect, whom I have seen and heard and probed as carefully as I possibly could in order to draw the truth from them." There is not a chapter of the *Examen* which does not bear witness to this; not a page, scarcely a paragraph that is not indicative of the most scrupulous inquiry, the most particular research, the minutest interrogations, all informed by a just if tempered zeal and the nicest conscientiousness, by candour, dignity, and most jealous loyalty to the truth. And so, although Bodin, Nicolas Remy, De Lancre had all written more copiously and were all three famous names, senators of no mean eminence and proved sagacity, it was the code of Henry Boguet, "The Manner of Procedure of a Judge in a Case of

Witchcraft,"—"a book precious as gold," it has been called—which was actually adopted in general practice by most local Parliaments and puisne courts, and that without any reflection upon or intended criticism of the digests and pandects compiled by most learned and most honourable legists and justiciaries, but because Boguet had in his seventy Articles codified the statutes and rulings, the methods and the regulations, most concisely, most clearly, and with the greater felicity.

Of the life of Henry Boguet, unfortunately very little is known. A native of Pierre-Court, which is a bailiwick of Gray in Franche-Comté, he was born about the middle of the sixteenth century, being descended from a good old stock of which several branches had long settled in the Dolonais district. From his writings it is clear that he was carefully and well educated, for he was widely read both in classical authors, especially the poets, and in the great historians. His bent, however, for the law was not long in discovering itself, and owing to his severe concentration upon the canonists and doctors, added to his acute and logical genius, he soon attained, by study and natural ability, high eminence in the legal profession. The modest piety and reverent orthodoxy of the rising advocate joined to a polished eloquence, could not fail to attract the notice of Ferdinand de Rye, Prince of the Holy Roman Empire, who had been appointed by Sixtus V to the Archbishopric of Besançon, in which Cathedral he was enthroned 13 November, 1587, and, owing to the favour of this magnificent prelate, Boguet was instituted Chief Justice of the whole district of Saint-Claude.

The city of Saint-Claude derives its name from S. Claudius, Abbot of Condat, whose life has been the subject of much controversy. Dom Benoît, *Histoire de l'abbaye et de la terre de S. Claude* (Montreuil-sur-Mer, 1890), tells us that the Saint had been Bishop of Besançon before being abbot; that he ruled his monastery for fifty-five years, and died in 694. The Abbey of Condat, which was founded between 425 and 430 by the hermits S. Romanus and S. Lupicinus, who had withdrawn into the desert where Saint-Claude now stands, became one of the most distinguished houses in Christendom. Originally the town which arose around the cloisters was known as S. Oyan de Joux from

S. Eugendus (Oyan or Oyand), a disciple of the two holy founders. S. Eugendus died 1 January, 510, at Condat, and his tomb was long a place of pilgrimage. When, however, the body of S. Claudius, which had been concealed at the time of the Saracen invasion, was discovered in 1260, visited in 1272 by Peter of Tarentaise (Blessed Innocent V), and borne in solemn procession throughout Burgundy before being brought back to the Shrine at Condat, the abbey and town formerly known as St. Oyan were thenceforward more generally called Saint-Claude, although actually the name Saint Oyan de Joux lingered until the seventeenth century.

As was natural, Henry Boguet had a very particular devotion to the great patron of the district, S. Claudius, and prominent among his published works is a life of the Saint, *Vie de Saint Claude,* 1591. This was reissued in 1607; and in 1627 at Lyons, C. Rigaud et Cobert printed what is termed the Second Edition of this most edifying study: "Les Actions de la vie et de la mort de Saint Claude avec des miracles et indulgences concédées aux Confrères de son nom, ensemble quelques mémoires des terres et ville de Saint Oyan de Joux, des abbés d'icelles . . . plus a esté adjousté le miracle faict au regard de deux hosties consacrées au lieu de Favernay . . . le 25 may, 1608." It will not escape notice that in Chapter V of his *Examen* Boguet fervently apostrophizes the glorious Saint Claude in a strain of glowing devotion, and declares his intention of writing an entire volume which shall celebrate the virtues, triumphs and honour of the Saint, and record the miracles daily wrought at his hallowed tomb. In an excess of criminal madness at the end of the eighteenth century the atrocious revolutionaries dared to profane the ancient shrine, and in March 1794 the body of Saint Claude, which had been venerated for so many hundreds of years by kings and prelates, by humble priest and simple artisan, by nobles and peasants, by pilgrims of every rank, high and low, and from every country, near and far, was sacrilegiously torn from its resting-place beneath the High Altar and burned to ashes in a mighty pyre.

A second work by Boguet which was highly esteemed was an exhaustive treatise upon the Burgundian code: *"In Consuetudines generales Comitatus Burgundiae obseruationes . . . authore Henrico Boguet.*

Lugduni, J. Pillehotte, 4to. 1604." These Commentaries long held their place as a legal text-book and a standard manual of reference. A second edition was published, octavo, at Besançon in 1725. But the book by which Henry Boguet is now generally known, although, curiously enough, as we shall have occasion to see a little later, it has become a volume of the very last rarity, is the famous *Discours des Sorciers; An Examen of Witches.*

The bibliography of the *Discours des Sorciers* is extremely intricate and difficult, so that the date of the first edition has not been exactly fixed even by such painstaking and eminent bibliographers as Albert Caillet,or Yve-Plessis in his *Bibliographie Française de la Sorcellerie.* We are, perhaps, fairly safe if we assign the *editio princeps* to Lyons, 1590, although the issue by Rigaud, Lyons, 8vo, 1590, is termed "3me édition." It should be noted that this impression of 1590 must have differed in many particulars from the treatise as it subsequently appeared, since the editions of 1602, 1603, and later commence with the bewitching of Loyse Maillat in June, 1598. In 1590 examples from the trials could not have been given. There is a Lyons edition, 8vo, 1602, "Par Jean Pillehotte, à l'enseigne du nom de Iesvs," and this would seem to be the first edition of the treatise as we now actually have it. In the following year, 1603, the same publishers issued the "Seconde Edition augmentee & enrichie par l'autheur de plusiers autres procez, Histoires & Chapitres," Lyons. This was "Acheué d'imprimer le xix Nouembre 1603," and a "Privilege du Roy" expressly forbids under strict penalties any other publisher save "Iean Pillehotte, marchand Libraire de Lyon," to print or to sell any copy (save those of Pillehotte's printing) for a term of ten years. This patent was "Donné à Fontaine-Bleau, le xxj d'Octobre, 1603," and signed by Henry IV in Council. It had been granted owing to the fact that in 1603 the *Discours des Sorciers* appeared both at Paris (D. Binet, *Seconde édition)* and at Rouen (Martin Ie Mesgissier). In spite of the prohibition the *Discours* was printed in duodecimo at Rouen twice during the year 1606, in the spring by Jean Osmont, and in the autumn by R. de Beauvais. At Lyons Pillehotte published new octavo editions in 1605 and 1607. At Lyons, again, Pierre Rigaud issued a "Seconde édition" in 1608, 3 volumes; and a "Troisième édition" in 1610, "trois parties en un tome"; both octavo. The last issue seems to have been that of Pillehotte, 8vo, Lyons, 1611.

When the *Discours des Sorciers* appeared it was prefaced in print by the approval and formal approbations of Doctors and Theologians not a few. No less a person than Père Coyssard, an influential member of the Society of Jesus and Rector of the Jesuit College at Besançon, vouched that the work contained nothing contrary to the Catholic Faith or hurtful to the soundest morality. Jean Dorothée signed the Imprimatur. De La Barre, Professor of Theology at the University of Dôle, unreservedly praised and recommended the book "auquel je n'ay rien treuué contraire à la Religion Catholique & Romaine, ny aux bonnes moeurs, ains plustost rempli de plusiers belles doctrines"; whilst two celebrated religious, most skilled theologians and canonists, Jean Le Comte, Prior of the old Augustinian convent at Lyons, and Amedée Besson, O.S.A., wrote that the *Discours* was an excellent treatise very necessary for the times, and finally the Vicar-General, Chalom, became lavish in his benedictions. Ushered into the world under such eminent auspices, dedicated to so august a prelate as the Archbishop of Besançon and to his all-powerful nephew, François de Rye, Dean of the Cathedral Chapter, it is hardly to be wondered at that Boguet's volume was at once accepted as an ultimate authority, whilst the book was straightway eulogized both in prose by the faculties of the Universities of Dôle and Lyons, and in verse by poets such as Jacques Michalet and Jean Heraudel. The learned Daniel Romanet, a doctor in theology and assessor of the High Court of Salins, who was known for his devotion to Notre-Dame-Libératries, addressed Boguet in the following sonnet:

L'impie abjurement, les offrandes, les voeux;
Les danses, les baisers, les viandes fardées,
Les poudres, les onguents, les grêles debandés,
Les Sabbats, les transports, les fascinements d'yeux:
Les charmes, les poisons, les couplements hideux,
Les souffles pestilents, les ocillades dardées,

Les bluëtans flambeaux, les paroles gardées,
Les caractères vains, les meurtres malhereux:
Les transmutations, les faits lycantropiques,
Les airs empoissonés, les spectres Plutoniques,
Les meurtriers touchements, la rage des esprits.
Entres aux corps humains, et bref ce qu'en la terre
Le Demon peut fournir pour nous dresser la guerre
Sont tracés par Boguet en ces doctes escrits.

The style of Boguet is nervous and concise; he is vivid and graphic in his details; keenly logical in his arguments; elegant in his expression; without prolixity, without periphrasis. Above all, his work is informed by the most patent and admirable sincerity. Perhaps one of the features which will most strangely strike the modern reader is his frequent appeal to and constant citation of classical examples and Latin authors. It cannot escape remark that he quotes repeatedly from Vergil, Horace, Ovid, Lucan, Pliny, Apuleius, and many more, often thus clinching a conclusion or driving home a syllogism in a way which to some readers now may appear a little too literary, even a little baroque. Yet a very strong case might be made out for such a line of thought and phrasing, but it must suffice to say that this stylistic mannerism, which in no way affects the solidity and essential truth either of his inquiry or his ratiocination, is a direct legacy from the Renaissance, that Renaissance which loved to subject theme to a formal purism of Vergilian Latinity. And so in his *Hymnus ad Diuum Stephanum* Cardinal Bembo wrote of Our Lord as "Magnanimus Hero," and of Our Lady

quem candida partu
Caelicolum regi tecto sub paupere Nympha,
Non ullam Uenerem, nullos experta hymenaeos,
Ediderat . . .

Jerome Vida, the pious Bishop of Cremona, in his *Christiad* when speaking of the Transfiguration nearly echoes the *Æneid:*

Uerus et aspectu patuit Deus.

After the Last Supper Holy Mass is thus described:

> Hunc semper ritum memores, arisque sacramus
> Sinceram cererem, et dulcem de uite liquorem,
> Pro ueterum tauris, pecudum pro pinguibus extis.
> Ipse, sacerdotum uerbis eductus ab astris,
> Frugibus insinuat sese regnator Olympi.

At any cost the Vergilian tradition must be preserved and accordingly there could be no keener shaft to wing an argument than an apt quotation from some classical source. We must not then be surprised to find that Boguet continually appeals to Roman story and repeatedly cites the Latin poets, although to us such allusion may seem far from germane to the matter in hand.

Henry Boguet, honoured and respected by all, died in 1619.

It has been said that the *Discours des Sorciers* in spite of its popularity, in spite of its wide and continued use, in spite of no less than a dozen known editions—and it is plain that several issues have completely vanished—has become a book of the last rarity, and the explanation of this is sufficiently remarkable. It appears that certain wealthy members of Boguet's family were of an exceedingly sceptical and hostile turn of mind. These persons united in a cabal, and pooling no small part of their several fortunes, they expended their utmost resources in buying up each impression of the *Discours des Sorciers* as it came from the Press. They then promptly consigned the copies to the flames. Owing to this deplorable mania, which they keenly pursued long after the death of the author, but a few exemplars remained in circulation, and the *Discours* is now actually one of the scarcest of the witchcraft manuals.

These insensate folk carried their hate even further, and did not hesitate to spread the most scandalous and opprobrious stories concerning their dead relative. So bitter was their animosity, so malevolent proved their designs, that it is almost to be suspected that they were themselves of that horrid craft and company which he had prosecuted with such lively energy. They actually rumoured that Henry Boguet had been a sorcerer, but secretly, and thus they explained his knowledge of the dark mysteries of that demoniacal society. It was further bruited in after years that he had been finally unmasked and sent to the stake as a warlock of long continuance. In England the case of Matthew Hopkins is hardly parallel. It will be remembered that this notorious "Witchfinder general" was popularly supposed to have stolen Satan's bead-roll at some Sabbat, and the vulgar legend went abroad that he was "swum as a wizard and went over the water like a cork." But we know that all this is utterly untrue. Hopkins died "peacibly, after a long sicknesse of a Consumption" at his old home in Manningtree, Essex, and was buried at Mistley, 12 August, 1647. On the other hand, far from impertinent is the instance of the lying legends which grew up around the name of that great and noble judge Nicolas Remy of Lorraine, whose *Dæmonolatriæ Libri Tres,* the fruit of the rich experience of fifteen years, was published at Lyons in 1595. Remy died at Nancy in 1600, and his enemies so vilely bespattered his reputation that the idlest and most preposterous stories concerning him won credence. We find these repeated in such compilations as Alexandre Erdan's *La France Mystique,* second edition, Amsterdam, 1858, Vol. I, p. 133, xl, where we are told of Remy: "Ce misérable parla tant et si ardemment du démon, qu'il finit par en perdre la tête; il alla, un beau jour, se dénoncer luimême comme sorcier, et *il fut brûlé publiquement."* These are the lies and malice of the Pharisees of old, and such accusations have received a divine answer: "If Satan cast out Satan, he is divided against himself: how then shall his kingdom stand?"

In the *Discours des Sorciers,* which has never before been translated from the French into any other tongue, we have a piece of altogether exceptional interest, one of the most valuable documents in the whole library of demonology. There is no doubt from the evidence that Boguet had to deal with a particularly noxious, well-organized, and essentially dangerous coven, and there is every indication that he did his work with a thoroughness and a practicality which alone could efficiently cope with so alarming and ominous a situation. It is a question whether in the background, behind those who were brought to trial, may not have lurked personages and influences justice could not, or at least did not, reach. When we consider the zeal of Bodin, of Henry Boguet, Nicolas Remy, and Pierre de Lancre, we must always remember the difficulties and hazards these brave men had to face. Already had the seeds of anarchy and revolution been widely sown. The wizard Troiseschelles openly boasted to King Charles IX that within the French coasts there were some thirty thousand witches, and, as Boguet himself writes, there was hardly a country which was not "infested with this miserable and damnable vermin." Their contest with the evil thing was hard and long; it was a struggle of which they could not hope to see the end; and yet they persevered, strengthened and sustained by the knowledge that their honour and their palm lay as much perhaps in the fight as in the victory.

MONTAGUE SUMMERS.
In Festo B.M.V. vulgo della Medaglia miracolosa.
1928.

To MONSEIGNEUR,

MONSEIGNEUR

the most Illustrious and Most Reverend Archbishop of Besançon, Monsieur Ferdinand de Rye, Prince of the Holy Roman Empire, Abbot of Saint Oyan de Joux commonly known as Saint Claude, Cherlieu, etc.

MONSEIGNEUR,

It is to you that the credit is due for the partial purging of your land of Saint Claude from witches, that vermin which had long been multiplying and would have infested many districts, but for the care you have taken to extirpate them. Messieurs your brethren, those three Bolts of Mars, have waged war upon the enemies of their Princes: but you have fought the deadliest enemies of Heaven that the world knows. So that just as their glory must live for ever by reason of their great and warlike exploits, so also can your glory never pass away by reason of your so pious care. Accordingly I have set down a little treatise concerning that which has been done with regard to this miserable sect of people, in order that all may know the zeal with which you have striven to bring them to the payment of their last debts; and I dedicate it to you as to the author, after God, of the good which has resulted, very humbly entreating you to accept it with an indulgent eye, even as it has pleased you always to honour with your favour him who offers it to you and will ever remain,

MONSEIGNEUR,

Your very humble servant,

HENRY BOGUET.

To MONSIEUR,

MONSIEUR

THE VICAR-GENERAL OF BESANÇON, MONSIEUR FRANÇOIS DE RYE, ABBOT OF ACEY, PRESEIGNE, ETC.

MONSIEUR, *I no longer marvel that there have formerly been witches who have said that, if as many if them were men as there were women, and if they had a great Lord as their leader, they would be strong enough to make war upon a King. For I have no doubt but that this would in such a case be easy for them, and that they would even overcome their enemies. I do not mean that they would do so by means of their spells and charms, although we read that this was done by Oddo, the great pirate and sea-rover, in Denmark, and by the Huns who by their magic arts defeated Sigisbert, King of Soissons, in the time of Chilperic, not to mention Haakon, Prince of Norway, who fought his enemies with storms of hail. But I mean that they could raise an army equal to that of Xerxes, although that was of eighteen hundred thousand men. For if it be true that Trois-eschelles, one of the best informed of their sect, declared in the time of Charles IX that there were in France alone three hundred thousand or, as some read, thirty thousand witches, at what figure can we estimate the number of those which could be found in all the different countries of the world? And must we not believe that since that time they have increased by more than half? For my part I have no doubt of it: for if we but look around among our own neighbours, we shall find them all infested with this miserable and damnable vermin. Germany is almost entirely occupied with building fires for them. Switzerland has been compelled to wipe out many of her villages on their account. Travellers in Lorraine may see thousands and thousands of the stakes to which witches are bound. We in Burgundy are no more exempt than other lands; for in many parts of our country we see that the execution of witches is a common occurrence. Returning again to our neighbours, Savoy has not escaped this pest; for every day she sends us a countless number of persons possessed of demons which, on being exorcised, say that they have been sent by witches into the bodies of these poor wretches: moreover, most of the witches whom we have burned here came originally from Savoy. And what shall we say of France? It is difficult to believe that she is purged of witches, considering the great number which she had in the time of Trois-eschelles. I say nothing of other more remote lands. No, no; there are witches by the thousand everywhere, multiplying upon the earth even as worms in a garden. And this is a shame to the Magistrates whose duty it is to punish felons and criminals; for if we had no more than the direct command of God to put them to death as being His bitterest enemies, why should we endure them any longer and thus disobey the Majesty of the Most High? In this we do even worse than the witches themselves; for disobedience is likened to Idolatry and Witchcraft by Samuel, speaking to Saul. And Saul found this to be true, to his own great damage; for, because he did not slay all the Amalekites and their cattle as he had been commanded, God was angry with him and caused him to be defeated and killed, with his sons, by the Philistines. Therefore we ought well to search our conscience, and fear lest it should happen to us as it did to Saul for that one disobedience. I pass over the fact that God at various times threatened cities and villages with destruction for this crime, and that He has sometimes brought them to utter ruin for the same crime of witchcraft. I say nothing, too, of the fact that the only delight of witches is to do ill, and that they gloat over the sickness and death of persons and cattle. This is but another reason why we should naturally be incited to punish them, provided that there is any humanity in us and if, to speak more strongly, we are at all worthy of the name of man. For even the most irrational beasts do not suffer amongst them those which league and conspire together against the rest, as we know from experience. Nature or, to speak more correctly, the Author of nature, naturally impresses this common duty on our minds; for otherwise the world could not continue. For these reasons, therefore, it is necessary that everybody should bear a hand in so good a work, and especially those in authority, so that we may show ourselves to be what we were created to be, namely, men and reasonable beings, and that we bring not upon us the destroying anger and indignation of the Living God. I know that there have before this been those who have not been able to believe that what is said of witches is true; but in these present days they are beginning to believe it, owing to a special grace of God, who has opened their eyes, which had been blinded by Satan that by this means he might, as he has done, increase his kingdom. These men, I say, are now busy in hunting down witches, so that not long ago they caused some to be put to death. And I take this as a sign that in a short time Satan and all his subjects will be overcome, and witches will no longer boast that they are able to make war upon a King, as they have done before now. I would have them to know that, if effect could be given to my wish, the earth would be immediately cleared of them; for I would that they should all be united in one single body, so that they might all be burned at once in a single fire. In the same way a certain Emperor wished, but wished wrongly, that all the Romans might have but a single head, so that he might slay them with one blow. Meanwhile I shall use every endeavour to make war upon them, both by bringing them to Justice, and by my humble writings, as I now do with this Treatise which I offer again to the public under your name, Monsieur, always presupposing that Monseigneur your Uncle, to whom I dedicated it in the first place, will agree that during his absence you should take his place in this new edition, and that on your own part you will be pleased to accept my offer as coming from one who has already devoted himself entirely to you and desires ever to be known,*

MONSIEUR,

as your very humble servant,

Henry Boguet.

AUTHOR'S PREFACE

It is astonishing that there should still be found to-day people who do not believe that there are witches. For my part I suspect that the truth is that such people really believe in their hearts, but will not admit it; for the Pagans have a lesson for them in this matter; they are refuted by the Canon and Civil Laws; Holy Scripture gives them the lie; the voluntary and repeated confessions of witches prove them wrong; and the sentences passed in various places against the accused must shut their mouths. I am not sure that I dare not go so far as to say that it seems more likely than not that such people are of the witches' party: in any case, I have no doubt this is true of some of them; and that the rest are unwilling to admit the existence of witches because, perhaps, they are descended from them and, in defence of their ancestors, would have men firmly believe that there are no witches in the world. Yet this is not a matter of such small moment as many people think; for it is a cause of the frequent immunity of witches, greatly to the mischief of the public and to the prejudice of the honour of God, which we should in all things have as our object, not allowing Satan to enlarge his kingdom further, as he does by means of the damnable plots of these his subjects.

Now I do not gainsay that the stories told of witches are very strange; for there is matter for much wonder in the form taken by Satan when he accosts them; their transvection to the Sabbat is astounding; we can but marvel at their oblations, their dances, their obscene kisses, their feasts, and their carnal couplings with their Master; it is beyond comprehension how they cause hail and tempests to spoil the fruits of the earth, and again how they cause the death of a man or the sickness of an animal; it would seem impossible for a witch to transport the corn from one field to another, and milk from the udder of one cow to that of another; it is beyond knowledge how they contrive to send demons and evil spirits into a man's body, or how they change themselves into wolves. In short, the deeds of witches have been considered as supernatural and miraculous, and therefore have men been unable to credit them.

But what then; Do we not know how great is the knowledge and experience of demons? It is certain that they have a deep knowledge of all things. For there is no Theologian who can interpret the Holy Scripture better than they; there is no Lawyer with a profounder knowledge of Testaments, Contracts and Actions; there is no physician or philosopher who better understands the composition of the human body, and the virtue of the Heavens, the Stars, Birds, and Fishes, of trees and herbs and metals and stones. Furthermore, since they are of the same nature as the Angels, all bodies must obey them in respect of local motion. Again, do we not know how great is the power which God in express words has given them upon earth. The Book of Job teaches us this so plainly that there is no need of other proofs; for God even says that there is no power upon earth which may be compared with that of Behemoth.

And if such be the power of Satan, why should he not be able to perform the works which we have mentioned? I will even say that it is all the easier for him to do so, in that all these works are due to natural causes. For the demons never work except through second and natural causes, although the speed and cunning which they employ make their actions appear to be miracles; whereas miracles can never be ascribed to them, since these belong to God only, as the Psalmist says: "He alone doeth great marvels."

At other times Satan has worked purely by means of illusion, by troubling and confusing man's eyes or fantasy. This is so in the case of Lycanthropes, and of those who believe that they see such creatures. Yet even this he contrives by natural means. So much for Satan in particular.

As for witches, although they cannot do such marvels as Satan, yet with his help they do terrible and shocking things. For they learn from him to compound a poison which they secretly pour into the broth of their enemy, who after tasting this poison sickens and languishes or suddenly dies, according to the might and virtue of the poison he has received: they strike people with headaches, pains in the feet and belly, with leprosy, epilepsy, swelling, and other such ills: guided by Satan they enter a man's house by night and cut his throat in his bed: they run about the fields and rocks in the form of wolves and so kill now a beast and now a child: in short they have ten thousand ways of harming men, beasts, and the fruits of the earth, with the help of the Devil.

For the most part the witch has only the intent to harm, whilst Satan actually performs that which he would have done. We have many proofs of this, as when a witch touches someone with his hand or, a wand, or melts a waxen image, or utters certain words, with the intent to cause the death or sickness of such a person. For neither the touch, nor the waxen image, nor the words are effective in anything save as a symbol of the pact formed by the witch with Satan; and it is Satan who, in this case, in some secret manner causes the death or sickness. It may be that he could not do this but for the wicked intent and wish of the witch; just as the body can do nothing without the soul, and the soul of itself can do nothing regarding the actions which belong to the body. And herein the witch is as guilty as if he had himself committed the deed, in accordance with the provisions of the Common Law which considers the author of a crime equally worthy of punishment as the man who actually commits it. And from this it will appear that the stories told of witches are no fable.

But to make this still clearer, I have founded the following Examen upon certain trials which I have myself conducted, during the last two years, of several members of this sect, whom I have seen and heard and probed as carefully as I possibly could in order to draw the truth from them. And although I have been at pains to be brief, I think that I have touched upon the chief points of my subject, as may be seen from a glance at the list of the chapter headings.

At the end of this Examen, I have added a short instruction for Judges who find themselves in the same case, since they must not conduct themselves in such trials as they do in those of other crimes. In this I have had the assistance of the works of the Inquisitors, of Bodin, Remy, Binsfeld, and others; but my chief help has been my own experience and my own observations of this damnable sect of people, who are the more difficult to convict in that they have always as their advocate that cunning Satan, who has the hardihood even to help and advise them when the Judge is speaking to them and questioning them.

And if anyone takes exception to my having disclosed the names of the witches who were accused, I answer that, since their trials have been accomplished, this does not seem to me to matter much; for their names can always be found by going to the registers. Further, it is better that their names should be known, so that men may be on their guard not only against them, but also against their children, who usually follow their manner of life, and to protect themselves either change their names or their place of abode. In short I am in this respect but imitating the example of most who have written before me. And although I have never in this book departed from the strictest standards of moderation, I would yet have it plainly known that I am a sworn enemy to witches, and that I shall never spare them, for their execrable abominations, and for the countless numbers of them which are seen to increase every day so that it seems that we are now in the time of Antichrist, since, among the signs that are given of his arrival, this is one of the chief, namely, that witchcraft shall then be rife throughout the world.

And truly it would be well that special Judges were appointed to cut off this Hydra's heads effectively so that they may not grow again. For the Ordinaries are so busy with their normal duties that they cannot give to witches the time they would like to give, and which such a matter requires. But let us come to our Examen.

The VARIOUS CHAPTERS
COMPRISING THE PRESENT EXAMEN

AN EXAMEN OF WITCHES

DRAWN from various trials of many of this sect in the district of SAINT OYAN DE JOUX commonly known as SAINT CLAUDE in the county of BURGUNDY *including the procedure necessary to a judge in trials for witchcraft*

CHAPTER I

Loyse Maillat, Eight Years Old, is Possessed of Five Devils and later delivered of them, and Françoise Secretain made Prisoner for Casting the Spell

ON Saturday the fifth of June in the year 1598 Loyse, the eight-years-old daughter of Claude Maillat and Humberte of Coyrieres in Perche, was struck helpless in all her limbs so that she had to go on all-fours; also she kept twisting her mouth about in a very strange manner. She continued thus afflicted for a number of days, until on the 19th of July her father and mother, judging from her appearance that she was possessed, took her to the Church of Our Saviour to be exorcised. There were then found five devils, whose names were Wolf, Cat, Dog, Jolly and Griffon; and when the priest asked the girl who had cast the spell on her, she answered that it was Françoise Secretain, whom she pointed out from among all those who were present at her exorcism. But as for that day, the devils did not go out of her.

But when the girl had been taken back to her parents' house, she begged them to pray God for her, assuring them that if they fell to their prayers she would quickly be delivered. Accordingly they did so at the approach of night, and as soon as her father and mother had done praying the girl told them that two of the devils were dead, and that if they persevered with their devotions they would kill the remaining ones also. Her father and mother were anxious for their daughter's health and did not cease praying all night. The next morning at dawn the girl was worse than usual and kept foaming at the mouth; but at last she was thrown to the ground and the devils came out of her mouth in the shape of balls as big as the fist and red as fire, except the Cat, which was black. The two which the girl thought to be dead came out last and with less violence than the three others; for they had given up the struggle from the first, and for this reason the girl had thought they were dead. When all these devils had come out, they danced three or four times round the fire and then vanished; and from that time the girl began to recover her health.

For the rest:—Late on the fourth of June Françoise Secretain had come to the house of Loyse Maillat's parents and had asked for lodging for that night. In the absence of her husband, Humberte had at first refused, but had in the end been forced by Françoise's insistence to give her lodging. When she had been received into the house, and Humberte had gone out to attend to her cattle, Françoise went up to Loyse and two of her younger sisters as they were warming themselves by the fire, gave Loyse a crust of bread resembling dung and made her eat it, strictly forbidding her to speak of it, or she would kill her and eat her (those were her words); and on the next day the girl was found to be possessed. Her mother bore witness to her refusal to give Françoise lodging, her father and mother together gave evidence of their daughter's malady, and this was confirmed by the girl, who gave evidence as to all the rest; and although she was so young she was so unshakable in her testimony that she compelled belief just as if she had been thirty or forty years old.

The Judge, being fully convinced as to what had happened, had Françoise Secretain seized and put into prison.

Chapter II.

The Means by which the Truth was drawn from Françoise Secretain.

FOR three days of her imprisonment Françoise Secretain refused to confess anything, saying that she was innocent of the crime of which she was accused and that they did her great wrong to detain her. To look at her, you would have thought she was the best woman in the world; for she was always talking of God, of the Virgin Mary, and of the Holy Saints of Paradise, and she had in her hand a long rosary which she pretended to say without interruption. But the truth is that the Cross of this rosary was defective, and it will be seen that this fact furnished evidence against her.

Further, it was observed that during her examination, although she strove her utmost to do so, she could not shed a single tear. For this reason she was more closely imprisoned, and certain threats were used to her. The following day she was pressed to tell the truth, but without success. Accordingly it was decided to shave off her hair and change her garments, and to search her to see if she were marked in any way. She was therefore stripped, but no mark was found; and when they came to cut the hair of her head she submitted with the utmost confidence. But no sooner was her hair cut than she grew perturbed and trembled all over her body, and at once confessed, adding to her first confessions from day to day. I shall set down only the principal points of her confession, following my undertaking to be brief.

Chapter III.

The Principal Points in the Confession of Françoise Secretain.

First, that she had wished five devils on Loyse Maillat.

Second, that she had long since given herself to the Devil, who at that time had the likeness of a big black man.

Third, that the Devil had four or five times known her carnally, in the form sometimes of a dog, sometimes of a cat, and sometimes of a fowl; and that his semen was very cold.

Fourth, that she had countless times been to the Sabbat and assembly of witches near the village of Coyrieres in a place called Combes by the water; and that she went there on a white staff which she placed between her legs.

Fifth, that at the Sabbat she had danced, and had beaten water to cause hail.

Sixth, that she and Groz-Jacques Bocquet had caused Loys Monneret to die by making her eat a piece of bread which they had dusted with a powder given to them by the Devil.

Seventh, that she had caused several cows to die, and that she did so by touching them with her hand or with a wand while saying certain words.

Chapter IV.

The Reasons for Imprisoning Françoise Secretain.

Above I have set down the principal points of Françoise Secretain's confession: she was further accused by Groz-Jacques of having changed herself into a wolf, but she would never speak openly of this matter. Before I examine each of these points, I must say that at first there was some doubt as to whether there was sufficient cause to seize and imprison this woman, on the ground that she should not be arrested on the strength of an accusation from a little girl that she had wished five devils on her; for it was considered that children are unstable and light-headed, and that it needs little to persuade them to say anything. Further, it was considered that no person should be lightly taken up when it is a question of his life or his honour; and that in a criminal process justice demands that the proofs should be clearer than daylight.

l. 1. de minorib. D. late per Tiraq. de pœn. caus. 7. l. fin. de probat. C.

However, the contrary view prevailed, and the accused was apprehended for several reasons: first, that there was evidence of witchcraft; second, that although the girl was only eight years old, her depositions were so very precise and never varied; third, that the mother substantiated the fact that Françoise had lodged at their house after having been at first refused; fourth, that the father and mother said that they had never had any quarrel with Françoise; fifth, that during her affliction the girl had always declared that it was no one but that woman who had bewitched her; sixth, that it was a question of the most abominable of all crimes, one which is usually committed at night and always in secret, and that therefore it did not call for such positive proof as would be required in the case of any other crime. For all the Doctors agree that less absolute proof is required in the case of grave, horrible and secret crimes. It was further considered that they were not asked to condemn the accused under the provisions of the said law, but only to commit her to prison so that she could more easily be brought to trial if the evidence should warrant such a course. Finally, it was reflected that a witch has the power to send devils into a person's body, and that therefore the accusation against Françoise Secretain was a possible one; namely, that she had wished five devils on Loyse Maillat. For all these reasons, therefore, this woman was thrown into prison.

Mascard. post alios tract. de probat. conclus. 1313, *num.* 2 *et seq.*, *vol.* 3.

Jacob. de Bell. vis. 7 *in sua practit. tit. de Inquisitio. num.* 52.

But they had not been able (as has since been the practice) to discover much against her beforehand; for they feared that she might make her escape if she were warned. And indeed the more recent usage in such cases is not altogether safe; and if it must be followed because no other course is possible, the witnesses must be sworn not to reveal their depositions, otherwise there is a danger that the matter may become known before all the information has been laid, and the accused may take to flight. But in this case the success of the event proved that Françoise Secretain had been deservedly imprisoned.

The secret judgement of God may be seen in this, when it is considered that numberless witches have been discovered and brought to their just punishment by means of a child: and in this the glory of God is made manifest, so that we may well say here, with His Royal Prophet: "Out of the mouth of babes and sucklings Thou hast ordained strength because of Thine enemies, that Thou mightest still the enemy and the avenger." In the following Examen we shall see that several other children have been the instrument by which not a few have been creditably judged guilty of this crime; and that one even, no more than twelve years old, convicted his own father of it, so unassailably that the matter was thought no less strange than pitiable. But let us return to the points of Françoise Secretain's confession.

CHAPTER V.

Whether it be Possible for One to send Demons into the Body of Another.

FRANÇOISE Secretain confessed in the first place that she had wished five devils on Loyse Maillat; and in the first chapter we have told of the means she used to this end. But it is no easy matter to determine whether a person has the power to send demons into the body of another: there are those who have considered it not to be possible, and it is even said that formerly some maintained this opinion before Pope Paul IV. The whole truth is that this thing is possible

Wier, de praestig. III. 16. Bodin.

with the permission of God; for we read that St.
Paul sent Satan into the body of the Corinthian *I Cor. 5.*
fornicator, and into Hymenæus and Alexander *I Tim. 1.*
the heretics. And David says in Psalm 78 that
God "cast upon them the fierceness of His anger,
wrath and indignation and trouble, by sending
evil angels among them:" a passage which Jean
Benedicti, the Franciscan Theologian, quotes in
his account of Perrenette Pinay in proof of my
contention. Thyræus is also of this opinion in *I. 16. 7*
his treatise on Demoniacs. *IV. 50. 12.*
There is no lack of examples. Simon Magus *IV. 58. 8 & 9*
frequently caused those to be possessed who
called him Sorcerer: Theodoret tells of a young
girl who was possessed by means of the spells and
enchantments of a sorcerer, though he adds that *Sect. 13.*
the Devil betrayed the sorcerer and revealed the *in Macedonia.*
whole secret of the matter: Jacques Bocquet
wished upon Rollande du Vernois two devils, of
whom one was named Cat and the other Devil;
and in this case Jacques confirmed the statement
which had previously been made by Rollande.
This woman was put in prison in the
year 1598 under a charge of witchcraft, and
after a long imprisonment was in the end burned.
Later we shall speak of her fully, as her case
deserves. Perrenette Pinay was found to be possessed *Cf. Benedict.*
by six devils, after having eaten at the
instigation of a witch an apple and a piece of
beef: another witch sent three devils into the
body of Catherine Pontet in the year 1554. The *Cf. Girard*
Jews of Rome caused eighty girls and women to *Grudius.*
be possessed by the Devil; and in the year 1552 *Bodin,*
the nuns of the Convent of Kendiorp were also *Demonom. III. 6.*
tormented in this manner by means of their *Marg. 1.*
cook: Caron in his "Antichrist Unmasked" nar-

rates that Catherine Boyraionne sent a number of demons into one Magdelaine, a woman of about twenty-two; and that another old woman cast a devil into one Marie; in each case the devils entered into the possessed by means of some nuts which they ate. Fernel also tells of a man who was thirsty and, for want of water, ate an apple, whereon he was at once possessed by a devil. But of what use is it to linger over such examples? Every day in our own town we continually meet with large numbers of persons who, for the most part, impute their possession to certain Vaudois or sorcerers. The truth is confessed by the devils themselves, being wrung from them by the might and virtue of exorcisms, and of the glorious body of St. Claude, who, being descended from the Counts Palatine of Salins, after having governed the Archbishopric of Besançon, came to this place to live the life of a hermit until his death in the year 650. By this he gained such favour with Heaven that from that time his body may be seen laid out whole upon the altar of the church in the eternal triumph of countless miracles which are performed upon those who resort to him; and demoniacs especially are every moment being healed by his prayers and intercessions.

De abdit. rer. caus. lib. 2.

O Blessed Soul! Here I could willingly fill several volumes with your praises, but I wait for another time when I shall have leisure to recount, with your help, your life and works. Do but lend me your hand now, that I may bring to a conclusion this little work in which I again take up the fight against the greatest enemies of God in this world; for I must now return to my subject. It is remarkable that as we have in this place those who are possessed just as they exist elsewhere, the devils who inhabit foreigners (of whom we have just spoken) have sometimes informed us how our own people have been possessed, very particularly explaining the methods used by witches to attain such a result, both as regards the seasons, and the food which they have caused them to eat; and of this fact we have already had several proofs and indications. For it is likely that God in His justice permits this, that such persons may be got rid of from the world, and punished according to their evil deserts.

As a further confirmation of my contention, I add that when witches are angry, they threaten those who have moved their anger that they will send devils into their bodies. Françoise Secretain acted in this manner towards several children whom she wished to take by force to the Sabbat, and namely towards a twelve-year-old girl named Christofle of the village of Aranthon. Loyse Maillat also stated that when this Françoise forced her to eat the piece of bread by means of which she was afterwards possessed, she threatened to wish evil spirits upon her.

And what is even stranger is that, if the witch has several devils under his control, he must find a lodging and employment for them all; for otherwise, according to Caron, he is in danger of his life.

Now the means usually employed by a witch to possess his victims with a devil is to offer them some sort of food; and I have remarked that he most often uses apples. In this Satan continually rehearses the means by which he tempted Adam and Eve in the earthly Paradise. And in this connection I cannot pass over what happened at Annecy in Savoy in the year 1585. On the edge of the Hasli Bridge there was seen for two hours an apple from which came so great and confused a noise that people were afraid to pass by there, although it was a much-used way. Everybody ran to see this thing, though no one dared to go near to it; until, as is always the case, at last one man more bold than the rest took a long stick and knocked the apple into the Thiou, a canal from the lake of Annecy which passes under the bridge; and after that nothing more was heard. It cannot be doubted that this apple was full of devils, and that a witch had been foiled in an attempt to give it to someone.

I have noticed also that demoniacs for the most part confess that the evil attacks them when they eat something; and from this it may be supposed that there is gluttony on their part; a sin abominable to God, who does not wish us to abuse the good things which it pleases Him to give us, or that instead of blessing and praising Him for His mercies, we should take the food He sends us immoderately or without remembering Him or thanking Him for it.

S. Jerome, epist. ad Eusto. Tertullian, de coro. milit.; et alii.

Let us learn, then, when we are about to eat and drink, to think of Him who is the author of all, and to bless our food with the sacred sign of the Cross as we have been taught by the Holy Fathers, who held the Cross in such reverence that they said it delivered us from devils and made them flee from before us; for the necessity of using this sign before we eat is such that St. Gregory writes of a Nun who, in eating a lettuce, swallowed the devil with the lettuce because she had not made the sign of the Cross.

But we shall speak more fully of the Cross in another place.

A point very worthy of examination here is how the Devil enters into the body of an innocent child who has committed no sin, as happened in the case of Loyse Maillat. This comes of the permission of God; for we see also that the witch has power over the health and life of children even to the extent of killing them in their mothers' wombs, as we shall show later. There must have been many innocent children among the first-born of Egypt; yet God put them all to the edge of the sword, even as He also caused the death of the child adulterously born to David and Bathsheba.

Thyr. in Demonom. II. 32.

Exod. 11.

II Sam. 12.

There is no doubt that the sins of the fathers are in some part the reason for this affliction; for the Holy Scriptures say that God punishes the children for the sins of their parents, unto the third and fourth generation of them that hate Him; and elsewhere God threatened to punish the Kings in their children, and this also has happened since those times. For some have had their sceptres taken from them, and others have been led into a miserable captivity.

Exod. 20.

II Sam. 2.
I Kings 14.
Eccles. 1.

Sometimes again God allows Innocents to be possessed and afflicted, not for any sin, but that His justice and His works may thereby shine the more gloriously. We have an excellent example of this in St. John's account of the man who was born blind, speaking of whom Jesus Christ said: "Neither hath this man sinned, nor his parents: but that the works of God should be made manifest in Him." And Loyse Maillat, at eight years old, was possessed of five devils; but what ensued from this? It led to the discovery of countless

John 9.

witches who have been punished as the gravity of their crimes deserved; and in this has God's justice been made manifest.

Canon 1. *de Calumnia. Canones cum illorum, de sentent., excommunic. atrox, de injuria. in Institutio. S. Thom.* 1. 2. *q.* 73. *art.* 9

It may further be said that, when the injured person is innocent the crime is all the greater; for the severity of the punishment is regulated by the quality of the party injured, and the greater the enormity of the crime, the greater punishment it deserves; and therefore, that Hell may be increased for witches, God permits them to harm and to possess children. I know that the Theologians distinguish five causes for the affliction of men by devils, but I leave such argument to them; for I would not enquire too closely into the judgements of God, and shall always content myself to believe that the great Master of the Universe does nothing without good reason,

Rom. 11.

since St. Paul speaks of "The depth of the riches both of the wisdom and knowledge of God."

Chapter VI.

Whether One Witch can Harm Another.

We have said that Groz-Jacques sent two devils into the body of the witch Rollande; and out of this arises the question whether one witch can harm another, to which I propose to devote a few words. It appears that the answer must be in the affirmative for several reasons, chiefly because, just as there are grades in the angelic Hierarchy, so among devils there is a sort of disordered order, which I would rather call a Cacarchy, whereby some are more potent than others. This may be verified by several passages of Holy Scripture; for in Job, speaking of Behemoth, it is said: "He is a king over all the children of pride." And in another place Beelzebub is called the Prince of the Devils; for the Jews reproached Jesus Christ because he cast out devils by Beelzebub the Prince of the Devils. But, more than this, our Lord clearly shows in St. Matthew that all devils have not the same power or might, in these words: "If Satan cast out Satan, he is divided against himself."

v. Peter Lombard, Sent. II., distinc. 6. Thyr. Job 41. *Matth.* 12. *Mark* 5. *Luke* 11. *Matth.* 12.

Our exorcists are well aware of this; for they sometimes command Lucifer and the other more potent devils to torment those which are inferior to them, when the latter prove stubborn in refusing to come out of the bodies of those whom they have possessed.

v. Flagell. Dæmon. Docum., 4.

If, then, it be true that one devil is more potent than another, as we have just shown, and as the Theologians are agreed, it follows that it will be easy for one witch to harm another, provided that he has control over a more powerful devil than that other; for a witch's power is governed by that of the devil which is his familiar.

St. August., Cass., St. Thomas., Perer., Binsfeld. de confession. malefic., dub. princip., conclusio 10.

Let us take some examples to confirm this statement. Sprenger tells that an old witch caused a younger witch to die, that she might heal a Bishop who had been stricken sick by the young witch. Nider writes that in Germany when a man is bewitched, he goes to an old witch, who pours molten lead into water until, with the help of the Devil, an image is formed of the lead; on which the old woman asks the sick man in which part of the body he wishes her to torture the

Mall. Malefic. II. 2. *Formic.* 3.

witch who has cast the spell on him; and if he agrees to her harming the witch, she takes a knife and strikes the image with it; and at the same instant the witch receives as many blows as were given to the image. I remember also that, when Antoine Tornier was confronted with Jaquema Paget, Jaquema accused her of having threatened her several times, and even of having often said that she would prevent her cows from yielding milk, although her own cows should yield abundantly. In this manner, therefore, it appears that one witch can harm another.

Chapter VII.

Of the Bodies of Spirits and Devils.

FRANÇOISE Secretain confessed in the second place that she had formerly given herself to the Devil, and that the Devil at that time had the appearance of a big black man. It is very certain that both good and bad spirits can make themselves a body from the elements; and this should not seem strange, if it is considered that the vapours which rise from the earth very often seem to us to take the form of men or animals. But these spirits, after the manner of a skilled painter, give whatever colour or form they please

I Sam. 28. to the bodies which they make themselves. The spirit which foretold his defeat and death to Saul had the exact likeness of Samuel, who had been dead for some years. Ezekiel was transported to

Azotus by an Angel who had the lips of a man, *Ezek.* 8.
whose face was the colour of amber, and from
the loins downward he had the appearance of
fire. The Angel who accompanied the young *Tob.* 5.
Tobias in his journey to Gabael had the form of
a young man, as also had the two Angels who *Gen.* 19.
visited Lot. We read in the Book of Maccabees *II Macc.* 3.
that, when Heliodorus was sent by his Prince to
despoil the Temple of Jerusalem, there appeared
unto him a horse with a terrible rider, together
with two other young men excellent in beauty,
who surrounded him and scourged him so that
his friends were constrained to run to the High
Priest, Onias, and to beg him to intercede for
him. And when Joshua entered into the prom-
ised land, he saw standing in a field an Angel in *Josh.* 5.
the form of a man, with his sword drawn, who
told him that he had been sent to guide and conduct the army of the children of Israel. Augustus
Cæsar, when he was about to proclaim himself
Emperor and Lord of the whole world, saw a
vision in the air of a Virgin holding a little child
in her arms, and for this reason he abandoned his
enterprise: similarly Attila, the King of the
Huns, departed from Italy, which he had deter-
mined to ruin and lay entirely waste, because he
saw standing on each side of Pope Leo I two
old men with flaming swords who threatened
him with death if he should advance any further:
it is said that these two old men were St. Peter
and St. Paul, who have always been the true
Tutelary Saints of Rome and Italy.

But I am particularly concerned with Satan, who *II Cor.* 2.
also adopts what shape he pleases, sometimes that
of a man, sometimes that of a beast, and sometimes even he transforms himself into an Angel

Spin. de Strigib. c. 15. *Anon. tract.* 3. *de credul. Dæm. adhib. Thyr. de loc. infest. part* 2. *c.* 26 *num.* 4. *Dan. au* 4. *point. Richer au disc. des images. cap.* 10. *num.* 1.

Plutarch, Brut.

Valer. Max. I. 55.

of Light. When he tried to tempt Jesus Christ and carried Him to the pinnacle of the Temple and to the top of a high mountain, he had the appearance of a man. When he addressed himself to Françoise Secretain, Jacques Bocquet, Clauda Jamprost, and several others of whom we shall speak later, it was under the shape of a man that he gained them. Of the same form was the demon which appeared to Brutus when he was about to pass out of Asia, and that which appeared to Cassius after the defeat of Mark Antony's army, which openly said that he was a devil. The devils which came out of the Idol of the Moon, which St. Jude broke in pieces, had the appearance of Ethiopians. Cynops, who cast himself into the sea at the prayers of St. John the Evangelist, was accompanied by three devils in the form of men newly raised from the dead. Satyrs, Fauns and Sylvans are nothing but devils bearing some resemblance to men.

Plutarch, Dion.

Plin. epist. 27. *lib.* 7.

Hector Boece. lib. 8.

Sometimes the Evil One takes the form of a woman, as we are taught in the stories of the lives of St. Anthony and St. Jerome, among others: and the two demons which appeared to Dion were in the form of women, as also seems to have been that which Curtius Rufus saw as he was walking late one day along a gallery. In Boethius also we have the story of a very beautiful young man who was burdened with a Succubus devil with a very fair face. What we know of Succubi is proof enough that the Devil often assumes the form of a woman, and that he chiefly does so at the Sabbat, as is evidenced by the words of Thievenne, of Jacquema Paget, and of several other witches.

We have said that the Devil sometimes assumes

the shape of a beast; and this we learn from St. Athanasius, who tells us in his Life of St. Anthony that the demons appeared to that holy man in the shape of Bulls, Wolves, Vipers, Scorpions, Leopards, Bears and horrible Dragons. Also George Gandillon confessed that, when the Devil appeared to them the first time, he had the form of a large horned Ram. At the Sabbat, too, he most often appears as a ram or a goat. Françoise Secretain confessed that he had lain with her four or five times, and that he was then in the form either of a dog or a cat or a fowl. Agrippa was followed by a black dog which was no other than a devil in disguise, as was clearly seen at his master's death; for being taken ill at an inn at Lyons, and finding himself at the point of death, he took from the dog a collar which it was wearing, all covered with certain characters, saying: "Begone, evil beast which have brought me to perdition." Upon this the dog threw itself into the Saône, and has never since been seen. The Devil which St. Philip cast out of the Idol of Death was in the form of a Dragon: and the seven devils which so tormented the passers-by, and were made to vanish by St. Andrew, were transformed into dogs. Thevet, again, tells us that in America they have a demon whom they call Agnan, which, like Proteus, appears now in one shape and now in another. And why should we not believe that the Dove and the Bull of Mahomet were no more than devils in that shape, just as it was with Agrippa's dog?

Rich. Discours des Images, c. 10. num. 8.

Paul. Jovi. in Elog.

Abdias, Bishop of Babylon.

Nevertheless, although Satan may take what shape he pleases, when he wishes to entice anyone into his net he most often appears to him in the form of a man; and I suppose that he does this so that he may not frighten him whom he approaches, or cause him to be amazed, as he would if he were to speak to him in the shape of a ram or a goat or any other beast. And in this we may see how very busy is this mortal enemy of the human race. But whenever he assumes the form of a man, he is, however, always black, as all witches bear witness. And for my part I hold that there are two principal reasons for this: first, that he who is the Father and Ruler of darkness may not be able to disguise himself so well that he may not always be known for what he is; secondly, as a proof that his study is only to do evil; for evil, as Pythagoras said, is symbolised by black. This is what Tamburlaine the Great had in mind when, while he was besieging a town, he set up black tents on the third day as a sign that he would put all the inhabitants to fire and the sword if they did not surrender. And long before him, the Greeks regarded it as a bad omen if, in drawing lots, one of the lots were black.

Ephes. 6.
Matth. 8.
Ovid, Fast. 5.

Furthermore, Satan does not always create for himself a body out of air, water or earth, but very often enters into a beast. We see this in St. Mark, where the Devil whose name was Legion prayed Jesus Christ to send him and his companions into the bodies of certain swine, and obtained his request. And, if we may believe Psellus, there are even demons which live under the earth, and sometimes enter into the body of a swine or other beast, not in order to harm it, but because the cold underneath the earth is so extreme that they cannot endure it, and, being equally unable to endure the rays of the sun, they

Alexander ab Alexandro, Genial. III. 12.
Mark 5.
Lib. de Dæmonibus.

are compelled to seek shelter and lodging in the bodies of beasts.

The Devil has also sometimes borrowed the body of a man who has been hanged; and this he does chiefly when he wishes to associate with a witch. It is for this reason, according to Cardan, that witches are usually ugly and stinking. *de subtil. lib.* 20.

Chapter VIII.

The Means Whereby Satan Wins Us to Him.

SATAN goes even further: for when he appears to us in the manner we have described, he invites us to give ourselves to him. This is how he acted in the case of Françoise Secretain, according to her own admission; and other witches say the same, and even that the Wicked One is so cunning that he knows how to choose the times and occasion most favourable to his designs. For he takes men when they are alone and in despair or misery because of hunger or some disaster which has befallen them. Eve was alone when *Genes.* 3.
she was seduced. Thievenne Paget was watching her cows in a field and lost one; and as she was sorrowing for this, Satan approached her and won her. It was the same with George Gandillon, who was irritated because he could not drive certain oxen. His father, Pierre Gandillon, was angry because his scythe did not cut so well as those of his companions, and wished himself to the Devil; whereupon Satan immediately ap-

peared to him and won his soul. Jacques Bocquet, Françoise Secretain, Clauda Jamprost, Antoine Gandillon and several others abandoned themselves to him because of their misery and poverty.

Furthermore, he makes fair promises. For to some he offers riches, assuring them that they will never lack for anything: to the vengeful he suggests the means to avenge themselves on their enemies: others he persuades that he will advance them in honour and rank: in short he so well suits himself to the character and humour of each one that he captures them at his will.

Yet it must be confessed that the fault lies wholly with the witch, for when he accosts them, Satan openly declares to them that he is the Devil, and makes them renounce God, Chrism and Baptism; and therefore such persons place themselves beyond forgiveness. For is there any man so foolish as not to know that the Devil is our mortal enemy, and that he desires nothing but the destruction of the human race? I have seen a deaf and dumb girl who, when she was angry, made an ugly grimace and pointed two fingers in the form of horns at those who had angered her, as if she wished to threaten them with the Devil; and this makes me think that she, and such as she, are well aware of his taking the form of a horned beast. Besides, who is ignorant that there is a God, and that He is above all the might of Satan? Even the Pagans are agreed that this truth is loudly proclaimed by Nature. Why, then, do we not turn to Him when we are tempted by the Devil, instead of yielding ourselves to the promises of our sworn enemy? Finally, if there were nothing else to be considered, are not witches condemned by the very nature of the rewards which they expect from Satan?

I have touched upon this point here to refute the opinion of those who try to excuse the greater number of witches on the ground that they are simple and ignorant. For it is clear that they are guilty of an offence against natural principles, of a crime which is severely and inexorably vindicated by the law. I may add that the infinite goodness of God towards them does but render them the more guilty; for He does not allow them to be taken by surprise. They know who it is with whom they are treating, they have time for deliberation as to whether or not they shall yield; it even appears that God takes no very strict count of their first renunciation of Him, of Chrism and of Baptism, as having been made in too great haste and without thought. Therefore the Devil in his subtlety and cunning makes them repeat their abnegation two or three times, and causes them to say that they do so with a willing heart. It is therefore apparent that they willingly cast themselves into Satan's net. But let us examine in more detail the witches' renunciation of God, Baptism and Chrism.

Can. qui ea 28. distinct. l. 2. de in jus. vocand. C.

Chapter IX.

Of the Witch's Renunciation of God, Baptism and Chrism.

AS the brave soldier disarms his enemy so that he may become his prisoner, having nothing with which to defend himself; so, when Satan wishes to become our master, he makes us renounce God, Baptism and Chrism, because these are the weapons with which we can guard and defend ourselves against him, and the Evil One well knows this.

For, considering God in general, did not Satan say to Him, speaking of Job: "Doth Job fear God for nought? Hast thou not made an hedge about him, and about his house, and about all that he hath on every side?" And the Royal Prophet says: "He that dwelleth in the secret place of the Most High shall abide under the shadow of the Almighty." And St. Paul, writing to the Romans, says: "If God be for us, who can be against us?" And notably it has been observed several times that, when one has pronounced the name of God or of Jesus Christ in the witches' assembly, everything has at once vanished, both devils and persons and meats.

Job 1. *Ps.* 91. *Rom.* 8. *v. Grillan.*

As for Baptism, it sets us out of Satan's power and is, as it were, a protection against all future ambushes and attacks. But here I must say that this Schemer causes the witch to renounce not only his first Baptism which he received in the name of the Holy and Undivided Trinity, but

Bodin, Demonom. II. c. 4. *Concil. Trid. Sessio* 4. *Bodin, ibid.*

makes him also be rebaptised in the name of the Devil and take another name. It would seem that he does this in order that the witch should be thereby persuaded that his first Baptism is wholly annulled, and that it can be of no more service to him.

For many witches, after they have fallen into the hands of justice, ask to be rebaptised: certainly Claude Coirieres, Christofle of Aranthon, Pierre Vuillermoz, and several others have made such a request. *Remy, lib.* 3. *Demonol.* c. 6.

Of Chrism we may say much the same as of Baptism, that it is a sovereign antidote against the power of the Devil: and this is confirmed by the statements of witches, who say that, when they have transformed themselves into wolves and wish to kill and eat children, they cannot touch that part which has been anointed with the Holy Chrism. This I know from the confessions of Jacques Bocquet, Clauda Jamprost and Thievenne Paget. The Chrism is of such worth and virtue that St. Cyril the Bishop speaks of it in these words: "Just as the bread in the Eucharist is no longer bread but the Body of Jesus Christ after the words have been pronounced, so also this Holy Unguent can no longer be called a simple or common ointment after it has been consecrated, but is a gift of grace which brings to us and gives us the presence of Jesus Christ and of the Holy Spirit, that is to say, His Divinity." And according to Pope Fabian this Holy Unguent was instituted by Jesus Christ after He had supped with His disciples. *Ræmond, Antichrist,* c. 39.

But the Devil exacts even more conditions; for sometimes he forbids those who give themselves to him to say the Apostles' Creed. He did so in the case of Pierre Bourgot, who confessed that the Devil required him to kiss his left hand, which was black, death-like, and quite cold. Antide Colas also revealed that Satan commanded her to pray to him night and morning before she set about any other work, and that afterwards she might go to church and pray as much as she pleased.

Chapter X.

Of the Voice of Demons.

THE matters we have discussed in the last two chapters lead me to speak of the manner of speech used by demons. For since they are purely spiritual, it would seem that they are incapable of speech, which is formed by the lungs, the palate, the tongue and the teeth, which are lacking in a spirit. Yet it is certain that demons do in some manner speak; for we see every day how they answer through the mouths of demoniacs. When Rollande du Vernois was possessed, her two devils so exactly imitated her own utterance at times, that we thought it was she who was speaking and answering us. But it has been observed that generally the Devil cannot control his voice so well as to imitate the human voice in such a way that it cannot be distinguished; for his voice is either harsh, or thin and penetrating, or like that of a man speaking in a tub. Psellus explains that the Devil speaks in this

de Dæmon.

manner so that, by not being clearly heard, he can the better disguise his subtleties and lies. Another reason is that it is impossible for art to imitate nature so closely but that there is always some difference between the two. And here it may be mentioned that, when George Gandillon was asked whether Satan spoke distinctly when he tempted him to give himself to the Devil, he answered that he did not, and that he could with difficulty understand what he said.

Now it is easy for the Devil to speak by the mouth of a demoniac, for then he uses the teeth, tongue and lungs of the possessed, just as he uses his other members in whatever manner he wishes; for he grimaces with the mouth, and uses the hands to push away the Cross and Holy Water, as I have seen in the case of Rollande du Vernois and several others who were possessed. This leads me to believe that, when the Devil enters into the body of a dog or a goat or a bird or any other animal, he can counterfeit the voice of a man, as he has several times done according to the statement of many witches. The first time he spoke to Rollande du Vernois, and to Pierre and George Gandillon, he was in the shape of a black ram; and it is known that he usually assumes this shape at the Sabbat when he speaks to his people, inciting them to evil either by soft words or by threats. This will not seem strange to any who have read the story of Balaam's ass, or who have seen jays and parrots counterfeit human speech so well that it seemed as if a man was speaking. The parrot given to Augustus, which he valued so greatly, is an example. I pass over the lamb which in human speech foretold good fortune to Egypt in the reign of Bochorus, and the ox which said to him who goaded it in ploughing that mankind would fail sooner than the crops; neither shall I pause over the dog and the serpent which spoke when Tarquinius Superbus was driven from Rome; and the rook which, some time before the death of the Emperor Domitian, prophesied in Greek great good to the Roman Republic; and the two oxen and the cock who spoke in the consulship of Quintus Fabius Maximus and Marcus Lepidus. All of these are mentioned by Fulgosus.

Fulgos. lib. 1. *c.* 4.

But it is far more difficult to believe that Satan can speak through the shameful parts of a woman, or when the person's mouth is shut, or when the tongue is thrust six inches out of the mouth; or that he can speak when he has no body at all, or one formed only of air. Yet this is known to happen; for we read that she who gave answer in the Delphic Oracle spoke through the lower and shameful parts, as did also a woman in Rhodige, an Italian town mentioned by Cœlius Rhodiginus in his disquisitions.

However, this thing is caused in a natural manner, just as if the voice were formed by an agitation and vibration of air; and it follows that Satan can in this way create a voice, seeing that he is well able to form a body out of air. The echo gives us an example of this, when we see valleys and hollow places reply articulately to the human voice so exactly that it seems as if those places were imitating our speech; and from this it is easy to understand that the human voice may be quite well counterfeited without the use of lungs, tongue or teeth.

Lib. 2. *de Incant. c.* 12.

Therefore Vair is right when he says that demons can counterfeit sounds like the human voice, and therewith express their meaning, and that although they have neither teeth nor tongue nor lungs, which are the instruments by which the voice is formed, they can yet present an artificial appearance of these organs, and by this means and by certain sounds they counterfeit some semblance of a voice which they cause to reach the ears of their hearers. So says Vair.

CHAPTER XI.

Of the Copulation of the Devil with Male and Female Witches.

THE third point in Françoise Secretain's confession was that she had had carnal relations with Satan. Clauda Jamprost, Jacquema Paget, Antoine Tornier, Antoine Gandillon, Clauda Janguillaume, Thievenne Paget, Rollande du Vernois, Janne Platet and Clauda Paget confessed the same thing; and it has been revealed in the examinations of witches that they all have this connexion with Satan. The Devil uses them so because he knows that women love carnal pleasures, and he means to bind them to his allegiance by such agreeable provocations. Moreover, there is nothing which makes a woman more subject and loyal to a man than that he should abuse her body.

And since male witches are addicted no less than female to this pleasure, the Devil also appears as a woman to satisfy them. This he does chiefly at the Sabbat, according to the reports of the father and son, George and Pierre Gandillon, and of those women whom I have several times named, who all agree in saying that in their assemblies there are many demons, of whom some take the form of women for the men, and others that of men for the women. These demons are called Incubi and Succubi. And it is no new thing for Satan to draw us to him by these means; for we read that, in order to tempt St. Anthony, St. Jerome and other devout persons, who passed their life in the solitude of the desert, he commonly appeared to them in the form of a courtesan.

There is also another reason for the coupling of the Devil with a witch, which is that the sin may thereby become the more grievous. For if God abominates the coupling of an infidel with a Christian, how much more shall He detest that of a man with the Devil? Moreover, by this means man's natural semen is wasted, with the result that the love between man and wife is often turned to hatred, than which no worse a misfortune could happen to the state of matrimony.

CHAPTER XII.

Whether such Copulation Exists in the Imagination Only.

BUT since there are some who maintain that the coupling of which we have just spoken exists in the imagination only, it will be well to say something here on this subject. For some treat the matter with derision, some are doubtful about it, and others firmly believe it to be a fact. St. Augustine appears to be among these last, as also St. Thomas Aquinas and several other later learned authorities. But the witches' confessions which I have had make me think that there is truth in this matter; for they have all admitted that they have coupled with the Devil, and that his semen was very cold; and this is confirmed by the reports of Paul Grilland and the Inquisitors of the Faith. Jacquema Paget added that she had several times taken in her hand the member of the Demon which lay with her, and that it was as cold as ice and a good finger's length, but not so thick as that of a man. Thievenne Paget and Antoine Tornier also added that the members of their demons were as long and big as one of their fingers; and Thievenne Paget said, moreover, that when Satan coupled with her she had as much pain as a woman in travail. Françoise Secretain said that, whilst she was in the act, she felt something burning in her stomach; and nearly all witches affirm that this coupling is by no means pleasurable to them, both because of

de Civitate Dei, V. 23.

Satan's ugliness and deformity, and because of the physical pain which it causes them, as we have just said.

The ugliness and deformity lies in the fact that Satan couples with witches sometimes in the form of a black man, sometimes in that of some animal, as a dog or a cat or a ram. With Thievenne Paget and Antoine Tornier he lay in the form of a black man; and when he coupled with Jacquema Paget and Antoine Gandillon he took the shape of a black ram with horns: Françoise Secretain confessed that her demon appeared sometimes as a dog, sometimes as a cat, and sometimes as a fowl when he wished to have carnal intercourse with her. For all these reasons I am convinced that there is real and actual copulation between a witch and a demon; for what is there to prevent the Devil, when he has taken the form of an animal, from coition with a witch? In Toulouse and Paris women have been known to make sexual abuse of a natural dog; and it seems to me quite to the point to refer here to the legends of Pasiphaë and other such women.

Bodin, Demonom. lib. 3. c. 6.

Another matter that I must mention, which is as strange as it is true, concerns one Antide Colas of Betoncourt in the district of Baume. She was imprisoned at that place for witchcraft, and it was found when visiting her that she had a hole beneath her navel, quite contrary to nature. This hole was examined on the eleventh of July, 1598, by Master Nicolas Milliere of Regnaucourt, Chirurgeon, who thrust his probe deeply into it in the presence of his servant, and of Antoinette Mongin, Jannette Bolet and Claudine Menestrey, who were required to be there as witnesses;

and then the witch confessed that her Devil, whom she called Lizabet, had sexual connexion with her through this hole, and her husband through the natural hole; but afterwards, when she was taken by order of the Court to the prison of Dôle, and they wished to examine this hole, it was found to be closed up, and there remained nothing but a scar. This woman was burned alive on the twentieth of February, 1599. But who would believe that Satan even lies with witches in prison? Yet this woman of whom we have just told confessed that he did so; as also did Thievenne Paget, who said that the Devil had lain with her three times while she was in prison.

When Satan means to lie with a witch in the form of a man, he takes to himself the body of some man who has been hanged. But even if he has only a body formed from the air, there is still nothing to prevent him from intercourse with a witch; for in that case he makes the body of air so dense that it is palpable (for air is, of itself, palpable), and consequently capable of coition with, and even defloration of a woman. And why should not this be easy for him, seeing that he is powerful enough to overthrow a town or a city or a kingdom? And as for his semen, he has but too plentiful a supply, even were there no other source of it, in that which he receives when he acts as a Succubus.

And therefore I thoroughly believe all that has been written of Fauns, Satyrs and woodland gods, which were no more than demons, and were inordinately lustful and lascivious. Also I think that we may consider under this head the stories we are told of the wantonnesses of Numa,

Vair, de Incant. II. 13.
Thyr. de loc. infest. I. 21.
Pliny, VII. 2.

and of the nymph Egeria, and of several others whom the poets have particularly mentioned. Similarly we find in the West Indies that their gods, which they call Cocoto, lay with women and had sexual intercourse with them; unless it was really certain lickerish men who abused them, as Decius Mundus, a Roman knight, whose story Josephus tells in his Antiquities, did to Paulina under pretence of being the God Anubis.

But to return to Françoise Secretain, it is a strange thing that Satan lay with her in the shape of a fowl. I am of opinion that she meant to say a gander instead of a fowl, for that is a form which Satan often takes, and therefore we have the proverb that Satan has feet like a goose. Yet it would be as easy for him to take the shape of a fowl as that of a gander. For we know that he has at different times assumed the shape of a dog for the same purpose, and we have two remarkable examples of this: one of a dog, said to be a demon, which used to lift up the robes of the nuns in a convent of the diocese of Cologne in order to abuse them; the other, of certain dogs found on the beds of the nuns of a convent on Mount Hesse in Germany.

Paracel. de Malefic. c. 15.

Wier.

Bodin, Demonom. III. 6.

CHAPTER XIII.

Whether the Copulation of Satan with a Witch can bring to Birth a Living Being.

IT is a matter of far greater doubt whether a living being can be born from the coupling of the Devil with a witch. I remember that, when Antoine Tornier and Antoine Gandillon were asked whether they were not afraid of becoming pregnant by the Devil, one answered that she was too old, and the other that God would not permit it. I have read, too, that Satan has sometimes asked a witch whether she wished to become pregnant by him, and that the witch has said that she did not wish it. It seems then that it is possible for issue to come of this coupling; and also there are many examples of such an occurrence, besides the proof which may be drawn from the Book of Genesis, where it is said that the Sons of God lay with the daughters of men, and that there sprang from them a race of giants, a passage which Josephus understands literally. As for examples, we have the English Merlin, who was said to have been born from the union of a demon with a woman: the Huns and the men of Cyprus are also said to spring from certain witches who had intercourse with the Devil: it is also said that Luther was born from the coupling of the Devil with his mother Marguerite: passing over what has been written of Plato, Servius Tullius, and of Florine and Ermeline, we

Genes. 6.

Antiqu. I. 3.

Remy, Demonol., I. 6.

Raemond, Antichrist, c. 6. *num.* 1.

read of women who have lain down to Satan and given birth to hideous and terrible monsters, as did the woman mentioned by Bodin in his Demonomania. Wier, again, says that the Germans maintain that from this diabolical copulation are born children that are puny and yet heavier than other children, that they milk three nurses dry without growing fat, cry when they are touched, laugh when any misfortune overtakes the house, and never live beyond seven years.

ib. 2. c. v.

If it be asked how such couplings can lead to procreation, I must refer to the opinion of St. Thomas Aquinas that Satan makes use of the male semen which he receives when acting as a Succubus; or that he so skilfully shoots it into the womb that, on meeting with the female ova, some result must necessarily follow; and even that this semen is kept in its original warmth by the Devil, who has but too many devices with which to harm and abuse the human race.

We know that there are many monsters born in the sea from the union of two fishes of different species; and that some even are found which resemble men, which are said by some naturalists and doctors to be procreated from the semen of a dead man; and therefore they advise us to bury the dead, whether men or women, so as to guard against such mischances. Then why should we think it strange that some issue should be born of the Devil and a witch, if their copulation is after the manner we have described? Binsfeld, Suffragan of Trèves, accepts the possibility of it, being in agreement with several learned authorities whom he quotes.

Paracel. in fragm. lib. de animalib.

De confess. malef., conclus. 5.

I may further add that it is the more easy to believe in such procreation, because even a virgin can conceive when the man's semen has been merely spent round about the natural place, without any loss of her virginity: this is vouched for by Navarro as being the opinion of St. Thomas. I have read also that, being rubbed by the herb called Nepeta, the cat conceives, and that this herb can supply the lack of a male. *Navar. consil. 3. num. 23. de frigid. & mal. lib. 4.*

Nevertheless, although all these reasons have some weight, I prefer to follow the opinion of those who believe that no issue can result from such connexions. For everyone knows that the abounding vitality and heat of the whole body is the cause of procreation: I mean the natural heat of a man. It is therefore impossible that an accidental heat, or one that is acquired merely by artifice, can be competent to produce such a result. Now this natural vitality and heat is lacking in a demon, as is also the heart which is its source; and I shall never believe that the Devil, after having borrowed a man's semen, can preserve its first heat, considering that it has to be carried to another place, and that semen becomes cold as soon as it is ejaculated from its ducts. Besides, all witches agree that the semen they receive from the Devil is as cold as ice. And further, can we think that God, who is jealous of His honour and is glorified in His works, would be willing to endow with life and a soul the fruit proceeding from so abominable a copulation? *Agrippa.*

I go even further, and maintain that nothing will be born if the witch has coupled with a ram, a cat, a dog, or any other animal, by reason of the disproportion between them: that if the contrary were true, there would not only be the case of the two women burned, one at Toulouse and the other at Paris, who were brought to bed by the *Bodin, Demonom. III. 6.*

natural dogs which had connexion with them; but the world would, if this thing were possible, be filled with the fruits of such couplings. For it was not only yesterday that such things were practised : the law of God long since punished with death the man and the beast who had sinned together. Therefore I conclude that if, because of the disproportion between man and a brute beast, no issue can come of any copulation between them, much less can there be any issue from the coupling of Satan with a witch, whether Satan take the body of a hanged man, or whether he make himself a body out of the elements.

Levit. 18 & 20.

This may seem to refute what we have said about sea monsters which are born from two fishes of different species; but there is great similarity between two such animals, in spite of the difference in their species; and there are parallel cases on land, where we know that a mule is born from an ass and a mare, and the Basilisk from a cock and a toad.

As for the Merman, it is difficult to believe that he is generated from the semen of a dead man, or that the corpse of a dead man is able to secrete semen competent for procreation. There can be no doubt that the Merman is generated of two fishes, and that Nature, which delights in variety, gives him the form of a man is the upper parts: in the same way on land she has brought forth animals which resemble man, such as the monkey, and the Brazilian beast called the sloth, which is about the size of a fox, and is like a woman about the face and hair, except for its much misshapen muzzle.

Raemond, Antichrist, c. 32.

With the leave of such eminent men, for whom I have the very highest respect and honour, I shall contradict the opinion of St. Thomas and Navarro; for how can their opinion be maintained, when all philosophers and naturalists agree that no generation is possible without the conjunction of the male and female seed? This argument will hold equally for that which has been said about cats, and for the stories that are told about Spanish mares being caused to conceive simply by a breath of wind in a certain place.

With regard to the monstrosities to which women give birth, these may be said to proceed either from a superfluity and excess of generative matter; or possibly from the force of imagination, which operates as a sort of seal stamping the image of a mother's fancy on the child she has conceived in her womb. Or perhaps we should rather believe that God, whose judgments are inscrutable, in this manner punishes mothers who abandon themselves to unnatural and abominable copulations. For we are not bound to believe the stories of Merlin, the Huns, the men of Cyprus, and others having sprung from demons: such stories are sometimes written by historians, but most often merely upon hearsay, and without corroboration of the truth.

It is said that Rhea, the mother of Romulus and Remus, was made pregnant by the God Mars; and Olympias, the mother of Alexander, by Jupiter in the form of a swan; but who is to believe that? Why should we not rather believe that these women used the Gods as a screen to cover their incests and adulteries? And therefore I maintain that the widow of whom Bodin speaks was made pregnant by a natural man, and not by a demon; and that God permitted her to give birth to a monster as a punishment for the unlawful and abominable fornication of which she was guilty in order to satisfy her wanton and unbridled appetite.

We have now but to explain the passage in Genesis where it says that "The sons of God lay with the daughters of men." But why should we pause over this, seeing how many learned men have interpreted it? There is no doubt that the sons of God are those who find favour with the living God; for in another place they are even called Gods by the Royal Prophet, just as certain names which are given to God may be applied to men.

Finally, since carnal desire is necessary only to those who need to supply a successor to continue their kind, and since Angels and demons are not subject to death, it follows that spirits are immune from the flames of love, and that they are without those members in which sensual desire is generated, namely, the lower parts of mankind.

CHAPTER XIV.

Of the Transvection of Witches to the Sabbat.

THE fourth point in Françoise Secretain's confession was that she had countless times been to the Sabbat; and this leads me to speak of the transvection of witches. There are those who have flatly denied the possibility of such a thing; and the Council of Aquileia even decreed that it

Ulric. Molit., de Lam. Vair, de Incant. II. 13.

was heresy to believe that witches are conveyed from one place to another in the manner they allege: Navarro, in fact, reckoned such a belief to be a mortal sin.

Wier, de praestig. VII. 29.
Can. episcop. 26. *q.* 5.

Nevertheless I have always been well persuaded of the contrary opinion, both because of the authority of those who have maintained this view, and by reason of the confession of nearly all witches that they have been conveyed to the Sabbat. There have even been cases of persons who were not witches, but have, following the example of and at the instigation of witches, rubbed themselves with a certain ointment, and of farmers, who have been transported to as much as a hundred or two hundred leagues from their homes, so that they have had great difficulty in finding their way back again.

Mall. Malefic. II. 1.
Bodin, Demonom. II. 3.
Remy, Dem. I. 14.
Grilland, de Sortileg. VII. 26.
Dan. Dialog. 4.
Bodin, ibid.

But I will come to what I have learned of this matter. Françoise Secretain said that, to go to the Sabbat, she placed a white staff between her legs and uttered certain words, and that she was then conveyed through the air to the witches' assembly. Rollande du Vernois confessed that she went there on a great black ram which carried her through the air so quickly that she was unconscious of the passage. Thievenne Paget said that the first time the Devil appeared to her, it was in full daylight in the form of a big black man, and that when she had given herself to him he embraced her and raised her in the air and conveyed her to the house in the field of Longchamois where he had carnal intercourse with her, and that he then brought her back to the place from where he had taken her. This field was the place where the witches of Longchamois and Orcieres held their Sabbat. Antide Colas said that the night Satan appeared to her as a gigantic man, black-bearded and clothed in black, he carried her to the Sabbat; and that at other times he used to come and take her on his back, and carried her like a cold wind, gripping her by the hair. It would take too long to write down all that other witches have said on this subject. But a fact which even more strongly inclines me to believe in the transvection of witches is that Jesus Christ Himself was carried by the Devil to the pinnacle of the temple of Jerusalem, and then to the top of a mountain; for if this could happen to our Lord, why should it not happen to witches? I pass over the transportations of St. Philip, Ezekiel, Habakkuk, Elijah, Enoch, St. Antide Archbishop of Besançon, St. Ambrose, Pythagoras, the Philosopher of Tyana, and countless others. But I cannot omit Simon Magus, who, in defiance of St. Peter, undertook to fly from the Capitol to the Aventine Hill, and was carried through the air with the help of Satan. It is true that at the end he fell and broke his legs; and this was by divine ordinance that God might be glorified in St. Peter. Similarly He was purposely glorified in Moses, when his rod was turned into a serpent and devoured those of Pharaoh's magicians. For it is in this manner that God raises up His enemies to cast them down, to their great confusion and His own honour.

Acts 8. *Ezek.* 8. *Philostr. Vair, Incant. II.* 13. *Spin. de strigib. c.* 5.

Exod. 7.

Neither shall I forget that, when the sons of France were hostages in Spain, there appeared a German magician who promised to convey these Princes home through the air, but that they would not trust themselves to him. For it was to be feared that, when the royal children were passing over some sea, the same fate might over-

Wier, de praestig. II. 29

take them as overtook Dædalus, after whom an arm of the sea was named because he lost his life in falling into it.

And as for the Council of Aquileia, those who admit the transvection of witches have sufficiently refuted its opinion. With regard to Navarro, it seems that he would entirely deny the existence of the Sabbat; but no one can rightly uphold such a denial, since there is nothing more certain than that witches assemble together; for otherwise they could not so perfectly agree in their reports of their Sabbats, even allowing for the fact that there are several Sabbats, held in different places. For we see that they all are unanimous in their accounts of the offerings of candles, the lewd kisses, the dances, the obscene couplings, the banquets, and the beating of water, which take place at their assemblies; and these are everywhere conducted in the same manner, since the Devil is always true to his nature, which is ever no more or less than that of an ape.

Again, how can we contradict those who have found themselves at the Sabbat, although they are not witches? Pierre Vuillermoz, Christofle of Aranthon in Savoy, the brothers Claude, Charloz, and Perrenette Molard have confessed that they were conveyed to the Sabbat near Coirieres at a place called és Combes, and that there they had seen done all that we have just said: yet the eldest of them could not have been more than ten years old. I mention their age to prove that they were not witches, and to show that the Devil had no power or authority to cause them to dream of these kisses and offerings and such matters. Finally, Antoine Tornier and Jacquema Paget have recorded that once, when they were coming home from gleaning and were passing along the field of Longchamois, they saw that the Sabbat was being held in that place, and set down their bundles and went and did as the others, and then took up their bundles and returned to their homes. I can hardly think that anyone will maintain that these two women were at that time asleep, and that it was only in their fancy and imagination that they went to the Sabbat.

CHAPTER XV.

How and in what Fashion Witches are Conveyed to the Sabbat.

Paracel. de Malefic. c. 16. Bodin. Demonon. II. 3. Remy, Demonol. I. 14.

FRANÇOISE Secretain was carried there upon a white staff; Rollande du Vernois on a big black ram which she rode horsewise. Satan was in the form of a black man when he bore Thievenne Paget and Antide Colas to the Sabbat: others go there sometimes on a goat, sometimes on a horse, and sometimes on a broom, and generally leave their house by the chimney. Some rub themselves first with a certain ointment, and others use none. There are also some who are not witches, but after anointing themselves do not fail to fly up through the chimney and to be carried away as if they were witches. Nevertheless it must not be thought that it is this ointment which causes their transvection; for we shall show later that neither ointment nor words nor symbols are, of themselves, of any use to witches. Those, therefore, of whom we have spoken are transported by the just permission of God, who in this manner punishes them for their too great curiosity.

There are some also who go to the Sabbat without either beast or staff to carry them; and again it should be known that a beast or a staff is of no more use than the ointment, but that it is the Devil, who of his own power, is as a wind which bears them along, just as a whirlwind uproots even the highest trees, and carried them two or three leagues away from the place where they grew. Even men have been known to be transported in this manner, as was Romulus, who, whilst he was among the Senators in the Field of Mars near the Goat's Pool, was lifted up into the air by a whirlwind and never returned. Again, Antide Colas said that when the Devil came to take her in her bed to carry her to the Sabbat, he was like a cold wind which took her by the head.

Paracel. de Malefic. cap 17.
Wier, de praestig. II. 29.
Plutarch, Romulus.

Chapter XVI.

Witches Sometimes go on Foot to the Sabbat.

Yet witches sometimes go on foot to the Sabbat, and this usually happens when the place of their assembly is not very distant from their homes. Pierre Gandillon, George Gandillon his son, and his daughter Antoine Gandillon went in this way to the Sabbat to a place called és Fontenailles, about two arquebus shots distant from Nezan, which was their native place and home. Clauda Jamprost, Clauda Janguillaume and Jacquema Paget of Orcieres also went on foot to the Sabbat in the field of Longchamois, about a quarter of a league from Orcieres. Groz-Jacques went by the same means to a Sabbat at Longchamois and another at a place called és Combes, near Coirieres, where also Pierre Vuillermoz of Aranthon, the brothers Claude Charloz, and Perrenette Molard went in like manner on foot. Pierre Vuillermoz added that, to get there, he had to pass a little stream. Jeanne Platet and Clauda Paget went to a place called au Mont; and I have read that many other places have thus been reached on foot. But there is no doubt that these witches were sometimes carried by the Devil to the Sabbat, as were those of whom we spoke in the last chapter; for they have themselves confessed it.

Chapter XVII.

Whether Witches go in Spirit to the Sabbat.

Bodin, Demonom. II. 5.

There are others who maintain that for the most part it is only in spirit that witches go to the Sabbat; and they substantiate their opinion by examples taken from certain witches, who after having remained in their houses as dead for the space of two or three hours have confessed that they were at that time at the Sabbat in spirit, and have given an exact account of all that took place there. In this connexion, Groz-Jacques said that it was quite possible to go to the Sabbat in spirit only; but Clauda Coirieres said that, if her spirit had been to the Sabbat, she knew nothing about it. One Holy Thursday night George Gandillon lay in his bed for three hours as if he were dead, and then suddenly came to himself; and he has since had to be burned in this place, together with his father and one of his sisters. Some little time ago there was a man of the village of Unau in the district of Orgelet, who brought his wife to this place and accused her of being a witch, saying among other things that when they were in bed together one Thursday night he noticed that his wife was absolutely still without even breathing; whereupon he began to shake her, but could not waken her, and became so frightened that he tried to get up to call his neighbours; but try as he might, he could not move from his bed, and he seemed to be caught fast by the legs, and was not even able to cry out. This lasted for two or three hours until the cock crew; and then his wife suddenly awoke, and when he asked her what was amiss, she answered that she was so tired from the work she had done the day before that she was weighed down with sleep and had felt nothing of what her husband had done to her. The man then supposed that she had been to the Sabbat, for he had already had some suspicion of her because the cattle of some of their neighbours, whom she had threatened, had been dying.

Indeed it appears very probable that this woman had been in spirit to the Sabbat. For first, the seizure of which we have told came to her on a Thursday night, which is the customary night for the Sabbat. Secondly, when the cock crew she awoke suddenly: now the Sabbat is held by night and lasts until the cock crows, but after it has crowed everything vanishes. Thirdly, the excuse she gave clearly proves that there was deceit on her part; for who has ever known a man to be so tired from his labour and toil that he could not easily be awakened? George Gandillon used the same excuse when he was asked why he had not been awakened even when he was frequently and violently shaken. Fourthly, it is obvious that there was devil's work, since the husband was as it were caught by the legs, and unable to cry out. And finally, the Magistrates of Unau who adjudicated for the husband stated that the woman was descended from parents who had already been suspected of witchcraft.

So much, then, for the contention that witches go to the Sabbat in spirit and soul only; a view which is in agreement with what Pliny wrote: "We have found it stated of Hermontinus of Clazomenæ that the soul used often to leave his body and go wandering here and there and bring back news of things that could only be known to such as were present to witness them, all the time leaving the body in a state resembling death, until his enemies, called the Cantarides, burned the body and so took away from the returning soul its casing, as it were."

But everyone will form his own opinion of this matter. For my part I have never been able to believe that such a thing is in any way possible; for if it is true that when the soul is separated from the body, death must necessarily follow, how can it be possible for a witch, after having been in spirit to the Sabbat, to return to life by

the help of the Devil? This cannot be except by *Ps.* 135.
a miracle, which belongs only to God and not *S. Thom.*
to Satan, who only works by secondary and *Grilland, de*
natural causes and therefore has no power to *Sortileg.* 10. 1.
raise the dead to life. For although one of the *Richer, des Images, c.* 38.
poets has written that Erichtho, a witch of Thessaly, brought to life a dead soldier who foretold to Sextus Pompeius the success of the Pharsalian war, this must not be believed as the truth: it was the Devil who had entered into the dead man's body and spoke through his mouth; or perhaps made use of some fantastic body as he did when Saul consulted the witch of Endor to summon the spirit of Samuel, that he might know whether he should give battle to the Philistines or postpone it to some other time.

I am aware also that it is written that at Rome Apollonius of Tyana raised from the dead a girl on the day of her wedding; but who shall say that this philosopher, who had no other object but to glorify himself, did not first cause the bride to fall into a sleep so deep that she seemed to be dead and that when the strength of the drug had been spent and the girl awoke, he gave out that it was he who had brought her to life?

I for my part stoutly maintain that in every case where it has been a plain question of raising the dead, witches have proved utterly powerless. We read of such as Simon Magus, Eunomianus and Polychronius Monothelita, who laboured to bring certain dead men to life, and lost their whole repute in the attempt. Certain heretics also have meddled in this matter, such as Luther, as Cochlæus tells us in his Life of him; but what are we to think when such men have effected the converse of what they set out to do? For we read that, in pretending to bring living men to life, they have caused the death of the men; and as examples of this we may quote Calvin, of whom Jerome Bolsecque speaks in his Life; and another Minister from the borders of Poland and Hungary, whom Alanus Copus mentions in the sixth book of his Dialogues, and, later, Cardinal Bellarmine in his Controversies. In this manner also Cyril the Patriarch of the Arians rendered one blind who was but pretending to be blind. But indeed how should heretics have power to raise the dead to life, seeing that the Prophets of Baal could not bring fire down from Heaven, and Mani could not heal the sick King's son, and Luther was brought into great danger when he wished to cast out the Devil from the body of a woman that was his disciple? I prefer, then, to say that sometimes witches are present at the Sabbat, and sometimes they are not; and that when they are so present they go there both in body and in spirit, and that Satan then places a fantom in their likeness so that a husband very often embraces an illusion instead of his wife, in just the same way that the poets pretend that Ixion embraced a cloud instead of Juno. Sometimes again Satan at that time makes himself a Succubus with whom the husband lies as if it were his wife. There can be no doubt that there are times when witches go to the Sabbat both in body and spirit without Satan putting any fantom in their place; but in such case the Devil induces so profound a sleep in those of the house, with mandragora or some other narcotic draught, that they cannot be awakened by any noise soever, and the husband, who has seen his wife come to bed before he

Grilland, de Sortileg. VII. 4.

Remy, Demonol. c. 4.

went to sleep, will think in the morning that she has not moved throughout the night, even though she has, in fact, been to the Sabbat for as long as two or three hours.

As for those witches who remain unconscious and as it were dead, it is probable that Satan sends them to sleep as he does those of whom we have just spoken, and reveals to them in their sleep what happens at the Sabbat so vividly that they think they have been there; and therefore they can give a marvellously accurate account of it. But I hold that this never happens except to such as have previously attended in person the witches' assembly, and have already enlisted beneath Satan's standard.

c. episcopi 26. *q.* 5. *Spina de Strigib. c.* 14. *Binsfeld, de confessio. malef. conclus.* 7. *dub.* 5.

Chapter XVIII.

The Sabbat is Generally Held at Night.

Françoise Secretain added that she used always to go to the Sabbat at about midnight; and Jacques Bocquet, Rollande du Vernois, Clauda Jamprost, Thievenne and Jacquema Paget, Antoine Tornier, Pierre Gandillon, George Gandillon, Antoine Gandillon—in fact all the other witches who have come into my hands have said the same. And it is no new or strange matter that Satan should hold his assemblies by night; for Jesus Christ tells us that the evil-doer hates the light; and in another place it is said that Satan is the ruler of darkness: moreover we find that he

Ephes. 6.

works chiefly by night, as when he slew the first-born of Egypt and the cattle at the stroke of mid-
Exod. 11. night. Again, the Evil One has clearly shown that he delights in darkness, for he has ever wished that anything which is offered to him should be black, as we are told by Ovid and
Fasti, 5. Alexander ab Alexandro. That which is white
Genial. III. 12. is, on the contrary, pleasing to God, according to
De legib. 1. Cicero; for white is symbolical of openness, cleanness, innocence, humbleness and chastity,
Rev. 3. and therefore it is written in the Apocalypse that he that overcometh shall be clothed in white raiment. In this connexion I shall mention that a little before peace was concluded between Louis XI, King of France, and the King of England on the 26th of August, 1475, at Pic-
Chap. 77. quigny, it is reported by Philippe de Commines in his History that a white pigeon came and rested on the English King's tent.

It is probable also that Satan assembles witches at night so that they may not be recognised; and for the same reason they dance, at their assem-
Grilland, de Sortileg. c. 4. *num.* 3. blies, back to back, and are now for the most part masked, as has been confirmed by Clauda Paget, who was called la Foulet.

But always it is a condition of these devilish assemblies at night, that as soon as the cock crows everything disappears. This I know from the statements of those whom I have mentioned, and especially of Clauda Jamguillaume, Antoine Tornier and Jacquema Paget, who said that they had spent hardly any time at the Sabbat because the cock crew as soon as they arrived. Some have thought that the sound of the cock is deadly to Satan, just as it is feared by lions; and in truth, if the Devil is afraid of a naked sword, he may well be afraid also of the crowing of a cock. But I am rather of opinion that God, being merciful, wishes by this means to draw to repentance those poor deluded ones who have renounced Him like St. Peter, who understood his sin when the cock had crowed thrice; and therefore this bird has remained as a warning to Bishops and Pastors to do their duty.

But let us speak now of the day of the Sabbat.

Chapter XIX.

Of the Day of the Sabbat.

I was formerly of the opinion that the Sabbat is held only on a Thursday night, since all the witches that I have examined have so reported it. But I have since read that some of the same sect have confessed that they have met together, sometimes on Monday night, sometimes on Friday or Wednesday or Sunday night; and therefore I have concluded that there is no fixed day for the Sabbat, but that witches go to it whenever they are so commanded by Satan. And here I shall add that, in this connexion, Antide Colas confessed that for a period of about seven years she had been to the Sabbat at each of the great Festivals of the year, as at Christmas, Easter, the Fête-Dieu and such days; and that the last time she had been there one Easter evening in the Valley of Saint Marie, where there were about forty persons assembled; and she said also that on the night of the preceding Christmas she had been there between the midnight Mass and the first Mass of the day. This is how the wicked one celebrates his assemblies on Holy Days, and seduces the creatures of God from His service.

Chapter XX.

Of the Place of the Sabbat.

Some have observed that the Sabbat is always held in some conspicuous place, marked by trees or a Cross; but for my part I do not know what to say about this. For the witches of Longchamois used to meet in a meadow on the highroad to Saint Claude, with the ruins of a house in sight; while those of Coirieres held their Sabbat by the village of Coirieres near the water, in a place called és Combes, where there are no roads at all. Pierre Gandillon, George Gandillon and Antoine Gandillon met at a place called és Fontenelles near the village of Nezan, which is a conspicuous enough place; and Jacquema Paget and Antoine Tornier said that the witches of Mouille held their Sabbat in the courtyard of the Priory of that place. So it will be seen that it is useless to consider too much of the place where witches hold their Sabbats and assemblies. For witches have no trouble in finding the place since Satan guides and conveys them to it. Yet I shall say that, according to Antoine Gandillon's statement, there must be water in that place; for when she was asked if she had been at la Georgiere, she answered that the Sabbat was not held there because there was no water. And I think that the reason for this is that, in order to cause it to hail, witches usually beat water with their wands; and, when there is no water, they make a hole in the ground and piss in it, and beat their piss.

CHAPTER XXI.

Of what Happens at the Sabbat, and of the Burning of Candles, the Kiss, the Dances, the Copulation of the Devil with Witches, the Feasts, the Accounts Rendered by Them to Him, the Beating of Water to produce Hail, the Mass which is said by Them, and how Satan Consumes Himself in Flames and Burns to Ashes.

THE fifth point in Françoise Secretain's confession is that she had danced at the Sabbat, and had beaten water to produce hail. I have no doubt that she did many other things, but witches never confess more than half of what they have done. But since I have learned from others nearly everything that is done at the Sabbat, I propose to set it down here in writing, since the occasion offers.

The witches, then, being assembled in their Synagogue, first worship Satan, who appears to them now in the shape of a big black man and now as a goat; and to do him the greater homage

Bodin, Demonom. II. 4.

they offer him candles, which burn with a blue flame; then they kiss him on the shameful parts behind. Some kiss him on the shoulder; and at other times he holds up a black image which he requires the witches to kiss, according to Antide Colas, who said that, on kissing it, they offered a candle or burning torch. Jeanne Platet and Clauda Paget said that the Devil gave them these candles, and that after they had offered them they did not know what became of them.

Caron, Antichrist, 1.

Remy, Demonol. I. 17.

Following this, they dance; and this they do in a ring back to back. Clauda Jamprost and Françoise Secretain have reported that the lame show more eagerness for these dances than do the others; for they said that the lame urged on the others to leap and dance. Now they dance in this manner back to back so that they may not be recognised; but in these days they make use of a different device for the same purpose, which is to mask themselves, according to the confessions of Clauda Paget, named la Foulet. There are also demons which join in these dances in the shape of goats or rams, as we learn from many witches besides those we have just mentioned; and particularly Antoine Tornier observed that, when she danced, a black ram held her up by the hands with his feet, which were, as she said, very hairy, that is to say, rough and rude.

They are not without pipes at these revels, for there are those whose duty it is to provide the dance music. Most often Satan plays upon the flute, and at other times the witches are content to sing with their voices; but they sing at haphazard and in such confusion that one cannot hear the other. Sometimes, but rarely, they dance in couples and at other times one here and another there, and always in confusion; for their dances are such as those of the fairies, which are truly devils in bodily form who had power no long time since.

After the dancing the witches begin to couple with each other; and in this matter the son does not spare his mother, nor the brother his sister, nor the father his daughter; but incest is commonly practised. The Persians also believed that, to be a competent and complete witch and magician, a person must be born of a mother by her son.

> Of son by mother is a witch conceived, *Catul. XC.*
> If the foul Persian creed may be believed.

I may safely leave to the imagination the question whether or not every other kind of lechery known to the world is practised at the Sabbat: what is even more remarkable is that Satan becomes an Incubus for the women and a Succubus for the men. This is a fact to which George and Antoine Gandillon have testified and, before them, Antoine Tornier, Jacquema Paget and several others.

These incests and lecheries bring to my mind the practices of the Euchites and Gnostics. They used to meet together on Good Friday evening with certain women, who were their sisters and aunts and cousins, and had carnal connexion with them. Nine months later, they again met at the same place and, taking the children that had been born of these incestuous couplings, they cut them about all over their bodies and collected their blood in phials, and afterwards burned the bodies. They then mixed the blood with ashes and made a sauce, with which they seasoned their food and drink.

After having abandoned themselves to such foul fleshly pleasures the witches fall to feasting and banqueting. In their banquets they have various kinds of meats, which differ according to the locality and the rank of those who are assembled. In our own district the table was covered with butter, cheese and flesh; Clauda Jamguillaume, Jacquema Paget and some others said that there was a great cauldron on the fire from which they all helped themselves to meat. Their drink is sometimes wine and sometimes water: Antoine Tornier said that she drank wine from a wooden cup, but the others mentioned nothing but water. But there is never any salt; for salt is a symbol of immortality, and is held in bitter abhorrence by the Devil. Moreover, God commanded that salt should be mingled with every sacrifice or oblation which is offered to Him; and therefore it is used in Baptism, which is a sovereign antidote against the power of the Devil. It may also be said that, since salt is symbolical of wisdom, God in His hidden purpose does not allow it to be used at the Sabbat, so that the witches may know that all that they do is sheer folly.

Levit. 2. *Mark* 9.

Some have written that in the same way they never use bread; but Christofle of the village of Aranthon has testified to the contrary, saying that she had eaten bread, meat and cheese at the Sabbat.

Remy, Demonol. I. 16.

But all witches are agreed that there is no taste at all in the dishes of which they eat at the Sabbat, and that the meat is nothing but horseflesh. And nearly all declare that when they leave the table they are as hungry as when they went to it. Antide Colas said that the food was cold; Clauda Vuillat, of the village of Mirebeau, that they ate nothing but wind at the Sabbat; Christofle of Aranthon that it seemed to her as if she had eaten nothing. All this shows how the Devil is always a deceiver, since he feeds his own people with wind instead of solid meat, as if they were chameleons. I have read that two Counts who were sorcerers followed his example, and treated their guests in such a way that they always came hungry away from their feasts; but Numa Pompilius and Pasetes had already acted in the same manner. But it must always be believed that, in most cases, those who eat at the Sabbat know very well what they are about.

Having finished the banquet, they render to Satan an account of what they have done since the last assembly; and those are the most welcome who have caused the death of the most persons and cattle, who have cast the most spells of illness, and spoiled the most fruit—in short, those who have done the most mischief and wickedness. Others, who have behaved rather more humanely, are hissed and derided by all, are set apart to one side, and are generally beaten and ill treated by their master; and from this arises the proverb that is common among them—"Do the worst you can, and the Devil will not know what to demand of you."

At this point Satan forms a league with his followers against Heaven, and plots the ruin of the human race. He makes these wretched creatures repeat their renunciation of God, Chrism and Baptism, and renew the solemn oath they have taken never to speak of God, the Virgin Mary, or the Saints except in the way of mockery and derision: he makes them abandon their share in Paradise and promise that they will, on the contrary, for ever hold to him as their sole master and be always faithful to him. He then urges them to do all the harm that they can, to afflict their neighbours with illnesses, to kill their cattle, and to avenge themselves upon their enemies, saying to them : "Avenge yourselves, or you shall die." Also he makes them promise to waste and spoil the fruits of the earth, and gives them a certain powder or ointment for that purpose—or so, at least, he persuades them to believe. Also he makes them take a solemn oath not to lay information against each other, and not to reveal anything that is done amongst them. This was part of the confession of Jacquema Paget, and the reason that she would say nothing against Antoine Tornier; and Judges should pay great attention to this point.

Remy, Demonol. I. 18.

Sixthly, the witches produce hail; but I shall explain later how this is done.

Sometimes, again, they say Mass at the Sabbat. But I cannot write without horror of the manner in which it is celebrated; for he who is to say the office is clothed in a black cope with no cross upon it, and after putting the water in the chalice he turns his back to the altar, and then elevates, in place of the Host, a round of turnip coloured black; and then all the witches cry aloud: "Master, help us." And to make Holy Water, the Devil pisses in a hole in the ground, and the worshippers are then sprinkled with his urine by the celebrant with a black asperge.

Raemond, Antichrist, c. 7. num. 5.

Finally, Satan takes the form of a goat, consumes himself in flames, and burns to ashes which the witches collect and secrete for use in the performance of their execrable and abominable designs.

Bodin, Demonom. II. 4.

Before ending this chapter I should like to point out how Satan in every way apes the living God. For to what purpose does he cause himself to be worshipped, if not to imitate Him? And are not his dances modelled upon those of the ancient Hebrews, who used to leap as a sign of eagerness whenever they offered anything to God or sang His praises? For thus did David when he played upon the harp before the Ark of the Old Testament. And further, may we not suppose that this cursed Serpent consumes and burns himself to ashes at the Sabbat in imitation of what Jesus Christ did at the Last Supper which He prepared for His disciples, when He gave them His body to eat and His blood to drink? I pass over the abominable sacrifice which they make; for the hair stands up on my head when I think of it. And indeed I should not have mentioned this matter at all were it not that I hold that we can draw from it a strong argument to uphold the reality of the body and blood of Jesus Christ at the Holy Sacrament of the Altar; for if we were in error concerning this, the Devil would never have troubled to bring pollution upon the Mass, but would have allowed us to slip further and further into a perpetual idolatry. He acts in the same way with regard to the Holy Relics which we venerate and adore; for in mockery of them he causes his disciples to kiss his most shameful parts.

Matth. 4. *Can. nec mirum*, 26. *q.* 5.

II Sam. 6.

Matth. 26. *Luke* 22. *Mark* 14.

But, that we may not wander from our subject, let us now consider whether witches can produce hail.

CHAPTER XXII.

Whether Witches can Produce Hail.

JACQUES Bocquet, Françoise Secretain, Clauda Jamguillaume, Clauda Jamprost, Thievenne Paget, Antoine Tornier, Pierre Gandillon, George Gandillon, Antoine Gandillon, Christofle of the village of Aranthon, and several others have confessed that they produced hail at the Sabbat for the purpose of ruining the fruits of the earth. To do this they beat water with a wand, as they said, and then threw into the air or into the water a certain powder which Satan had given them, and this caused a cloud to arise which afterwards turned to hail and fell on the land according to the witches' wish. So we may conclude that such persons do produce hail. This conclusion is substantiated by what we read of a certain Haakon, Prince of Norway, who fought his enemies with hailstones: of the Brachmanes, who could cause the weather to be either fair or rainy: of one Julian, who caused it to rain and brought relief to Mark Antony's Roman army suffering from thirst: of certain priest sorcerers who did the like for the French when they were beseiged by the Spanish in a town in the Kingdom of Naples: of a King Henry of Sweden and Finland who had control of the winds, so that the Finns used to sell them to merchants. And there was also that pirate of the seas, Oddo, who passed over the water without any ship, and destroyed and sank his enemies'

Vair, de Incant. II. 14.

Remy, Demonol. III. 12.

Bodin, Demonom. II. 8.

Olaus, III. 4.

ships beneath the waves by means of the storms which he raised with his charms and witchcraft. I pass by the report that was spread to the effect that the Norse Princes of Denmark, Sweden and Norway sent to Queen Elizabeth of England two sorcerers who by their magic arts caused squalls to arise which, in the year 1588, scattered in one moment that great Spanish Armada the like of which had never been seen before.

Florimond de Raemond, Antichrist, c. 26.

The Romans also had certain priests who were charged with the raising and allaying of thunder and lightning; and their laws on this matter are to be found among those of the Twelve Tablets. Now I have no doubt that Satan can produce hail; yet there are those who maintain that, when the Devil foresees the approach of a storm, he deceives witches into the belief that it is they who cause it; while others have written that Satan keeps hail clouds in certain caverns which are, as it were, his magazines, and that he brings them thence when he is invoked by his disciples. But granting that this last be true, as I well believe it may be, it does not therefore follow that all hailstorms are caused by Satan. For hail is caused naturally by a mingling of vapours and exhalations raised into the middle region of the air. But these matters, like all other natural phenomena, are at Satan's commandment. This we fully learn from the Book of Job, where it is said that when the Devil had received from God power to afflict and injure Job, the lightning fell at once from Heaven and struck his flocks, the winds immediately arose and smote down his houses and overwhelmed his sons; in short, the Heavens so rose against him by Satan's contrivance that in one moment he lost

Bodin, Demonom. II. 2.

Paracel. de Malefic. c. 4.

all his wealth, although he was the richest man in the East.

Exod. 8.

It will not be inappropriate to quote here in confirmation of our contention the frogs and serpents of Pharaoh's magicians; for there is no doubt that those animals were created by an apt application of active to passive principles; this being the opinion of St. Thomas, which is based on logical argument, since it is a fact that frogs are generated by corruption, and there is no reason why a rotten rod or wand should not be turned into a serpent; for certain naturalists have observed that the same result comes from a woman's hair hidden in a dung-heap.

Vair, de Incant. II. 12.

There need be no difficulty in the fact that these matters of which we have spoken were done in an instant, for Satan and the demons perform all their actions with such speed that they seem miraculous. And when it is considered that Nature can be assisted and helped forward by Art, it will not seem strange that Satan can accomplish in a moment that which naturally involves the passage of a considerable time; for it must be remembered that the Alchemists also, if we may believe them, can by a turn of the hand create gold, although in the process of Nature this takes a thousand years.

Again, it is easy to understand that the hail falls just where the witches wish; for Satan's power in the air is so great that he can dispose the cloud just where he wishes. Nevertheless, God does not always permit this to happen, as I know from the testimony of Rollande du Vernois, Françoise Secretain and other witches, who said that they had often wished it to hail upon the fruits of certain villages, but that the hail had fallen upon rocks and high mountains without doing any damage.

Some witches also are poor, and have no wish for hail, through fear that it may cause a famine and that they will die; and therefore they contend at the Sabbat with those who are rich. There was one burned in this country who witnessed to the truth of this, saying that when the rich wished to cause hail and the poor opposed them, they had to throw dice to see which party should prevail. Antide Colas of Betoncourt also confessed that the poor are often at difference with the rich at the Sabbat over the question of destroying the crops; and she said that on one occasion the poor had defeated the rich in the Valley of Saint Marie, where the Devil, in the shape of a big black man, made them dance round a sheaf of corn turned upside down with the ears towards the ground.

But I have often marvelled at one thing which Satan does to witches when they assemble to produce hail :—he requires them to give him of their hair. I do not know whether he may be amorous of women's hair; but I may say that there are Theologians who have maintained that the bad angels are amorous of women's hair, and *Paracel. de Malefic. c. 7.* the Suffragan of Trèves even says that the Incubus devils attach themselves chiefly to women *Binsfeld, de confess. malef. conclus. 5.* who have beautiful hair; and it is contended that St. Paul had this in mind when he wrote to the Corinthians that woman should go with her head *I Cor. 11.* covered because of the Angels.

Yet I prefer to believe that witches give their hair to Satan as pledges of their contract with him. But the Evil One does not waste this hair; for he cuts it up small and mingles it with the exhalations from which he forms hail; and therefore it is that we ordinarily find little hairs in this hail. It may also be that the Devil uses these hairs to weave the spells and charms which we see cast upon those who are possessed.

Furthermore, it appears from what we have said in this chapter that neither the beating of water nor the powder which they throw in is of any avail to witches in producing hail; for it is rather probable that all this is only a symbol of their pact with Satan. Yet it might be possible for this powder to possess some virtue or property by which it could raise up storms. For we know by experiment that saltpetre mixed with alum engenders clouds and causes thunder and lightning in the air; and Democritus said that if you took the head and gullet of the Sancus, a fish that is found in Egypt, and burned them with oak wood, or if you roasted its liver on a red tile, it caused it to thunder and rain.

Paracel. de Malefic. c. 5. Mattioli on Dioscor. I. 60.

Chapter XXIII.

Of the Powder Used by Witches.

THE sixth and seventh points of Françoise Secretain's confession were that she had caused the death of Loys Monneret and of several cows; and this brings me to speak of the calamities occasioned by witches. For they afflict persons, cattle and the fruits of the earth; but since the means they use for such purposes are innumerable and for the most part unknown, I shall confine myself to treating of the more obvious of them.

And first there is the powder which they use. This is sometimes black, sometimes white or of an ashen colour, and sometimes of some other colour. They use it when they produce hail, as we saw in the last chapter; and they also use it against persons or cattle, to kill them or make them ill. When Jacques Bocquet and Françoise Secretain wished to kill Loys Monneret they made her eat a crust of bread dusted with a white powder which their master had given them. When Thievenne Paget wanted to be revenged on Claude Roy she mixed the powder in a cheese which she made him eat, and he died immediately afterwards. Michel Udon and Pierre Burgot confessed that their masters, who were named Moyset and Guillemin, gave them an ashen powder with which they rubbed their left arms and hands, and that by this means they killed every animal that they touched.

There are others who bury some of this powder under the threshold of a door or in some other place, and those who pass over that spot are taken ill. This is what Groz-Jacques did to a man of Mi-joux, of whom we shall speak later. Some have thought that the powder thus given to witches is veritable poison, and others have not held this opinion. But my own belief is that both these opinions may be right. For since the Devil has knowledge of the properties of every herb, it is easy for him to compound a poison and give it to his disciples to cause, by this means, the death or illness of a person or beast. And it is likely that the bread which Loys Monneret ate was poisoned. On the other hand, I believe that the powder in the cheese which Claude Roy ate was not poison; for several persons ate of the same cheese, but none was ill except Claude: moreover, when Thievenne Paget was questioned on this matter, she said that she had been quite certain that the cheese would harm no one except Claude Roy, since it was her intention to kill him only. In such a case, then, it is Satan who secretly procures death or illness; and this he does by invisibly mingling some venomous juice with the food of those whom the witch wishes to injure.

I shall quote two examples to make this more evident. When Jacques Bocquet was beaten by the man of Mi-joux and proposed to revenge himself for the wrong which he thought had been done him, he put some powder under the threshold of a shed where the man kept seven calves, five of which belonged to him, and the other two to one of his neighbours. The seven calves, on returning from the fields, passed over the threshold, and the five which belonged to the man died at once, while the other two remained healthy and unharmed.

Early one morning Antoine Tornier threw some powder into the fountain of Orcieres, wishing by this means to kill the cattle of Big Claude Fontaine; and she commanded her son Antoine David not to water his cattle before those of Big Claude had drunk. Her son, forgetting what his mother had said, or not thinking about the spell she had cast, watered his cattle first, became blind after a few days and remained so till his death; while neither Big Claude's cattle nor those of others which drank at the fountain after Antoine

David took the least hurt. Now if the powder which Antoine Tornier threw into the fountain of Orcieres had been poison, there is no doubt that all the cattle which drank there would have died at once. Similarly it is certain that all seven of the calves which the man of Mi-joux kept in his shed would have died if the powder which Groz-Jacques buried under the threshold had been poisonous. But we should further consider that it was impossible for this last powder, being buried as we have said, to have the power to penetrate through the earth and reach the animals so as to harm them.

Chapter XXIV.

Of the Unguents and Ointments Used by Witches.

There are unguents and ointments which witches make, if they have not already been given to them by Satan; and of these there are several kinds. An Italian author, in his *Porta, II. 26.* "Natural Magic," has described the composition of some of them; but these ointments are for the most part made of the fat of little children whom the Devil has instigated witches to murder. The witches anoint themselves with it when they go to the Sabbat, or when they change themselves into wolves; but I do not see that these ointments can have any other effect in such cases than to deaden and stupefy the witches' senses so that Satan may the more easily have his *Dan. Dialog. 4.* will of them. At other times also the Evil Spirit

mixes with it some ingredient which causes deep
Dioscor. V. 115. sleep, such as mandragora or the Memphite stone and such things, as it happened to the old women of whom Giovanni Battista Porta speaks,
c. 26. who after being rubbed with a certain ointment
De subtil. lib. 18. fell to the earth as dead. Cardan adds that the ointment made from little children first sends these old hags to sleep, and afterwards makes them dream marvellous dreams.

This fat also helped François Gaillard of Longchamois to escape from prison, when we had him in custody in the year 1600 for the murder of a German stranger. Claude Coirieres was a prisoner for witchcraft at the same time, and had a grease with which she rubbed François Gaillard's hands; whereupon the latter at once went out by a window and jumped on to a rod stretched along the windows, on which it was impossible to set foot except by the help of the devilish arts; from there he climbed on to the roof and, after having climbed down, fled to the château of Esprel, two leagues from Saint Claude, where he was retaken. But he has since confessed that as he was fleeing he went at a quite incredible speed, and that on escaping from the prison he seemed to be without any feeling; and he added that he had never felt the least tired until, to be rid of the grease with which his hands were anointed, he washed them in the snow which was plentiful at that time.

I am well aware that many will find this matter strange for several reasons, but chiefly because it is thought that Satan has no power over those who are cast into prison. But let them read what I have set down in Chapter 46, and then they will easily be persuaded of the contrary.

Another use to which witches put the grease of which we are speaking is to cause the death, or at least the illness, of men and beasts. Christofle of the village of Aranthon confessed that Groz-Jacques and Françoise Secretain made her rub a certain ointment on the hinder parts of a cow, and that the cow died the next day. And we read that in the year 1536 there were at Casale, a town in the Marquisate of Saluzzo, forty men and women who smeared the door latches with some ointment, as a result of which several people died. A rumour has reached us here that the same thing happened a year ago at Geneva; and this is no new experience to those of that city, for they suffered in the same way in the year 1536, when the ointment with which the doors were smeared caused so great a plague in the city that the greater part of the inhabitants died of it. But we need not go so far afield, for let us take what happened in this town of Saint Claude in the year 1564. There was a man of Orgelet, whom I shall not name, who put the plague in twenty-five houses by cunningly smearing with a grease, which he carried in a box, some spoons which belonged to the masters of the houses; but in another box he carried an antidote which he used every morning to protect and guard himself against the evil which he brought to others. He was executed for it at Annecy, where he confessed, among other things, what I have just said, and especially repented of having caused the death of the mistress of his own house. I have the story from the Sieur Millet, who was then Syndic and Magistrate at Saint Claude and witnessed his trial. There can, then, be no doubt that such ointments are actual poison.

Vair, de Incant. II. 5.

Bodin, Demonom. IV. 4.

But in connexion with the statement we have just made, that witches sometimes cause the plague by means of their ointments, I shall add that they most usually poison and infect the air and the water. We have seen how Antoine Tornier meant to poison the fountain of Orcieres so as *Riol. ad Fernel. de abdit. rer. caus. II. 12.* to kill Big Claude Fontaine and his cattle. The great plague described by Thucydides, which so miserably afflicted Greece, was caused, according to Aratus, by the Peloponnesians poisoning several *Fulgos. IX. 11.* wells in the district of the Piraeus. And when the son of Philip the Fair was reigning in France there were several lepers in the countries of Languedoc and Dauphine, who surreptitiously bathed in the springs and so infected them that in a short time all the people of those countries were stained with the same disease; and therefore those first lepers were burned alive.

IV. 18. And as for the air, Nicephorus Calixtus recounts that the Persian magicians, in order to bring our religion into bad repute, caused an evil and disgusting stench to emanate from the *de Divinat.* place where Christians were. And St. Augustine says: "Sorcerers have the power to transmit diseases, and to corrupt and infect the air."

In either case it is easy for them to achieve their object. For what can be easier than to poison the water supply? And if the air is sometimes corrupted by the odour from a dung-heap so as to cause a plague throughout a whole district, why should we not believe that witches can infect it by the heavy and loathsome stenches which they draw from a poison that they know how to compose with the help of their master? We read, in fact, that after the soldiers of Marcus Avidius Cassius, Mark Antony's lieutenant, had opened a chest found in the temple of Apollo at Selancia, a town of Babylon, the air which came from it was so poisonous that it wasted the whole country with the pestilence; and being brought from there to Greece, and from Greece to Rome, it provoked such a plague that almost a third of the human race died of it. *Card. de subtil. lib. 2.*

While I am treating of this subject, I wish to set down the strange story of one of the so-called Reformed Religion, who was executed at Nyon not fifteen months ago. This man was returning from Berne in a state of despair because his only brother had caused him to lose the greater part of his goods in a lawsuit. The Devil appeared to him in the shape of a big black man, and said to him that, if he would give himself to him, he would cause him not only to recover his goods, but also to gain possession of all his brother's goods, and told him how to proceed so as to secure such a result. "Here is a box," he said, "in which there is some grease. Take it, and go to your brother, and beg him to settle matters with you in return for a sum of money. Invite him to dinner, and mix some of this grease in his broth, and you will see him die in a few days. As he has two sons, you will be appointed their guardian. You will send the older to school, and keep the younger in your house and in like manner make him eat of this grease, and he will die like his father. Then you will bring back the elder son and do to him as you did the younger; and so you will be left master of all their goods as well as of your own, for they will leave no nearer kin than yourself to succeed them." The poor man, hearing this speech and knowing that he who spoke to him was the Devil (for he had so declared himself), refused to take the box or to give himself to him. The Devil pressed him, and said to him for the last time: "See, here is the box. When you have done what I have told you, you will dedicate yourself to me." And he placed the box on a stone and disappeared. The poor man was for a long time troubled in spirit, but in the end he took the box, and then followed Satan's advice so well that in less than a year he caused the death of his brother and his two nephews, and so succeeded to all their property. But he did not long enjoy his wealth, for Satan played him a trick after his own heart. He at once began to urge him to dedicate himself to him; and as the man had no wish to do so, he so tormented and beat him that his cries reached the ears of his neighbours, and then those of the Judge. He was then seized and, after he had confessed, was executed. This story teaches us among other things how the Devil provides his disciples with greases and ointments to cause the death of people. This was also confessed by Jeanne Platet, otherwise known as la Berche; for she said that, in order to kill persons and beasts, she touched them with her hand, which she had previously anointed with a grease given her by her master. And why should we not give credit to this, seeing that the Barbarians of old used to poison their arrows with toxicum and the Napellus, as we may read in the work of Pietro Andrea Mattioli.

CHAPTER XXV.

Whether Witches Kill by their Blowings and their Breaths.

THIRDLY, witches cause death and affliction by their blowings and their breath; and Claudа Gaillard, called la Fribolette, will serve as witness to the truth of this. For meeting Clauda Perrier in the church of Ebouchoux, she breathed upon her, and the woman was at once stricken with an illness and was made impotent and died after having lingered for a year in poverty and weakness. And again, because Marie Perrier had once refused her alms, she blew strongly upon her so that Marie fell to the earth and, being with difficulty raised up, was ill for some days, until her nephew Pierre Perrier threatened the witch. Sprenger also recounts that a witch of the diocese of Constance breathed upon a man and so afflicted him with leprosy all over his body that he died soon after : he has many other examples of this sort of thing, to which the reader may refer. Now there are some who think that, when witches do this sort of offence, they have in their mouth some evil drug or root by the strength and reek of which they cast the spell. And in my opinion this is possible, and I do not think it needful to linger over Bodin's argument that the witches would, in that case, be the first to die; for they have the antidote and countercharm to protect them

Mall. Malefic. II. I. *c.* II.

Dan. Point 4.

against their drugs and poisons, as was the case with Mithridates, who, because of the precautionary drugs which he had before taken, could not find any poison that would kill him; and the King Nicomedes also used an antidote whenever he went to any place where he suspected poison;
VI. 5. and this countercharm has been described by Mattioli in his notes upon Dioscorides.

And certainly it is necessary that they who compound the poisons should have drugs to protect themselves from them. Here I may recount what Nicolas Nicole says of a certain Duke who knew the use of a poison so subtle that, if it were thrown on burning coals, the smoke of it would kill all who were in the room except himself, who was protected by a certain antidote which he took beforehand. And we spoke in the last chapter of a man of Orgelet who carried two boxes, one filled with an ointment with which he spread the plague, the other of an antidote which he used every morning to safeguard himself against the malady: this story serves as a corroboration of my contention.

Nevertheless I hold that in most cases witches have no drug or herbs in their mouths, but that Satan alone causes the death or sickness in the secret manner which we have before described.

CHAPTER XXVI.

Whether Witches Afflict with Words.

FOURTHLY, witches cause harm and mischief by their words. A Jew named Zambares by uttering certain words made a bull fall stark dead at the feet of St. Sylvester in the time of Constantine the Great. Nider tells that he saw a witch who, by pronouncing a single word, caused people to die suddenly; and he tells also that he likewise saw another who, with one word made her neighbour's chin turn upside down. When Françoise Secretain wished to kill certain beasts, she struck them with a wand, saying these words: "I touch thee to kill thee," etc. I have seen many other witches who did likewise. Moreover, we find in Homer that Circe changed the companions of Ulysses into swine by the power of words.

Raemond, Antichrist, 26. 6.

Circe did with her chants accursed and strange
The wretched comrades of Ulysses change.

And Aristophanes writes that the witches of Thessaly performed marvellous things by their words:

Vile witches can with magic utterance
Free wretched souls of all the ills that chance;
Or charm the remnants of their wits away
From those who dote on loving all the day;
Or stay a river in its onward flowing
So as to set its waters backward going.

I. 7. And Ovid, in his "Amores":

Charms change corn to grass and make it die:
By charms are running springs and fountains dry.
By charms mast falls from oaks, from vines grapes fall,
And fruit from trees when there's no wind at all.
Why might not then my sinews be enchanted,
And I grow faint as with some spirit haunted?

And Vergil says:

Poisonous snakes burst at a witch's chant.

And Lucan:

With no more venom than a magic song
They turn man's sounder judgment out headlong.

Touching this matter the Romans made a law: "That he who hath bewitched the fruits of the earth shall be punished; and that it shall not be lawful for any person soever to remove the corn from one man's field to another by enchantment." We know the verses which make it impossible to churn butter; and for those who
Ecl. VIII. 77 "tie the points"(causing sexual impotence and frigidity) Vergil says:

Three strands of divers colours, in three knots
Knot them; and say: "Here bind I Venus' fetters."

Nec mirum. 8. Magi. 26. q. 5. The Canon also allows that witches can cause injury by their mere words.

But how are we to account for the fact that even when they praise and compliment you, they injure you? Yet this is no new thing; for there were formerly in Africa and Italy certain families which, by praising people, caused them to die, thereby proving themselves altogether devilish. Yet other strange matters do they accomplish by their uttered spells. To go to the Sabbat, they place a staff between their legs and say these words: *White staff, black staff*, etc. The Ephesians, by means of certain magic words which they used, brought all their undertakings to a successful issue. Pythagoras enchanted the eagle with his words. It was by the force of her words that Medea seized the moon from the sky and brought it down to the earth. The great magician Mahomet did likewise, and put the moon in his sleeve: at least he himself wrote that he did so. *El-phurkan.*

Yet, in spite of all this, who will believe that mere words have the power to hurt? For my part I am of opinion that they are no more than a symbol of the pact between the witch and Satan; for it is certain that words have no other purpose than to denote the thing for which they were ordained and to express the passions of the soul and the affections of the spirit. Besides, if words had the power to kill, they would do so when uttered by anyone who was not a witch. And again, of what possible effect could be the strange unknown words used by witches: such as *Gaber siloc fandu*, which they say when they wish to prevent a chicken, whose head has been pierced with a knife, from dying? Or *Malaton malatas dinor*, which they use to prevent one from shooting with an arquebus? There are countless others which I purposely omit. I have the same opinion of the numbers and characters which have been only too curiously quoted by certain authors, even by Paracelsus in his Celestial Medicine, who, as well as Pico, Prince of Mirandola, is to be censured for saying that barbaric and meaningless words have more magic power than those which are understood. For in such cases it is Satan who secretly causes death or casts the evil spell. And if we find it written that Medea and Mahomet brought the moon down from the sky, we must not take this for the truth; but rather we should think that these witches cast a glamour over peoples' eyes and made them see what was not. For Satan and his witches are wont to act in this way, as we have remarked in another place.

Chapter XXVII.

Whether Witches Afflict with Looking.

FIFTHLY, witches cause injury by their looking.
l. 2. Sprenger observes that little children are
ll. 1. *c.* 12. more liable to be hurt in this way than are grown people; and he adds further that witches, by merely looking at them, can corrupt and soften the hearts of their judges. Cattle also are subject to this evil:

Verg. Eclog. Some evil eye has witched my lambs.

It is so also with the crops and trees. And this should not seem strange, seeing that there were formerly families in Africa which caused death by their looking. And we read the same of certain tribes about Pontus, Scythia, Transylvania, and Muscovy. Again, Philostratus in his life of Apollonius mentions a certain Saturnius of Ephesus who, by his mere looking, killed all those at whom he looked. Further, we read that the witch Eriphile looked at a beast, and that soon afterwards some evil came to the beast. And the proverb which the Italians keep to this day, *Di gratia non gli diate mal d'ochio*, shows that the same practice was rife in Italy. Similarly there are animals which kill by their looking, such as the Basilisk, and the serpent Catoblepas which lives about the spring Nigris in Ethiopia, which many believe to be the source of the Nile. There are other animals which, by looking at a man, take away his speech: such as the wolf.

Vair, de Incant. II. 9. *Wier, de praestig. II.* 49.

Moeris was first beheld by wolves.

Verg. Eclog.

Notwithstanding this, I have never believed that witches had the power to cause injury by their looking. For whence should such power come to them? Either it must be born with them, or it must be acquired by art. Now the former alternative is impossible; for it cannot be that God, who created man to be a civilised animal, would have endowed him with a deadly power to kill those with whom he consorted. I could almost brand such a belief as a detestable impiety, seeing how strictly the Law of God punishes a murderer. Also it should be considered that, if witches were born with this power of killing, all indifferently at whom they looked would die; but this is not the case.

And if this power is acquired by art, I should like to be shown of what nature it is in witches; whether it consists in some poison emanating from them, or whether it is due to something else. But how would they not themselves be hurt by the poison which they emanated? Or how comes it that the force of the poison dwells in their eyes only, and that it hurts only the enemies of the witches, and not all sorts of people indifferently? Nothing is more certain than that, in such cases, it is Satan who kills or causes injury.

And if there have been families in Africa and Italy and Scythia and elsewhere which claimed to be able to kill by their looking, who can doubt that such people were witches and that Satan performed the murders which they wished to commit? We should think the same of the shepherd who bewitched the lambs in Vergil, and of those who injure the crops and the trees by looking at them.

Touching their effect on a Judge, I may well believe that a witch can, by looking at him, soften his heart by causing him to feel pity and compassion for her misery. For since the eyes are the messengers of the soul, they tell the Judge the inner torments and perplexity which the witch suffers. But I cannot be persuaded that a Judge can be corrupted by this means, for the eyes have no power to bribe. And of this I am the more assured, since it has been proved that a witch can in no way injure the Officers of Justice; for Justice comes directly from God, and can by no means be confounded.

Passing to the matter of the Basilisk and the serpent Catoblepas, I shall say that the most learned scholars hold what has been written of them to be a fable. And Mattioli has asked how it has been possible to examine these serpents

without dying, seeing that they are very small, *Vair, de*
and that Catoblepas stands with half its body *Incant. II.* 9.
upright the better to infect the air and those who *Dioscor. VI.* 55.
look at it from near by? For this purpose it would be necessary to have the power to charm them, as did the witch of the town of Thene in Thessaly whom Aristotle mentions.

And even if that which is reported of these animals were true, we should have no warrant to draw a parallel between them and mankind. The Basilisk and the Catoblepas were born with such poison as to be able to kill with their looking, just as we know that serpents kill with their teeth, and scorpions with their tails. They are animals which God has placed in the world to punish men, for He avenges Himself in countless ways. But man is not born in the same manner. And as for wolves, there are those who
flatly deny what has been said of them; and in *Scal. Riola*
any case we should hold the same opinion of *ad Fernel. II.*
them as of the Basilisk, the Catoblepas, the *17. de abdit. rer. caus.*
Scorpion and the Serpent. Yet I shall always rather believe that the fright which a man experiences on suddenly seeing a wolf freezes his limbs and nerves so that his voice becomes a
hoarse whisper. Cardan says that there is some- *De subtil. lib.*
thing inimical to man in the eyes of a wolf, which 18.
prevents his breathing, and therefore his speech.

CHAPTER XXVIII.

How Witches Afflict with the Hand.

SIXTHLY, witches cause hurt and injury by a touch of the hand. I have seen a witch cast an evil spell upon a man by pulling him three times by his coat. Another time, on passing a herd of cattle, she struck a calf on the flank with her hand and the calf died a few days later; and when they came to skin it they had great difficulty in separating the hide from the flesh at the place where it had been touched, and also they found the imprint of a hand marked upon the same place.

Jeanne Platet confessed that, in order to cause the death of persons or cattle, she used to rub her hands with an ointment given her by the Devil. Similarly Michel Udon and Pierre Burgot confessed that they rubbed their left arms and hands with a certain powdered ash, and that when they then touched an animal they caused it to die. Moreover, the Inquisitors have written that if a Judge lets himself be touched on the bare arm and hand by the witch, he thereby becomes her advocate.

But whatever may be said, I do not believe that the witch can cause injury simply by her hand; but that if he who has been touched becomes ill, it is undoubtedly Satan who strikes the blow. And when a witch anoints his hand, it may still be that Satan plays his part in the work: or else the ointment may be veritable poison which on being applied to the skin penetrates it and passes into the inner parts of the person or beast, which is thus killed or made ill by the witch. For doctors write that poisons and venom need not necessarily be taken through the mouth, but can be applied externally; and this can be seen any day in the foam of a rabid dog, for if it falls upon a wound or any place from which the skin has been rubbed off, it generally causes death. The herb Scilla is similarly injurious when rubbed against the skin: and if a man hold Cantharides in his hand it constrains him to piss blood.

Wier, de praestig. III. 27.

Card. de Subtilit. lib. 2.

The difficulty lies in the question whether the witch can protect himself from the poison of the ointment with which he anoints himself But if the reader will refer to Chapter 25 he will find that this may easily be done. Similarly, in Chapters 27 and 37 he will find the answer to what I have said concerning Officers of Justice.

Chapter XXIX.

How Witches Afflict with a Wand.

Seventhly, witches cause injury by striking with a wand. Françoise Secretain and Thievenne Paget confessed that they had killed several animals, both cows and horses, by striking them with a wand and uttering certain words. Cardan also tells that he saw at Pavia a witch who caused a child to die by gently touching its back with a rod. But it seems to me that there is no difference between this touching with a wand and the touch with the hand of which we have just spoken.

CHAPTER XXX.

Of the Images Used by Witches.

l. multi de malefic. C. & ibi Binsfeld., Grilland, de Sortileg. q. 5. *num.* 9.

FURTHERMORE, witches make use of certain waxen images, which they melt and pierce, and so cause their enemies to pine away even as the images waste away. And this agrees with what has been written of Meleager, who was burned commensurately with the burning of the fatal brand by the witch Althea. And we have Ovid as our authority that Medea used this practice.

Amor. III. 6.
Boet. lib. 11.

The waxen likeness of her absent foes
She pierced and injured with a hundred blows.

Wier, de praestig. IV. 9.

And again:

Images of wax with magic art
She made, and killed them, piercing to the heart.

Duffus, King of Scotland, was in this manner afflicted for a long time, until the witches who were melting his image were found in the town of Forres in Moravia. It is believed that Charles IX of France, in whose reign the slaying of Huguenots on St. Bartholomew took place, died through the means of such an image. Many similar stories are told. One witch will even harm another by means of a certain image made from molten lead, as is often found in Germany, as I have remarked elsewhere. They make images, too, so as to hang their companions by the hair. There are other images made in order to gain the love of a woman. Most of these images are mentioned by Plato in the eleventh book of his "Laws." Our own witches for the most part have their images baptised. But who will doubt that it is Satan alone who works in these cases? for it is not possible for a witch, by means of his images, to kill a man who is two hundred leagues distant from him. *Bodin, Demonom. II. 8.*

Similarly it is Satan who operated in the case of the execrable witch who on Good Friday pierced the Crucifix with his arrows, and was thus enabled to kill every day three men, provided that he had seen and recognised them. Later we shall see that these wretches generally use images when they wish to perform an act of healing.

The thing would be easier to believe if they sent some gift; for if the gift were poisoned it could injure its recipient, as did the shirt which Medea sent to Jason's new wife, Creusa: for as soon as Creusa had put on this shirt her body began to burn all over so that she died. Hercules burned in the same manner. I have in our prison a woman charged with almost the same thing: for she gave a neighbouring woman a shirt as a gift, and as soon as the woman put it on she began to feel ill.

CHAPTER XXXI.

How Midwives, if they are Witches, Kill the Children they Deliver.

Bodin, Demonom. IV. 6.

IN the ninth place, those midwives and wise women who are witches are in the habit of offering to Satan the little children which they deliver, and then of killing them, before they have been baptised, by thrusting a large pin into their brains. There have been those who have confessed to having killed more than forty children in this way.

Sprenger, II. I. 13.

They do even worse; for they kill them while they are yet in their mothers' wombs. This practice is common to all witches, as we find in Nider, who writes that one named Stadlin in the Diocese of Lausanne confessed that he had killed seven children in their mothers' womb by means of an animal which he had buried under the threshold of the house. Parent witches do not spare even their own children; for we read of a Baron of Rays who, after having confessed to the murder of eight children, added that he wished to kill in its mother's womb the ninth, which was his own son, and to sacrifice it to the Devil.

Bodin, Demonom. II. 5.

I do not doubt that this is done at the suggestion of the Devil; for he generally demands their children from parents who are witches, as he did from Groz-Jacques, from whom he demanded one of his daughters. Pierre Vuillermoz also deposed that, when he was only eight years old, his father Guillaume Vuillermoz took him to the Sabbat. Claude and Clauda Charloz and Perrenette Molard likewise said that when they were very young they were taken to the Sabbat by Clauda Gindre, their maternal grandmother. It is probable that these children had been dedicated to Satan by Guillaume Vuillermoz and Clauda Gindre; yet it is true that they have not been convicted of any act of witchcraft.

Here I cannot refrain from reprimanding parents who, through waiting for suitable godparents, leave their children so long unbaptised. For it is evident from what I have said in what danger these children are until they have received this Holy Sacrament; seeing that, if through the ministry of a witch they die before baptism, they are eternally deprived of the sight and glory of God, which is the greatest joy with which the souls of the blessed are rewarded.

Finally, witches change themselves into wolves, and in this shape kill and eat both men and beasts. But of this I shall more fittingly speak elsewhere.

Chapter XXXII.

By what Ills Witches Particularly Afflict People.

Let us now examine by what ills witches afflict mankind particularly. I maintain that they afflict people with all kinds of ills of the stomach and the head and the feet, with cholic,

Dan. the 3rd point.

paralysis, apoplexy, leprosy, epilepsy, dropsy, strangury, etc. And this they do easily with the help of Satan, who secretly causes persons to swallow certain poisons and drugs; or perhaps the witches themselves mix them with their food and drink. And according to the composition of the poison it will spread over the whole body or attack only one member; for, says Cardan, there are poisons which do not cause death, but continually attack one of the victims' members. Again, according to Theophrastus, the poison may take two, three, or six months to prepare, and the illness of him who is bewitched will continue for a longer or shorter time according to the time taken to collect the ingredients of the drug. Witches very frequently dry up the milk of nurses, apparently by making them swallow a certain powder which they throw in their broth, unless it is Satan himself who plays this trick. Jannette Gresson, wife of Jean Liegeard des Granges, who was burned at Dôle some thirty years ago, in this way deprived of her milk, although it was very abundant, Clauda, the widow of the late Etienne Goguel, and Nicole Clauderey of Mossans.

Sprenger, II. I. I.

de Subtil.

Mattioli. Pref. to Book 6 of Diosc.

Dan. ibid.

Bodin, Demonom. IV. 5.

They also cause a man's virile member to disappear and be concealed, and then to reappear at their own pleasure. This is widely practised in Germany.

At times also they prevent carnal copulation between a man and a woman by relaxing the nerves and depriving the member of rigidity: at other times they prevent procreation by turning aside or blocking up the seminal ducts so that the semen does not reach the generative cells. And they hold a married couple thus bound for as long as it

Wier, de Praestig. III. 18.

Sprenger, II. I. 7.

Can. Si per sortilegias, 33. q. 8.

pleases them, sowing ten thousand other seeds of discord between them besides. And this binding spell of impotence is no new thing; for St. Augustine and the Canons speak of it, and, before them, Vergil:

Three strands of divers colours, in three knots *Eclog.* 8.
Knot them; and say: "Here bind I Venus' fetters."

And Ovid:

Is not my body languishing with poison? *Amor. III.* 7.

And elsewhere:

Why might not then my sinews be enchanted,
And I grow faint as with some spirit haunted?

This practice is to-day more common than ever. For even children meddle with charms for tying the points—a thing which deserves exemplary punishment; for, rightly understood, such charms are of no avail, since it is Satan who is working in such a case, relying merely upon the witch's consent.

Furthermore, witches cause him whom they have bewitched to void, sometimes from the mouth and sometimes from the bottom parts, needles, hairs, iron tools, stones and papers. There are several examples of this; for I myself have seen an infinite number of such articles, among other things stones and balls and locks of hair and pigs' bristles. But I will content myself with a single example which I have from a gentleman of this country who may be believed. Some time ago one of his sons, a boy of fifteen or sixteen, voided by the penis five or six paper notes and some peas. The notes were covered with strange characters and the peas were wrapped in hair. The boy told his father that his schoolmaster was in the habit of stretching himself upon his body, placing his mouth on the boy's mouth, which he made him open, and muttering into it I know not what words. It appears from this that the pupil had been bewitched by his master.

Wier, de praestig. III. 5.
Grilland, de Sortileg. q. 3. num. 28.
De Variet. XV. 80.

Nevertheless the more curious will be in some perplexity as to whether these matters are imaginary or not. For some have maintained that they are not natural articles which appear in such shapes; while others have said that Satan brings these things from elsewhere. Cardan writes that all this is a mere glamour and illusion. Yet I would have it known that the peas and the notes of which we have spoken are still in existence, although it is eight years since the thing happened; and this serves to refute the dictum of Paul Grilland, who holds that the matters which come from the bodies of those who are bewitched melt and dissolve in a short time.

Mattioli, Dioscor. lib. 5 (Prefa.).

I will go further, and say that I believe that these matters most often do really proceed from the bodies of the bewitched, even if they are stones, balls of hair, or other such things. For if it is true that stones and gravel grow naturally in the bladder and kidneys from heavy and sluggish humours, and in the course of time are baked and hardened by the heat of the body; and if the retention of the urine is a sufficient cause of the growth of the stone; why should we find it strange for a stone to be engendered in the body of a bewitched person through the agency of Satan, seeing that the Evil One can cause not only retention of urine but as many humours and fevers of the body as he pleases? And as for the balls of hair, the Devil causes the victim to swallow these hairs separately; and then, since he can insinuate himself into all parts of the body, he makes with them such balls and tresses inside the body.

But with regard to other matters which the body is not capable of receiving, such as knives, iron tools, and nails, I have no doubt that the Devil brings them from elsewhere and mingles them with that which the bewitched person vomits or voids, so skilfully that it appears to us that they come from the person's body.

These matters are also found on bed mattresses, or elsewhere in some corner of the house, or under the threshold of the door. Some say that these are charms, sortileges, or magic spells, and will not be satisfied until they are found, holding that until then the illness or devil will not leave the bewitched person. But although I would not deny that it is well done to search for such matters, and chiefly to purge the sick man of them, yet I confidently assert that it is superstition to believe that the patient cannot be healed if they are not found. And I prove this by the example of St. Hilarion, who, having a possessed girl in hand, would not allow anyone to remove the blade which a young man had, at the suggestion of Satan, buried under the threshold of a door, although the Devil cried out that he would not depart until this blade was removed; and yet the girl did not fail to be delivered.

I would add here that it is a great sign that the person is bewitched when he thus voids iron tools, stones, hairs and other such matters. So is it also when a person languishes to death. For we see that those who are bewitched pine and waste away little by little, remaining in such a state for a long time before they die. Such was the case with Claude Perrier, Mathieu Andrey and several others, as we have remarked elsewhere. Yet I would not conclude from that that witches do not sometimes cause men to die suddenly; but I speak of what usually happens.

Paul Grilland, de Sortileg. q. 3. *nu.* 9. & *q.* 8. *nu.* 1. *Remy, Demonol. I.* 4. *Binsfeld,* 1. 4. *q.* 8., *de Malefic. C.*

Finally, witches are the more to be feared in that they come by night and find people in their houses or their beds, being guided by their Master, who opens and shuts doors for them so secretly that it may not be guarded against, and for the most part even makes them invisible.

Chapter XXXIII.

How Witches Afflict the Herds.

What we have said in the foregoing chapters principally concerns mankind; but we must to some extent treat in particular of Cattle, the Crops, and the Fruits of the earth. Let us start, then, with Cattle

Witches have many and various ways of injuring cattle, and these methods are in some part the same as those of which we have already spoken. For with a powder, an ointment, a glance of the eye, a word, a touch with the hand or a wand, they will make the beast ill or cause it to die; and of this we have recounted several examples in Chapters 23, 24 and the following chapters.

At other times they deprive the animal of milk; and this they do with the help of Satan by giving it certain noxious herbs to eat, which dry up and keep back its milk. Or else, at the moment when the animal begins to give milk, Satan takes it from its teat. Also they cause the milk of one cow to go into the udder of another, as it is said. Clauda Vernier, known as la Montagne, wife of Pierre Vernier, known as Billet des Granges, who was burned at Dôle about thirty years ago, confessed that she used to cause the milk of her neighbour's cows to flow in this way into the udders of her own. And this is why Antoine Tornier, when she was threatening Jacquema Paget, said that her cows were yielding twice as much milk as her own. But we can only believe that in this case Satan, in the manner we have said, causes one of the cows to lose its milk, and on the contrary causes that of the other to increase twofold by the means of certain beneficial herbs which he gives it to eat, such as Cytisus and other such. Or else he takes the milk from one cow, and when the other is being milked he comes with his milk, which he pours so skilfully into the pail that it appears to come from the second cow's teats.

For such is commonly his practice in the matter of wine according to Sprenger, who says that once the bottles of a witch, which were empty, became full of wine in a moment; for it is likely that Satan had taken that wine from some cellar to fill the bottles with it.

Here I must recount a strange and devilish remedy used by Christine, the chambermaid of Theodore Lopers, Vicar of the Hospital of Kreveld, when three of her cows had lost their milk. She sent them in front of the house of the woman whom she suspected of having caused the loss of their milk, having first bidden them to go in the name of, etc.; and when they were in front of the house they remained there for some time lowing continually, and then came back with their milk restored.

Now there is one sign, among others, by which it may be known whether an animal has been bewitched, namely, when it dies in a state of frenzy. This is what happened to a hen belonging to Rollande du Vernois: for this woman had two hens, and one day she refused Groz-Jacques Bocquet an egg; whereupon Groz-Jacques, meaning to kill her hens, threw them some crumbs of bread which he had dusted with a powder; and when they had eaten them, the two hens at once died. But one of them, before dying, threw itself to the ground and leaped and climbed against the walls in such a way that it was thought to be mad. The same thing happened to several horses which Antoine Tornier and Clauda Coirieres had bewitched. Vegece also says that a bewitched animal is sad and heavy, and that it grows thin and falls ill if it be not helped by natural remedies.

CHAPTER XXXIV.

How Witches do Hurt to the Fruits of the Earth.

WITCHES also do hurt to the fruits of the earth in several ways. For they raise hailstorms and tempests to ruin them when they have ripened, as we have already said. Secondly, with the help of Satan they cause cankerworms, rats and other vermin to waste and devour the fruit: such vermin being either created by Satan or brought from elsewhere; for it is certain that devils can bring animals together wherever they please. *St. Augusti. St. Thom. Binsfeld ad* 1. 4. *de malefic. & q.* 9. *conclus.* 4.

Thirdly, at the prayer of witches Satan procures the loss and waste of the two principal causes of the fertilisation of the soil and its preservation in its natural condition, namely, moisture and heat. Lastly, it is said that witches, with the help of their Master, strip the fruit from one field and cause it to be transferred to another. The Germans Hoppo and Stadlin, according to Sprenger, *II.* 1. 15. boasted of having done this. And Pliny records *XVIII.* 6. that Caius Furius was formerly brought to trial for the same reason. Vergil himself saw it practised:

I saw the crops pass over from one field *Eclog.* 8.
To another.

And long before him the law of the Twelve Tables punished such witches with death: *Let him who hath bewitched the fruits of the earth be put to death; neither shall it be lawful for a man to transfer the corn from one field to another.* It is my opinion that this is done, not by Satan transporting the corn from one field to another, but by his changing the fields themselves. For it is the opinion of the Theologians that the devils are able to move all inferior bodies; and therefore it cannot be any more difficult for Satan to transport a field from one place to another than it is for him to remove a mountain or a rock. For we read that there are whole lands and countries which have been transported from their place by the agency of the Devil and his magic, so that rocks which were facing to the north have in an instant been turned towards the south. This I take from Florimond de Raemond.

Vair, de Incant. III. 1.

Antichrist, c. 26, *n.* 2.

Chapter XXXV.

Whether Witches are Able to Heal.

WE have treated of the hurts which witches do to man and beast. Let us now consider whether they are able also to heal. It appears that they are able, since we have many examples to prove it. The Emperor Hadrian was by witchcraft cured of a dropsy into which he had fallen, as Dion relates in his Life. We read that Apollonius of Tyana gave sight to the blind and made the lame to walk, and that he delivered the town of Ephesus from a great pestilence which was afflicting it. Marie Perrier was restored to health after her nephew Pierre Perrier had threatened Clauda Gaillard, who was suspected of having cast the spell upon her. Jacques Bocquet, one of the great witches of his time, told Françoise Secretain that she would heal Loyse Maillat, into whose body she had sent five devils, if she gave her some bread which she had had from Loyse's house and had kept for three days. I have seen another woman who healed several kinds of sickness by her prayers; but I noticed that all these prayers were full of superstition and impiety. For example, if a horse had been stung, she would say certain words in the form of a prayer, and would plant in the ground a nail which she would not draw out again; but what virtue could there be in a nail so planted? I find that the Romans, who were as superstitious as any nation in the world, when they wished to drive away the plague used to fix a nail into a stone on the right-hand side of the temple of Jupiter, and that they did the same as a remedy against charms and when any faction arose between the citizens. There are also others who, in order to prevail over their enemies in battle, drive a nail into a tree.

Vair, de Incant. I. 4.

Wier, de praestig. IV. 9.

When this woman of whom I speak wished to still a storm or tempest, she first came out of her house muttering I know not what between her teeth, and then went forward little by little, never taking the least step backward; for, she said, she must not do so on pain of her life. Then she gave to some poor person a just alms, that is to say, as much bread as the poor person could eat at one meal; and to Satan she gave the largest pine in the neighbouring forest. In thus sacrificing to Satan she did neither more nor less than the ancients, who used to sacrifice to him in the name of Hercules *Canopianus* in order to rid themselves of lice, and in the name of Acor *Cyrenaicus* to free themselves of flies, and in the name of Apollo *Parnopianus* that they might not be plagued with rats. The Romans also used to sacrifice to Fever, and the Indians to the Evil Spirit, so that they might not be invisible and harmful to them.

When this woman said the prayer for the foaling of horses, she raised herself upon her right hand and usually turned herself towards the church. And when she came to heal certain cows, before saying her prayer she used to ask the owner of the animals for bread and salt; but she never made the cows eat of either the bread or the salt. She used to practise countless other similar prayers.

A neighbour of mine was cured in this superstitious manner by an old woman who was suspected of being a witch. He was in his cradle taken with a very strange illness; for he had the hiccups so badly that at each spasm (and these were almost continuous) he could be heard at a distance of twenty-five or thirty paces, and also his eyes were so bleared and covered with wax that he could hardly see. They had recourse to doctors, but without any avail; and so it was thought that the sickness was due to witchcraft. They then consulted the old woman of whom I spoke, because she had previously used certain threats to the child's father, and so prevailed upon her with their words that she promised to heal the child. She had herself shut in a room alone with him, after having asked for a tile, a salt-cat, and a blanket. They watched what she did through a window which gave on to the room; and she warmed the salt-cat and the tile, and then took the child from the cradle into her arms and completely covered herself and it with the blanket so that no part of their bodies could be seen, and remained so for half an hour; then she arose and recalled those whom she had caused to leave the room, and the child was healed from that time. It is likely that the old woman, when she was under the blanket, used certain other words and ceremonies which she did not wish to be seen.

Now all these superstitions make me believe that when witches heal it is entirely due to the help of Satan. Among other indications that this is the true opinion is the fact that it is necessary to believe firmly that the witch will cure you, or you will never recover your health; for it is always necessary for the sick man to have complete faith in his doctor. Do we not see many who have no trust at all in their doctor, and yet they do not fail to regain their health?

I do not deny that it is a great help to the sick that he should have faith in his doctor. For Galen and Avicenna said that the doctor who cured most sick men was he in whom they felt most faith. But such faith is not a necessary condition in medicine: yet in a case of witchcraft all the witch's brews and remedies are useless without it. This point has, in my opinion, been brought out by the physician Auger Ferrier better than anyone else in the following words: "If it so happen that the sick man has no faith in the sorcerer, but considers the remedy to be ridiculous; or if he is prevented from having such faith by the bystanders who in his presence make mock of the

Riol. ad Fernel. de abdit. rer. caus. II. 18.

Metho. II. 11.

remedy; the sorcerer will accomplish nothing, because there is present a spirit at enmity to that of which he is persuaded. For the cause of the healing lies in the virtue of the trusting spirit being in agreement with that of the patient." So says Auger Ferrier.

Again, witches make use of characters and words when they heal, and yet nothing can be more certain than that such words and characters have no healing property. For who will maintain that the letters P and A are good for the malady of the eyes? Who will believe that the words *Abracadabra Abracadabra*, etc. drive away the fever? Who will assert that the verses *Gaspar fert myrrham*, etc. preserve the patient from the falling sickness? Who will believe that the verse which Cæsar pronounced had the power to prevent his bed from being overset? Or that Ulysses was cured of his bloody flux by saying certain words? It enrages me to speak of the other obscure and barbaric words which these people use for the scrofula, for dislocated bones, for the bite of a mad dog, for the toothache and the gout. For they claim to cure all sorts of ills by their words and characters. This may be seen from the case of Paracelsus, who should have made himself the richest man in Europe; but perhaps he took no payment in money. For that is the common practice of witches, who are content to receive as payment the soul of him who consults them for their Master, from whom they have learned this trick, so that by this means the number of those who have recourse to their remedies may be increased. No, no:

It is but vain to think that words can cure
The aches and pains our mortal frames endure.

In this matter Pericles showed his wisdom. For on recovering from a sickness and being asked if his malady had been great, he answered: "You may judge how great it was from the fact that it took half my sense from me: for if I had been in my right mind, I would never have allowed them to tie round my neck these charms which you see hanging there." And indeed I think that this Captain was more in the right than Galen and the Platonists who put so much faith in charms and amulets, which were condemned by even the Emperor Caracalla and derided by Lucian in his "Dialogue of the Philosophers."

In the same class I consider the numbers observed by witches in their healing. For they make the sick man fast for so many days, or offer so many candles, or say so many Paternosters; and if he fail in but one point he will never be healed. For in Magic it is a maxim that if a man fails in the smallest possible point, he can derive no benefit at all.

v. Concil. Trid. Sess. 22. in Decret. de Observat. & Aut. in celeb. miss. sub. fin.

Furthermore, witches in their healing sometimes make use of matters which are contrary to God and Nature; as the Chaldeans did in the case of a gladiator whom they caused to be killed and then gave his blood to drink to Faustina, the wife of the Emperor Marcus Aurelius, so that she might lose the love which she bore to that gladiator. Democritus also prescribed as the cure for the dropsy, that a man's throat should be cut and his blood given to the patient to drink while it was still warm; or else that he should be given certain forbidden and unlawful matters to eat. Apollonius of Tyana, to cleanse the town of Ephesus from the plague, caused an old man to be stoned by the people. To pass to the Master of

Riol. ad. Fernel. de abdit. rer. caus. II. 13.

witches, the Oracle of Delphi once replied to
Wier, de the Ionians, who were seeking some remedy
praestig. I. 6. against the plague, that they must sacrifice every year before the altar of Diana a beautiful youth for one Melanippus, and a maiden for one Comethone whom Melanippus had raped in the temple of Diana; and the Ionians did so thereafter. Another Oracle told the Emperor Hadrian that he would never bring his charms to a successful issue until he found a man who would voluntarily sacrifice himself; and Antinous, his chief favourite, freely gave himself up to die. All this conforms with the religion, or rather irreligion, of the Gauls, who according to the teaching of their
Caes. lib. 6. Druids believed that a man's life could only be
Suet. Claud. redeemed by the life of another man, and there-
Wier, ibid. fore they did not scruple, when they were seriously ill, to sacrifice men as victims, so that they might recover their health. This practice was forbidden to them under Augustus. Later, Constantine the Great made a most humane use of this custom; for when he was tortured with a leprosy which was the despair of his physicians, there were certain Greeks who advised him to make a bath of the blood of several newly-killed children; but this good Emperor would never agree to this, but on the contrary had himself and one of his sons baptised by the Pope St. Sylvester, and was immediately healed by this sacred bath. For the rest, it should not appear strange that Satan causes men to be sacrificed in order to cure a person. For in every case he acts in the same way, as we read of Creon's son, of Iphigeneia,
Plin. V. 36. and Quintus Curtius. The Thracians also and the Carthaginians, and the tribes of Brittany, used to sacrifice men under the pretext of secur-

ing good fortune. The *Cymbri* had nuns with white hair and white robes who, in time of war, used to cut the throat of one of their prisoners of war over a cauldron, and then poured the blood into a tankard, and as it dripped they foretold what was to happen; while others opened his belly and, after examining his entrails, announced that their people would gain the victory. And the people of Temistitan, before the Spaniards conquered that town, used to immolate more than 2000 persons every year, and all of them innocent of any crime; but what is even more strange is that they had two chief idols of an enormous size, which they renewed each year, on a certain day, made of a flour composed from every vegetable and seed which can be used for human purposes, and mixed with the blood of those whom they had immolated. Julian the Apostate, in order to know the future, delighted in cutting people's throats; so that after his death they found the bodies of several of those whom he had murdered in his wells and cisterns and drains; and in another town, after having performed horrible sacrifices to the Devil, he had a woman hanged by her hair, after he had first had her cut open while she was alive.

Strab. VII.

Vigener. Comment. on Cæsar.

Niceph. X. 35.

Again, consider how Satan caused the mother of Vitellius to die. Through the mouth of Aurinia he gave this Emperor to understand that he would have a long and secure reign if he survived his mother. Vitellius believed this, and hastened his mother's end. But I am weary of these bloody examples: let us continue after our former method, and consider less violent matters than those of which we have just spoken, by which none the less we may conclude that it is

Satan, and not the witches, who effects such cures.

Witches claim to heal by means of a messenger, that is to say, by contriving that the messenger shall take the medicine prepared for his master.

Dioscor. VI. 46. The hermit of whom Mattioli speaks acted in this manner. He asked the messenger if he would take a medicine for his master; and when the messenger said that he would, he made him take off his right shoe and place his bare foot upon the ground, and then took a knife and with the point traced the form of the messenger's foot all round, and then told him to raise his foot. Then with the same knife he scratched within the tracing of the foot the following words: *Caro Caruse, etc.* After this, always with the same knife, he raked up the earth where the words had been scratched until there remained no trace of a letter, and cast the earth into a little earthen pot filled with water. After it had remained for some time in the pot, he strained it through the messenger's shirt and gave it to him to drink, after having made the sign of the Cross; and by this means the patient was cured without any further mystery. Mattioli adds that he who used this cure was his friend, and that he had seen him use it several times, and that he had even assured him that this cure was the greatest secret of those who boast that they are of the race of St. Paul.

The following examples are similar. When a man is wounded, his doublet is fetched from a distance and a plaster is applied to the opening of it, and the patient is made to drink clear water, and is immediately healed. And if a man is wounded by the *Tareronde*, they take its tail and apply it to an oak, which withers and dies, and by this means the patient is cured. But who can doubt that in such cases it is the Devil who heals, just as he does mischief and hurt by means of the images of which we have treated above?

I wish also to mention certain more ridiculous matters, which nevertheless go to prove the same conclusion. In order to cure the falling sickness, witches would have a man use the powder from the skull of a robber who had been hanged. This is an altogether detestable practice. And when they wish to cure someone of sexual impotence, they make him piss, etc. Or else they make him go into a forest and look at the nest of a pie, etc. Also, in such a case, they make him who has been prevented from lying with his wife piss through the wedding ring, etc. Again, when a man is in doubt whether he is a victim of witchcraft, they send him to take bread and salt in the house of the suspected witch; as if the bread and salt thus taken without the witch's knowledge had the power to heal him. I was forgetting to say that sometimes in their cures they make use of the brain of a cat or a raven's head, which are true poisons.

In the cases which we are considering, therefore, it is Satan who effects the cure. And he does so by making use of second and natural causes, and the methods used by physicians. For, as the learned Cardinal Bellarmine says, when a sickness is naturally curable the Devil can bring remedies to the sick man. Or else it is merely a case of the Devil ceasing to do ill, as Tertullian says, speaking of the blind and the lame whom the Emperor Vespasian caused to see and walk, according to Suetonius: "The Devil insinuates himself into the eyes of the blind and the legs of

Bodin, Demonom. III. 2. de not. Eccl. lib. 4. c. 14.

In Apolog. c. 22.

the lame so that they may not use these members, in order that, when he ceases to torment them, he may appear to heal them."

Nevertheless there is always this evil in cures effected by witches, or rather by the Devil: the cure is only effective for a limited time, or else it is necessary for the sickness to be transferred to someone else; and sometimes we find both these conditions operating at the same time.

The first point is proved in the case of those who have their wounds charmed away; for this only lasts for a time. I knew a French gentleman who, because he had had some wounds received in battle charmed away, thought that he was entirely healed; but three years later, after making a slight effort in spurring his horse, the wounds opened again and he died.

The second point can be proved by the example of Mumol, Grand Master of France, whose life the witches saved by causing the death of the grandson of King Childebert. Several similar examples may be found in Bodin. But it has been noticed that in such cases Satan never loses by the exchange; for if the witch wishes to heal an old man, he will wish the sickness upon a younger man; or if the person bewitched is of low rank, he will transfer the spell to one who is of higher rank and quality. At other times the witch, having failed to give the sickness to someone else, has himself had to suffer the pain of it: this happened to the scholar of whom Bodin speaks, who wished to cause the death of a child who was still at the breast, so as to heal its father. For as he ran after the nurse who had run away with the child on learning of the plot formed by the witch and the father, and was crossing the

Demonom. III. 2.

Ibid.

threshold of the room where the sick man was, he fell stark dead. In nearly the same way the Devil caused the death of Jeanne Platet, whom we held in our prisons not long since. This woman was accused of having sent devils into the body of a girl named Guillauma Blondan; Guillauma's parents importuned the witch to cure the girl, and she at last consented, and told the girl that she must keep a nine days' fast, during which she must every day go to stool; and that she, on her own part, would observe the same novena, which was to be begun on a Friday. The girl obeyed and kept her novena; but it happened that on the night of the last day the witch died in prison; but nevertheless the girl was shortly afterwards healed, having voided by the back passage several little animals in the form of lizards, as the witch had told her. Also she vomited through her mouth a deal of green matter in which was found a piece of coal as big as a nut; and then there were found two little holes going right through the floor of the room. The witch confessed when she died.

Yet I maintain that such matters are entirely concerned with the pact formed between the witch and Satan. For I know for a fact that a witch who wishes to heal a person sometimes casts the spell upon a beast, as was done in the case of a man named Mathieu Andrey of the village of Pierrecourt. For when he could find no cure for the sickness which was consuming him, he at last consulted a passer-by, who asked him if he was willing that his sickness should be cast upon a cock which he had in his house. The patient agreed, whereupon the stranger had the cock buried in Mathieu's garden, and he was healed. But not for long, for two or three years later he fell ill again and died.

This example will serve as a proof of the last point on which we touched, namely, that a witch's cure is sometimes only temporary, and also is conditional upon the ailment being transferred to another creature.

I shall here set down one more example to show that when witches wish to heal a person they often cast the spell upon a beast. I know a man who, at the age of ten or twelve, became as it were frenzied. It was at once believed that he had been bewitched by a man who was suspected because he had threatened the father that he would harm him in that which he loved best. One day it happened that the father's husbandman was passing with a hen in his hands before the house of the suspected man, who asked him where he was going. The husbandman answered that he was going to see his master's son, who was sick; and the other replied that he was very sorry for it, but that he had the means of healing him, and told the husbandman that, on arriving at his master's house, he must put the hen he was carrying on the ground, and that if the boy killed it he would be cured; but that they were to take great care not to eat this hen. When the husbandman reached his master's house he did as he had been told, and put the hen on the ground. The hen went straight up to the sick boy, who took it by the neck and killed it, and was immediately cured. Who, then, can doubt that the spell was cast upon this hen?

Chapter XXXVI.

That for the Cure of these Maladies Satan and his Demons must on no Account be Appealed to, but God Only.

IT is obvious from what we have said in the last chapter that the methods used by witches in their cures are by no means certain, nor the cure itself when it is accomplished. And from this I would conclude that it is best for us not to consult them when we are sick, even if it is they who have cast the sickness upon us. Moreover, it is not lawful for us to do so, seeing that we are strictly forbidden by Holy Scripture to have recourse to Satan or his demons, whatever advice or help they may promise us. The Canon Law excommunicates us in such case; and the civil Law has made similar provision by the penalties which it imposes on those who have recourse to such people, thus righteously amending the constitution of the Emperor Constantine, which permitted the use of magic for a good purpose, such as to heal the sick or to still tempests. And yet this Emperor was in some sort to be excused, for when he drew up his constitution he was still plunged in paganism and did not know that, according to St. Paul, we must never do evil that good may come of it.

Navarr. in Manua. c. 11. *num.* 29. *Deut.* 18. *Levit.* 20. *C.* 2. *de sortileg. C. admoneant* 26 *q.* 7. 1. *cæteræ famil. Ercis.* 1. *item apud Labeonem si quis astrologus de injur.* 1. *nullus aruspex* 1. *nemo de malefic. C.* 1. *eorum de malefic. C.*

Rom. 3.

Experience has proved also that they who have consulted the Devil and his demons have never prospered. Ochozias, King of Israel, being sick from a fall, had recourse to Beelzebub, for which Elias foretold his death: "What," said the prophet, "is there no God in Israel? And because thou hast nevertheless taken counsel with Beelzebub, thou shalt therefore die." And so it happened to him immediately afterwards. The Emperor Heliogabalus, while consulting a necromancer, was cruelly murdered and dragged through the sewers with his mother. Pompey wished to enlist the support of certain witches against Cæsar, and lost both the victory and his life. The same happened to Ariovistus: and within living memory one of the great Kings of Christendom lost his reason through having consulted a necromancer in order to know the issue of his fortunes. Similarly Sanchez d'Avila, being wounded by a horse's kick, neglected the chirurgeon's art and relied upon the treatment of a soldier who practised certain benedictions; and, according to the history of Portugal, died for his superstition. When Adrian VI held the Papal See, a Greek named Demetrio Spartiano allayed a very severe plague which ravaged the city of Rome by unlawful and superstitious means; for having cut off half the right horn of a wild bull which the people had given up to him, and after placing certain charms in its right ear, he at once made it so tame that, after throwing a thread over its whole horn, he led it about wherever he liked, till he brought it to the Coliseum, where he immolated it; and at once the plague began to abate. But soon afterwards the Bourbon army sacked Rome, which was justly permitted by God because, as Florimond de Raemond says, the Romans in seeking a remedy for the plague which afflicted them rather put their faith in

Bodin, Demonom. II. 3.

Lib. 10.

Antichrist, c. 26. *num.* 6.

Satan and one of his witches, against the wish of the Pope, who in no way desired to allow this magician and conjurer to exercise his art.

But how can it be that the wrath of God is not kindled against those who have recourse to witches, since it is His will that they should not be left to live on the earth? "Thou shalt not permit a witch to live," He says in Exodus; and elsewhere certain men are expressly commanded to stone the Pythoness woman. Even the Persians, who were superstitious enough, used to crush their witches' heads between two stones. It was therefore well said by St. John Chrysostom that it is better to die than to seek the help of the Devil or witches to be cured: "It is better for a Christian man to die than to redeem his life by means of witchcraft and sorcery." It was for this reason that St. Hilarion would not permit anyone to remove a strip of leather which a young man had, at the suggestion of Satan, placed under the house door of a girl whom he loved; although Satan had entered into the girl's body and said that he would not leave it until the strip was removed: nevertheless the girl did not fail to be delivered by the prayers of St. Hilarion. The case of Rollande du Vernois was similar: she was possessed of two demons which Groz-Jacques had sent into her body, and asked that Groz-Jacques should be sent for, making signs that the demons would then depart from her; but I was in no mind to send for this man, but called in the Priest who conjured her diligently and pursued his exorcisms; and this was done in such a manner that the demons left Rollande. I hold that it was not she who asked for Groz-Jacques, but the demon, who wished

Exod. 22.

Homil. 8. *sup. Epist. ad Coloss.*

S. Jerome, in vita Hilario.

one spell of witchcraft to be driven away by means of another. In this matter we may learn a lesson from the Roman Senate; for in the time of Marius it refused to use the services of a witch named Martha, although she promised victory, as we read in Dio Cassius.

In such cases, then, we must have recourse to God alone, following the advice which Elias gave to King Ochozias, whether we wish to prevent a misfortune or to be delivered from one. "He who is helped by the Almighty," says David, "shall ever abide in the protection of God, etc." And Satan reproached God because He kept Job in His protection, so that he could not harm him: "Doth Job fear God for nought?"
Job 1. he said. "Hast not thou made an hedge about him, and about his house, and about all that he hath on every side?"

> But words there are with power to ease,
> And our chief sufferings appease.

It is the prayers which we offer to God that are our protection from the Evil Spirit and his
Matth. 15. snares. Jesus Christ drove the Devil from the Canaanite woman's daughter at the prayer of her
Luke 9. mother: He delivered the lunatic from the devil which tormented him at the prayer of the
Mark 2. demoniac's father: He healed Miriam the sister of Moses of the leprosy at her brother's prayer. Therefore it is God alone, as He Himself says in Isaiah, who sends life and death, health and sickness, and there is no salvation save in Him.

CHAPTER XXXVII.

Whether it is Permitted to Menace a Witch in order to Heal or Ward Off Harm.

I AM aware that there are those who are agreed that it is not lawful to have recourse to witches in order to induce them by prayers and fair words to effect a cure; for they hold that this shows an abject and humble spirit, and has some appearance of adoration; and they add that St. Paul very expressly forbids us to have communication with the Devil: "I would not that ye have intercourse with devils." But they maintain that it is permissible if a man approaches the witch with force and threats; and they even assert that there is no better method than that to compel a witch to remove the spell which she has cast. We have noted an example of this in the case of Clauda Gaillard, who struck Marie Perrier ill by breathing in her face; and yet, as soon as she was threatened by Pierre Perrier, the evil at once left Marie. But I would not say that this practice is common to-day; yet indeed it seems to have some sound base if one considers that he who threatens a witch does so in a disdainful spirit and, as it were, commanding the witch.

Yet I doubt whether this latter method may be any more conscientiously used than the former; for in each case a man gives the witch the occasion to consult Satan for a remedy, and this is directly against the law of God, as we have more fully argued elsewhere in the preceding chapter. Yet I will concede that, in order to ward off an evil, there is no offence in a man's bearing himself proudly and fiercely towards witches, so that these may fear them who behave towards them in such a manner, and may feel some dread for those who command them and might harm them. The Emperor Frederic Barbarossa made this clear to the Arab sorcerer who was sent by the Milanese to poison him; for when he was caught, and was threatening to kill the Emperor by his words if he did not let him go, the Emperor caused the man himself to be punished with death as he deserved.

But the best example of this is provided by the Officers and Ministers of Justice; for all are agreed that no witch, however wicked, can do harm to their persons. I may add that Satan himself holds them in fear and dread. I know this from the depositions of Rollande du Vernois. This woman was possessed of two devils, and yet was suspected of witchcraft. When I approached the guard-room to hear her statement she was tormented more violently than usual, and said that her devils felt my approach and for that reason tormented her in that manner.

Bodin, Demonom. III. 4. Remy, Demonol. I. 2.

Herein there is certainly a secret judgement of God, who will not permit the wicked, such as are witches, to have power over the persons of Judges, so that justice, which, as King Joram said, is of Him, shall be executed.

II. I. 11. Yet I have read in Sprenger that a witch who was about to be thrown on to the fire said to the gaoler that she would pay him, and blew into his face, and struck him with leprosy all over his body so that he died after a few days. This gaoler was perhaps not performing his duty well.

It is not out of place to say here that there are many who, to ward off spells and enchantments, make use of date stones, and the stone called alum, feathers, Squills, Moly, St. John's wort, madwort, the root of the female Satyrion, rue, the herb called Our Lady's gloves, the root of the herb called Baaras of which Josephus speaks in the "Jewish War." But it is very difficult to believe that these stones and roots, which are corporeal matters, can have any power against the Devil, who is purely spiritual; and it is more probable that they can only operate in the manner which we shall explain in Chapter 57.

Plin. XIII. 4. Dioscor. 113. Mattioli, pref. to Dioscor. 1. Dioscor. III. 89. VII. 25.

Yet it may be that we should believe that God, the more to manifest the glory of His Majesty, consents to combat and overcome the Devil by means of the least of His creatures. For He acted so in the case of Pharaoh's magicians, who easily in imitation of Moses made frogs and serpents and dragons, and turned the water into blood; but when they tried to make flies they were powerless and ashamed.

The people of the West Indies behaved very abominably on this account when the Spaniards came to their country. For as a protection against charms they wore round their necks an image of Pederasty, a *Sodomite* and his *Ingle*—matters which a Christian cannot hear spoken of without loss to his sense of shame and modesty.

Chapter XXXVIII.

That He Who is Bewitched can Avail Himself of Physicians.

WE have said above that he who is bewitched must have recourse to God alone, and not to Satan or his demons, but I would not therefore infer that the patient may not consult with physicians for his cure. For in availing himself of medicine he makes use of a means granted to us by the Almighty with an honourable title to preserve and recover our health; and besides, the Majesty of God is far more gloriously manifested in effecting such work by means of His creatures than if He were to do it Himself.

I cannot, moreover, agree with Philo Judæus and others who maintain that a man whose sickness is due to witchcraft cannot be healed by physicians. For we have shown that witches afflict persons with all sorts of sickness, such as cholic, paralysis, apoplexy, epilepsy, etc., which proceed from putrefaction or some other natural cause, and can be cured naturally according to the science of medicine: so that there is nothing to prevent physicians from healing such maladies.

Cf. chap. 32.

Even stranger things have been known; for certain bewitched persons have, with the help of physicians, voided needles, iron tools, stones, hairs, and other such matters. This was so in the case of the gentleman's son whom we mentioned in Chapter 32; and Wier, too, recounts several examples of it.

I make no doubt that certain witches have boasted that no physician could remove the spell of witchcraft cast by them; but what of that? Must we believe them? The Devil puts this claim in their mouths so that we may give honour to a witch rather than have recourse to medicine.

And if the maladies of which we have spoken continue for a long time and appear to be incurable, this comes of the obstructions caused by Satan, who sometimes renews the causes of the sickness and sometimes, in his own subtle and occult manner, contrives that the sickness shall be outside the physicians' knowledge.

But let us come to the other points which concern Françoise Secretain.

Chapter XXXIX.

The Rosaries Used by Witches generally lack the Cross; but in any Case the Cross is always Imperfect in some Particular.

When this woman was examined the first time, it was noted that there was no Cross on her rosary, and that she did not shed a single tear although she tried her hardest to weep. Now all the authorities agree that the presumption is heavily against those who are accused of witchcraft when they cannot shed tears.

See the following chapter.

Art. 40. I would not draw quite so definite a conclusion from the fact of their rosary being without a Cross; yet I will say that this must tell strongly against them. For the Cross is one of the chief flails of Satan, as is fully witnessed by the
S. Greg. l. 3. memorable example of Julian the Apostate,
Dialog. c. 7. who, having met with several devils in the temple of an idol, and having made the sign of the Cross, caused all the devils to disappear at once. Everybody knows that, although this unhappy Emperor held the Christians in deadly hatred and was good for nothing, yet he drove away devils with the Cross; for so powerful is this sign against demons that they could not conceal their fear of it from Julian. For they reproached him that, although he was but an empty vessel, yet he was sealed with the sign of the Cross.

We read also of certain persons who have come unexpectedly or out of curiosity into the assembly of witches, and have made the sign of the Cross; and that then everything, devils and viands and witches, have vanished. I shall leave what I
Chap. 55. have to say concerning the Cross until later. It is enough to say here that nearly all the rosaries of those who have been executed in this place have been examined and have been found to be without a Cross, or at least to be defective in some detail of the Cross, as in one of the arms or some other particular. Such were the rosaries of Groz-Jacques Bocquet, Clauda Jamprost, Claude Jamguillaume, and many others.

Chapter XL.

Witches are Unable to Shed Tears in the Presence of the Judge.

Let us return to the presumption taken against those accused of witchcraft when they cannot shed tears. I have read of a woman who confessed that witches can shed only three tears from the right eye. And it is a fact that the learned Doctors hold this to be one of the strongest presumptive evidences of witchcraft that there are. But I wish to recount my own experience in this matter. All the witches that I have examined in my capacity of Judge have never been able to shed tears in my presence, or if they have shed them it has been so slightly as not to be noticed. I say this although I have seen them who appeared to weep, but I have no doubt that it was only pretence; and even if their tears were not feigned, I am at least quite certain that it was with the greatest difficulty that they were called up. I am led to this opinion by the great effort which the accused make to weep, and the scarcity of tears which they are then able to shed.

Bodin, Demonom. IV. 4.

But if I spoke particularly to them, they wept as copiously and plentifully as possible. The same happened when they had confessed; but then their tears seemed lighter and happier than before, as if they had been rid of a heavy burden.

In conclusion, it is probable that the reason for the inability of witches to shed tears is that tears are chiefly proper to penitents for washing and cleansing their sins. For tears, as St. Bernard says, penetrate to Heaven and soften the wrath of God Almighty; and therefore they cannot be welcome to the Enemy of our salvation, who consequently prevents them as much as he can. Similarly, Satan holds bells in extreme detestation; for by their ringing the people are warned to prepare to observe their duty and pray to God. Also they drive away storms and tempests.

Sprenger, III. 15.

And whenever you ask witches why it is that they cannot shed tears, they answer that it is impossible for them to weep because their hearts have been so hardened and straitened by being accused of so detestable a crime as witchcraft. I discuss in another place how much weight a Judge should give to this plea.

Art. 39

Chapter XLI.

The Eyes of Witches are Continually Bent upon the Ground when in the Presence of the Judge.

IT was further noted that, when Françoise Secretain was being examined, she always kept her eyes bent upon the ground so that the Judge had great difficulty in making her look him in the face. I find that this is usual with witches, and have noticed it in many who have been

Bodin, Demonom. IV. 4.

burned: therefore this also is an indication of the guilt of the accused. *v. Art.* 35.

It is said that the reason why they thus bend their eyes upon the ground is that they are ashamed to look the Judge in the face because of the enormity to their crime. But I rather incline to the belief that they are then consulting with Satan as to the answers they shall give to the questions put to them by the Judge; for at the same time as they look upon the ground, they mutter I know not what between their teeth; and when they are asked what they are doing, they answer that they are saying their paternosters.

But it is not only at such times that witches look upon the ground; for if you watch them in their chambers and their prisons you will generally find them stretched out face downwards. This was their custom in the time of Apuleius, who recounts that they said their prayers in holes in the ground. We read that Moses, Joshua, Elias and the other Prophets used to turn their faces towards the ground when they would appease the wrath of God: and it may be that this is why Satan, who always tries to ape God, wishes his witches to pray to him in this manner.

Chapter XLII.

Witches when they Renounce the Devil Spit Three Times upon the Ground.

Françoise Secretain did another thing. When, at various times, she renounced the Devil, she spat three times upon the ground. This was also done by Groz-Jacques, Antoine Tornier, Jacquema Paget, Clauda Jamguillaume, Pierre Gandillon and several others. I used to think that this was a sign of the pact between the witch and Satan, and that this spitting signified that the witch was not willingly renouncing Satan; but I have since found that it was a custom amongst the Ancients to spit three times in their bosom to ward off spells and charms. Wherefore Theocritus writes:

Vair, de Incant. IV. 18.

> He shall spit three times in my bosom.

And Ovid:

> Each of you spits in his bosom.

And this superstition has been handed down to us, so that these persons who spit thus three times on renouncing Satan still retain the custom. For when they are asked the reason for this spitting, they answer that they have always heard that if you spit three times upon the ground when you renounce Satan, the Evil One cannot harm you in any way. Nevertheless I prefer to retain my former opinion; for witches spit in this manner also in certain similar circumstances, as when they heal the king's evil, and at the elevation of the Host at the Mass, as we learn from the Inquisitors.

Chapter XLIII.

Witches must be Shaved and their Clothes Changed.

IT remains for us to consider two other points concerning this witch: first, why her hair was cut; and secondly, why she was stripped to see if there was any mark upon her.

As for the first, it has always been the custom to take this precaution against witches, and to shave off all their hair when they fall into the hands of justice, in order to draw the truth from them more easily. The Emperor Domitian did so to the Philosopher of Tyana, and several after him have done the same with advantage. There have even been witches who have begged the Judge to have their hair cut, saying that otherwise it would be impossible for them to confess the truth.

Philost. vita Apollo. Aemig. Demon. III. 9.

Now this is because witches have drugs which procure taciturnity, which is otherwise called the Spell of Silence, which they hide in their hair; and as long as they carry them they will never confess; and they feel no pain when they are tortured, when it is chiefly necessary to shave them. And since they frequently conceal

v. Marsil. in pract. d. nunc vivendum nu. 52. Bodin, Demonom. IV. 1.

these spells in their clothing, for this reason they are required to change their clothes.

Remy.

Yet there are those who have condemned this practice as superstitious; but for my part I see no harm in it. For although the Spell of Silence is in itself of no profit to witches, yet it is a fact that they themselves firmly believe it to be so; and this it is which causes them to lose all feeling, in exactly the same sort as we find that some men die and others are cured, merely through their lively expectation of death or of health. Ovid writes:

I have seen a dying man revived by hope.

This presentiment or imagination was the cause of the death of a priest named Jean de Jean at the time when Strozzi was defeated with his army of *Terceres* in the Isle of S. Michel. For this priest, being the Maréchal de Camp's chaplain, and finding himself aboard the galleon *S. Matthieu*, driven back to the last line of defence, died without being hurt at all through sheer terror and fear induced by the sight of the fires thrown by the French and the sound of the cannon, as I learn from the history of Portugal.

De occult. philoso. c. 6.

Again, Paracelsus says that it is imagination alone which causes the plague, or a man's bravery or cowardice. And therefore, in my opinion, it is permissible to shave the hair of witches and to change their clothes, in order to deprive them of the firm faith which they have in this spell which may be hidden in their hair or their clothing.

Another reason which persuades me that there is no harm in this practice is that it is certain that witches, when they are shaved, are much tenderer and more susceptible to pain than those who are not shaved.

There have been cases of more cunning witches who have swallowed drugs to deaden their senses. And this is an easy matter for them to do, for even salt dissolved in clear water is unhappily productive of this result. Criminals nowadays are so well aware of this ruse that torture has become almost useless as a means of wresting the truth from them; and therefore it is necessary to keep a strict watch upon the gaolers, since it is usually they who procure such drugs for their prisoners in the hope of reaping some profit thereby.

There are others who use Characters and Prayers, and even certain verses and passages of Holy Scripture which I care not to quote here, seeing that they mingle with them the milk of the Holy Virgin Mary, making God as it were the author of their impunity for their witchcrafts: God, I say, who only commands us to punish the wicked, and to whom the sacrifice which the Magistrate and Justice make of such persons is pleasant and agreeable. But there can be no doubt that such witches also swallow drugs to deaden their senses, just as do those of whom we have just spoken. For we have shown *Chap. 26.* elsewhere that no words or characters are of any virtue as spells or charms.

I hold also that it is no more permissible to use such words, as some do, to cause the accused to confess when he is at the torture, than it is to use them for any other purpose. The reader is referred to my Instruction to Judges.

Chapter XLIV.

The Marks Borne by Witches.

Let us pass on to the other point. Françoise Secretain was stripped, that it might be known whether she had any mark upon her. For all witches have a mark some on the shoulder, some on the eyelid, some on the tongue or the lip, and others on the shameful parts; in short it is said that there is no witch who is not marked in some part of her body. Satan marks them thus to show them that they are in the future to become his slaves; for we read that slaves are usually branded, as is chiefly the case in Spain and Barbary, where they are branded on the face: and at all times Princes and Captains have had certain signs by which they could know their own subjects and soldiers. It is then but reasonable that Antichrist also should mark his own with a distinct sign by which he may know them.

Dan. the 4th point.

Further, I would say that just as Jesus Christ wished the faithful to be distinguished by the venerable sign of the Cross, so this Ape of God has imitated this by marking his subjects with some sign and character.

Raemond in his "Antichrist" says that he has seen witches who recognised each other by some little spot in the eye, and that Trois-eschelles was especially proficient in this. I do not doubt this; for it has been remarked that witches usually have two pupils in one of their eyes, just as the Tibians of Pontus had a double pupil in one eye and the image of a horse in the other, and could bewitch by their looking, as it is said that every woman can who has a double pupil.

Now the mark of a witch is generally some sort of blemish or hare's foot, or some such thing. There was one who had a face of the size of a farthing, from the centre of which extended several threads of hair to the circumference. Yet the place where they bear these marks is so insensitive that they do not shrink even if they are probed to the bone in that place.

Bodin, Demonom. IV. 4.

Caron, Antichrist, Part I.

But they are very difficult to find, because they are very inconspicuous; and also the Devil most often effaces them as soon as the witch has fallen into the hands of Justice, as he did to George Gandillon, who showed me where the Devil had touched him on the left shoulder, which is the place where he usually touches witches. Caron the physician writes that when he and his colleagues were once searching for the mark upon a witch named la Boyraionne, Satan, who was possessing a young girl by means of this woman, told them the place where it was, mocking them for not having been able to find it.

Ibid.

Yet there are witches who say that they have never been marked. Among such was Groz-Jacques, who, on dying contrite, assured me of this. Therefore I hold that there are witches who are not marked; and I am of opinion that Satan marks only those of whose loyalty he is a little doubtful. And in this he does neither more nor less than those who lend money; for if they trust their debtor they are content with his word; but if not, they tie him strictly down in writing. We have read, also, of witches who have given the Devil schedules written and signed in their own blood, as did the Advocate of Paris of whom Bodin speaks.

Demonom. III. 2.

Therefore I conclude that they are wrong who are so scrupulous as to be unwilling to condemn a witch to death unless a mark can be found, as is the practice in a certain Republic which I shall not name. For what, then, would be the point of what we have just said, namely, that the Devil most often removes the mark from a witch as soon as he is made a prisoner?

Finally, these marks are of great importance in dealing with witchcraft; for they constitute an extremely strong presumptive evidence of guilt, so much so that, when they are joined to other indications, it is lawful to proceed to an immediate condemnation.

CHAPTER XLV.

Satan often Kills Witches when they are in Prison, or else he Inspires them to Kill Themselves. Sometimes he Reveals what will Happen to them at their Deaths.

SO much for Françoise Secretain. I am sure that all will agree that she was worthy of death, and of a witch's death by burning. But this she forestalled; for when we were on the point of pronouncing her sentence, she was found dead in prison.

In other instances witches have strangled themselves, and it seems that they have done so at the instigation of Satan. For, fearing lest witches, in dying at the hands of Justice, should be induced to repent, he either kills them or impels them to kill themselves, so that they may not escape him. In this manner he urged Antide Colas to hurl herself out of a window, or to hang herself from a window four days after she had been incarcerated at the Château de Betoncourt, appearing to her in the shape of a big black man. And I have no doubt that the Devil suffocated Françoise Secretain; for she had reported to us that they had tried four or five times to burn her in prison, to the extent of thrusting fire down her throat.

I must add that, when she was questioned about these threatened burnings, she always answered that they might do what they would with her, but that they would never burn her. It may be that Satan had revealed to her that she would die in prison; for I have read of the same in the case of a witch of Biévres. This woman said to her Judge that he would play her a scurvy trick; and before her sentence was pronounced she told him that he would cause her to be burned alive. The Judge sentenced her to be first strangled and then burned; but owing to a mistake on the part of the executioner, she was burned alive. When Clauda Jamguillaume who was executed in this place, was at the stake ready to be burned alive, she also said to the executioner that she knew that he would serve her ill and cause her to die slowly. And so it happened; for she broke loose and jumped out of the fire three times, so that in order to control

Bodin, Demonom. IV. 4.

her the executioner was forced to stun her. I remember also that, when sentence of death had been passed on Antoine Gandillon, she repeatedly entreated us not to let her die a slow death; and orders were accordingly given to the executioner, and yet she died more hardly than six others who were executed with her, among whom were her father and brother. It is obvious then that this foreknowledge of witches comes of the Devil. Nevertheless these last two died penitent. What then? It may be that Satan revealed to them that they would die a slow death with a view to bringing them to despair at the prospect of the pain they would have to suffer.

We read of another witch named Ascletario, who, although he was not a prisoner, told the Emperor Domitian that he would be eaten by dogs; and this happened to him although the Emperor had caused him to be put to death, for he was accidentally eaten by dogs after his death.

Chapter XLVI.

That Satan companies with his Witches when they are in Prison and even Assists them in the Presence of the Judge.

NOw because there are those who believe that, once witches are made prisoners and are fallen into the hands of Justice, the Devil deserts them and assists them no more, I wish to rid them of this opinion by what I shall here shortly set forth.

The examples I have quoted in the last chapter are entirely relevant to this point. For in them we see that for one thing Françoise Secretain confessed that they tried five or six times to burn her in prison, to the extent of thrusting fire down her throat; and although she did not assert that it was the Devil who made this attempt, it is impossible for us to suppose that it was anyone else. Again, we read that four days after Antide Colas was imprisoned at Betoncourt the Devil appeared to her in the shape of a big black man and incited her to throw herself from a window or to hang herself from it; and for this reason. For here I may add that he then lay with her and abode with her for about an hour, being all the time quite cold; and since she would in no respect follow his evil advice he tormented her throughout her whole body and caused her to shiver, and stung her on the left side as he had already done before, and also on the right arm.

I cannot omit to record that when the Devil was urging her to hang herself, there was a Voice which counselled her not to do so and showed her that, by hanging herself, she would dishonour her parents, and that it would be better for her to die another death. It is to be supposed that this was the voice of her good Angel, who wished to prevent her from hanging herself, so that by dying at the hands of Justice she might come to repentance; as she did.

Another time, on the first and second days of her imprisonment at the Château of Betoncourt, there appeared to her a little white dog which advised her to let herself be ducked, telling her that she would sink to the bottom of the water unless anything prevented her; and that if they wanted to hang her she should permit it, because the rope would break and she would fall on her feet without hurting herself; and soon afterwards he beat her all over, on the head and arms and shoulders and other parts, and stung her in the left side when he wished to go away. A witch of S. Preuve removed the fetters from her arms in the presence of the Judge, a feat which, says Bodin, was humanly impossible.

Denomon. III. Apollonius of Tyana did the same at Rome in sight of all his fellow-prisoners; and he did much more. For when, in the reign of Nero, he was shown the text of his accusation, which was held in the hands of Tigellinus, nothing was found written on the scroll; and another time, being accused before the Emperor Domitian, he vanished, and was seen the same day at Pozzuoli.

Thievenne Paget, who was burned in this place, confessed that the Devil had three times carnally known her in prison: a thing which I should never have believed if this confession had not been made before me, and if others as well as she had not confessed the same thing, especially that Antide Colas of whom we have spoken.

Clauda Coirieres, who was likewise burned in this place for witchcraft, gave an ointment to François Gaillard, who was detained in prison with her on a charge of murder; and when François had smeared his hands with this ointment, he escaped from prison as by a miracle: I have touched upon this matter elsewhere.

But what stronger confirmation of our contention could we wish than that which happens when the Judge examines witches? For at that time the Devil assists them and advises them what to answer, as they themselves have confessed. Also at this time they always keep their eyes bent upon the ground, and continually mutter I know not what between their teeth, so that the Judge has difficulty in making them answer and look him in the face.

Now whatever may be the truth of this matter, it will not appear very strange to those who have studied the story of Job. For there we read that when God was assembled with His Angels (which are called the Sons of God), Satan also came, and God asked him from whence he had come. And he answered that he came from going to and fro in the earth, etc. Now if the Proud Spirit dared to present himself at the assembly of God and His Angels, why should he not be found in a prison to assist his own followers, even though the Judge be present?

For these reasons it seems to me that, in a case of which Bodin speaks, the liberation of the *Demonom. II. 5.* prisoner by the Judge was no necessary concomitant of what followed. The witch rubbed some ointment upon herself, fell down as if she were dead and without any feeling, and five hours later recovered consciousness and arose and related many matters of different places, which were afterwards verified. For she could have done as much even if she had not been liberated. And I am the more persuaded of this by the fact that, although the Judge liberated her, he did not allow her to go far away, so that she was all the time rather in the hands of Justice than actually free and out of prison.

It is obvious, therefore, that Satan frequents

witches in prison. And therefore they should be carefully watched and often visited, so as to prevent such a meeting as far as it is possible, and to obviate the inconveniences and misfortunes which may result from it.

Yet I must say that although we have shown that witches and other prisoners sometimes escape from prison through the magic arts of the Devil, it is nevertheless known that they have all been quickly recaptured. So it was in the case of Apollonius of Tyana, and of François Gaillard, of whom we have spoken. And this comes of the just permission of God, who wills not that they who are worthy of death should escape from the hands of Justice.

Chapter XLVII.

Of the Metamorphosis of Men into Beasts, and Especially of Lycanthropes or Loups-garoux.

THE same method of procedure which was used in the case of Françoise Secretain was followed in those of Jacques Bocquet, Clauda Jamprost, Clauda Jamguillaume, Thievenne Paget and Clauda Gaillard. Jacques Bocquet, otherwise known as Groz-Jacques, came from Savoy, and was apprehended on the accusation of Françoise Secretain. Clauda Jamprost was from Orcieres, and was accused by Groz-Jacques. Clauda Jamguillaume and Thievenne Paget were also from Orcieres, and were accused by Groz-Jacques and Clauda Jamprost. Claude Gaillard was from Ebouchoux, and was imprisoned as the result of information arising from the preceding trials.

The first four of these confessed that they had turned themselves into wolves and that, in this shape, they had killed several children, namely, a child of Anathoile Cochet of Longchamois, one of Thievent Bondieu known as the rebel of Orcieres, four or five years old; another of big Claude Godard, and another of Claude the son of Antoine Gindre. Finally, they confessed that in the year 1597 they met in the neighbourhood of Longchamois two children of Claude Bault, a boy and a girl, who were gathering strawberries; that they killed the girl, and the boy saved himself by running away. They confessed also that they had eaten part of the children which we have mentioned, but that they never touched the right side. These murders were verified both by the evidence of the parents, and by that of several others in the villages of Longchamois and Orcieres, who deposed that all these children had been caught and eaten by wolves at such a time and such a place.

Clauda Jamguillaume added that she had nearly killed two other children, and that with the intent to do so she had hidden behind a hut in the mountains for about an hour, but had been prevented by a dog, which she killed in spite; but that nevertheless she contrived to wound one of the children in the thigh.

Jeanne Perrin also gave evidence that Clauda Gaillard had turned herself into a wolf, and had attacked her in that shape in a wood called

Froidecombe. It was therefore very convenient that all these witches should have been tried together, since they had all turned themselves into wolves. Pierre Gandillon and his son George Gandillon would also have been tried with them, but that they were hurried too quickly to their execution; for these last two also confessed that they had turned themselves into wolves. Yet the son averred that he had never meddled with any children, but that, in company with his aunt Perrenette Gandillon, he had only killed certain goats, among them one belonging to his father, which, as he said, they had done by mistake.

All these witches confessed besides that they had many times been to the Sabbat, that there they had copulated, danced, eaten and made their ointment; and also that they had caused the death of countless persons and beasts. But since we have dealt in detail with these last matters in their proper place, I shall here confine myself to the consideration of the first of them, namely, lycanthropy and the metamorphosis of men into beasts.

There is much disputing as to whether it is possible for men to be changed into beasts, some affirming the possibility, whilst others deny it; and there are ample grounds for both views. For we have many examples of the fact. The family of Antæus in Arcadia used to become wolves at a certain season of the year. After Demenetus Parrasius had tasted the entrails of a child, he
Sigeb. was changed into a wolf. Baianus, the son of a certain Simeon who was a chieftain of the Bulgarians, used to change himself into a wolf when he wished, as did Mœris, of whom Vergil speaks:

Mœris I often saw changed to a wolf
And prowling in the woods.

Eclog. 8.

Ovid reports that Lycaon did the same:

He was amazed, and howled in loneliness,
Nor could he speak as he was wont to do.

Job Fincel relates that he saw a Lycanthrope at Padua. Herodotus tells that the inhabitants of a district in Scythia used to turn into wolves; and this is also common among the peoples of the North. When the Romans were trying to prevent Hannibal from crossing the Alps, a wolf came amongst their army, rent those whom it met, and finally escaped without being hurt. In the year 1042 the people of Constantinople were much embarrassed by the appearance of more than 150 wolves at the same time. And in 1148 in the land of Geneva there was seen a wolf of unusual size, which killed thirty persons of both sexes and various ages. Who, then, can doubt but that these wolves were Lycanthropes?

Lib. 11. *mirab. Cf. Jean Bauhund, a physician of a Duke of Wurttemberg, in his story of the raging of wolves.*

Again, there are the three wolves which were seen on the 18th of July, 1603, in the district of Douvres and Jeurre about half an hour after a hailstorm had very strangely ruined all the fruit of that country. These wolves had no tails; and, moreover, as they ran through herds of cows and goats they touched none of them except one little kid, which one of them carried a little distance away without doing it any harm at all. It is apparent from this that these were not natural wolves, but were rather witches who had helped to cause the hailstorm, and had come to witness the damage which they had caused.

Also there was one which was larger than the others, and always went in front; and Groz-Jacques Bocquet, Thievenne Paget, la Michollette and several others said that, when they ran about in the shape of wolves, Satan used also to assume the form of a wolf and led and guided them.

The people of this country ought to know as much as any others about were-wolves; for they have always been known here. In the year 1521 three witches were executed:—Michael Udon of Plane, which is a little village near Poligny; Philibert Montot; and one called Gros Pierre. These men confessed that they had changed themselves into wolves and in that form had killed and eaten several people. While he was in the shape of a wolf, Michael Udon was wounded by a gentleman, who followed and found him in his hut where his wife was bathing his wound; but he had then resumed the form of a man. There have for a long time been pictures of these three witches in the Church of the Jacobins at Poligny. And in 1573 Gilles Garnier also confessed that he had made himself into a wolf, and in that form had killed and eaten several children, and was burned alive at Dôle by order of the Court. Here it will be relevant to recount what happened in the year 1588 in a village about two leagues from Apchon in the highlands of Auvergne. One evening a gentleman, standing at the window of his château, saw a huntsman whom he knew passing by, and asked him to bring him some of his bag on his return. As the huntsman went his way along a valley, he was attacked by a large wolf and discharged his arquebus at it without hurting it.

He was therefore compelled to grapple with the wolf, and caught it by the ears; but at length, growing weary, he let go of the wolf, drew back and took his big hunting knife, and with it cut off one of the wolf's paws, which he put in his pouch after the wolf had run away. He then returned to the gentleman's château, in sight of which he had fought the wolf. The gentleman asked him to give him part of his bag; and the huntsman, wishing to do so and intending to take the paw from his pouch, drew from it a hand wearing a gold ring on one of the fingers, which the gentleman recognised as belonging to his wife. This caused him to entertain an evil suspicion of her; and going into the kitchen, he found his wife nursing her arm in her apron, which he took away, and found that her hand had been cut off. Thereupon the gentleman seized hold of her; but immediately, and as soon as she had been confronted with her hand, she confessed that it was no other than she who, in the form of a wolf, had attacked the hunter; and she was afterwards burned at Ryon. This was told me by one who may be believed, who went that way fifteen days after this thing had happened. So much for men being changed into the shape of wolves.

But they are sometimes also changed into the shapes of other animals. For we read that Circe changed the companions of Ulysses into swine:

Circe did with her chants accursed and strange
The wretched comrades of Ulysses change.

And Lucian and Apuleius confessed that they were formerly changed into asses. It is probable that this is what happened to certain pilgrims who were crossing the Alps, according to the evidence of St. Augustine: as also to an Englishman who, says Guillaume Archbishop of Tyre, was thus metamorphosed by a witch of Cyprus while kneeling in a church; and to another mentioned by Vincent of Beauvais in his "Mirror," and by Baptista Fulgosus, who after he had been dipped in water returned to his former shape. Others also have held that the ass which Belon in his "Observations" says that he saw in Cairo in Egypt was none other than a transformed man.

De Civit. XVIII. 17.

VII. 11.

Bodin.

Others have been changed into cats. In our own time one named Charcot of the bailiwick of Gez was attacked by night in a wood by a number of cats; but when he made the sign of the Cross they all vanished. And more recently a horseman was passing by the Château de Joux and saw several cats up a tree: he approached and discharged a carbine which he was carrying, thereby causing a ring with several keys attached to it to fall from the tree. These he took to the village, and when he asked for dinner at the inn, neither the hostess nor the keys of the cellar could be found. He showed the bunch of keys which he was carrying, and the host recognised them as his wife's, who meanwhile came up, wounded in the right hip. Her husband seized her, and she confessed that she had just come from the Sabbat, where she had lost her keys after having been wounded in the hip by a shot from a carbine.

Cf. Bart. de Spin. de Strig. c. 19.

The Inquisitors also tell that in their time there were seen three large cats near the town of Strasbourg, which afterwards resumed the shape of women.

At other times men have been seen in the shape of a horse. Præstantius took the form of a horse; *Fulg. VIII. 2.* and an Egyptian's wife cured by St. Macharius that of a mare.

Again, there have been those who have been accused of changing themselves into hares, as was Pierre Gandillon, who was burned alive in this place.

But even if we had no other proof than the history of Nabuchodonosor, that would suffice *Dan. 4.* for us to believe that the metamorphosis of a man into a beast is possible. For it is said that this Prince was changed into an ox, and lived for seven years like a beast, eating straw.

The fact of transformation can again be proved from the example of Lot's wife, who was turned *Gen. 19.* into a pillar of salt which was still to be seen in *Luke 17.* the time of Josephus, as he himself testifies in *I. 19.* his "Antiquities." It is again instanced in the transmutation of all sorts of herbs and plants into various kinds of worms and serpents, which are all endowed with their appropriate forms and qualities, as we read in Cardan. Also we observe *De Subtil. XVIII.* that if a woman's hair be hidden in dung, it is changed to a serpent, as also is a rotten rod or wand. And in the town of Darien, a Province *Ibid.* of the New World, drops of water are in summer turned to little green frogs.

Nevertheless it has always been my opinion that Lycanthropy is an illusion, and that the metamorphosis of a man into a beast is impossible. For it would necessitate one of two things:—either the man who is changed into a beast must keep his soul and power of reason, or he must lose this at the moment of metamorphosis. Now the first point cannot be admitted, since it is impossible for the body of a brute beast to contain a reasoning soul. We know by experience that the wisdom or folly of a man is governed by the temperature of his brain, and that those with small heads are not usually very wise: then how can we believe that a soul gifted with reason can make its lodging in the head of a wolf or an ass or a cat or a horse or a hare? Besides, it is said in Genesis that man was created in the image and likeness of God, and this principally refers to the soul; and would it not be unspeakably absurd to maintain that so beautiful and holy a likeness should inhabit the body of a beast? Therefore I think that Homer was in error when, speaking of the companions of Ulysses who were changed into swine by Circe, he says that they had the hair, head and body of swine, but that their reason remained intact.

Gen. 1.

But if, on the other hand, a man loses his reasoning soul when he is metamorphosed, how is it possible for him to recover it, and for it to return into him when he resumes the shape of a man? If this were possible we should have to admit that the Devil can perform miracles, if we grant the truth of the maxim of the Philosophers, that "That which is lost can never be recovered." But then I ask, Where does Satan put the soul when it is separated from its body? Does he cause it to wander in the air, or does he shut it up somewhere until the Lycanthrope has resumed his human shape? Certainly I cannot think that God permits him who has sworn our utter ruin to play such tricks with us. Aristotle was far nearer the truth when he said that the soul no more leaves its body than a pilot leaves his ship. In conclusion I believe that the trans-

Cf. Richard, Discours des Miracles, c. 38.

mutation of a man into a beast in the manner we speak of is so much the less possible in that the truth is that He alone to whom creation belongs can change the forms of things. And it would be a shameful thing for man, to whom all the beasts of the earth are subject, to be clothed in the form of a beast. For the Law has so much respect for the human face, since it was formed in the likeness of celestial beauty, that it has not permitted it to be disfigured even by branding or otherwise as a punishment for any crime. A Council has even pronounced those to be infidels who believe in Lycanthropy and the metamorphosis of a man into a beast.

St. August. St. Thom. Binsfeld, de Confess. malef., 3. dub. princip. post præclud. conclud. 2. Psal. 8.

C. Episopi 26. q. 5.

As for Nabuchodonosor, he was never changed into an ox; but he thought he was so changed, and therefore went with the brute beasts and lived as they did. This is very clearly shown by the words of the Holy Scripture, which are repeated three times in the same chapter: "Thou shalt eat grass *as oxen.*" But even if we were to admit that this Prince was truly changed into an ox, it would not follow from that that witches have the power, with the help of Satan, to change themselves into wolves. For as to the former case, we must say with the magicians of Pharaoh: "This is the finger of God." In the same light I would regard what I have said of Lot's wife.

St. Jerome, Epipha. and many others quoted by Binsfeld, d. 3. dub. conclus. 3.

Dan. 4.

Exod. 8.

As for the herbs, and drops of water, and woman's hair which are changed into worms and serpents and frogs, this comes about through corruption and putrefaction, by which imperfect animals are engendered; but this does not apply in the case of Lycanthropes.

There have been those who have flatly contradicted the changing of a man into a beast, holding that the Lycanthrope did its work in the spirit only, whilst its body lay lifeless behind some bush. But there is no more truth in this than in the former opinion; for if it be true that, when the soul is separated from the body, death must necessarily ensue, how is it possible for Satan to bring the witch back to life, seeing that *Chap.* 17. to do so is possible with God only, as we have fully shown elsewhere?

My own opinion is that Satan sometimes leaves the witch asleep behind a bush, and himself goes and performs that which the witch has in mind to do, giving himself the appearance of a wolf; but that he so confuses the witch's imagination that he believes he has really been a wolf and has run about and killed men and beasts. He acts in just the same way as when he causes witches to believe firmly that they have been to the Sabbat, although they have really been lying in their beds; and it is likely that the ointment with which they rub themselves only serves to deaden their senses so that they do not awake for a long time. And when it happens that they find themselves wounded, it is Satan who immediately transfers to them the blow which he has received in his assumed body.

Notwithstanding, I maintain that for the most part it is the witch himself who runs about slaying: not that he is metamorphosed into a wolf, but that it appears to him that he is so. And this comes from the Devil confusing the four Humours of which he is composed, so that he represents whatever he will to his fantasy and imagination. This will be easier to believe when it is considered that there are natural maladies of such a nature that they cause the sick to believe that they are cocks, or pigs, or oxen. And here I shall set down what Cardan relates of André Osiander of Nuremberg, a man well versed in theology. This man was in his youth afflicted with a quartan fever; and when it attacked him, he thought that he was in a forest and that many serpents and other savage beasts attacked him; and there was no means of persuading him that he was only imagining this, and that he was all the time in his father's house. And whenever his father came to him, he always came back to his senses and recognised the house, the room and his friends; but when his father went away again, he again fell into his former sickness and imaginings, which continued for as long as the fever lasted. It is in the same way that those who are feverish, having their palates out of order, cannot correctly discriminate between different dishes. And when people see the witch in this shape, and think that it is really a wolf, the fact is that the Devil befogs and deceives their sight so that they think they see what is not; for such fascination is commonly used by the Devil and his demons, as we know from several examples. Simon Magus told the Emperor Nero that he might cut off his head, and he would come to life again on the third day; but he substituted a sheep, which they beheaded thinking that it was he. He also so troubled the eyes of St. Clement and several other holy persons that they mistook Simon for Faustinian. Again, there was once brought to St. Macharius a young woman whom everybody took to be a mare. About twelve years ago at Uzelle, which is a village in the department of Baume in our country, a certain man's house

de Subtil. lib. 18.

Clem. de recogn. lib. 10.

appeared to be all on fire, so that all the inhabitants ran to extinguish it as they usually do in such cases; but after about an hour they saw the house standing whole and quite undamaged; and this happened on three separate occasions, and was contrived by a certain chambermaid, as I was told by Monsieur Jean Cretenet, the Lord of Thalenay, a Canon of the Metropolitan Church of Besançon, who was himself present on one of these occasions. I also know of this from the report of the trial sent to me by the Lord Ayme Morel of Besançon. Consider also our card manipulators. I have seen an Italian Count named l'Escot, who practised this marvellously: he would put a ten of spades in your hand, and you would always end by finding that it was the king of hearts, or some other different card. Those in whose presence he did these tricks were men of wit who were very careful to make sure whether it was only a matter of sleight of hand. There is no doubt but that he cast some glamour over their eyes; for he also turned his back to them and muttered I know not what between his teeth when he did these sleight-of-hand tricks.

But why should we find anything very strange in this fascination by which Satan makes a man appear like a wolf to us? For, among other naturalists, Albert, Cardan and Giovanni Battista Porta of Naples have taught us how to cause men's heads to seem like those of horses and asses and other animals, and their snouts like a dog's. They even have means to make men appear like angels. And therefore I am the less surprised at the formulas which they also give for causing a house to appear silvery, luminous, green, full of serpents, and to assume other terrible forms. This is consonant with what we have just said of the house at Uzelle.

The following examples also are pertinent to our subject with regard to the last point which we have just touched upon.

About three years ago Benoist Bidel of Naizan, a lad of fifteen or sixteen, climbed a tree to pick some fruit, leaving his younger sister at the foot of the tree. The girl was then attacked by a wolf without a tail; whereupon the brother quickly climbed down from the tree. The wolf then left the girl and turned to the boy, and took from him a knife which he was carrying, and wounded him in the neck with it. People ran to the boy's assistance, and led him into his father's house, where he died of his wounds in a few days. But before he died he declared that the wolf which had wounded him had its two forefeet like a man's hands covered on the top with hair. They knew then that it was Perrenette Gandillon who had killed him; for she tried to make her escape after striking the blow, and was killed by the peasants.

Similarly Jeanne Perrin deposed that while she was going through a wood with Clauda Gaillard, Clauda said to her that she had received more alms than she; and then she went behind a bush, and Jeanne saw come from it a wolf without a tail, which pranced round her and so frightened her that she let fall her alms and ran away, after having protected herself with the sign of the Cross; and she added that this wolf had toes on its hind feet like a human being. There is a strong presumption that this wolf was no other than Clauda Gaillard; for she afterwards told

Jeanne that the wolf which attacked her would not have done her any harm. And as for the hands and the toes which were recognised by Benoist Bidel and Jeanne Perrin, are they not evidence that Perrenette Gandillon and Clauda Gaillard were not really transformed into wolves? We may say the same of the wife of the gentleman of Auvergne, of whom we wrote above, whose hand was found in the hunter's pouch instead of a paw. This agrees also with what Job Fincel says of his Lycanthrope of Padua, namely, that, when its paws were cut off, the man was found with his hands and feet cut off.

The confessions of Jacques Bocquet, Françoise Secretain, Clauda Jamguillaume, Clauda Jamprost, Thievenne Paget, Pierre Gandillon and George Gandillon are very relevant to our argument; for they said that, in order to turn themselves into wolves, they first rubbed themselves with an ointment, and then Satan clothed them in a wolf's skin which completely covered them, and that they then went on all-fours and ran about the country chasing now a person and now an animal according to the guidance of their appetite. They confessed also that they tired themselves with running. I remember once asking Clauda Jamprost how she was so well able to follow the others, even when they had to climb up rocks, seeing that she was both old and lame; and she answered me that she was borne along by Satan. But this in no way renders them immune from fatigue. For they who are carried by the Devil to the Sabbat say that when they arrive there, or when they return to their houses, they are quite weary and fatigued.

Remy, Demonol. I. 24.

In company with the Lord Claude Meynier, our Recorder, I have seen those I have named go on all-fours in a room just as they did when they were in the fields; but they said that it was impossible for them to turn themselves into wolves, since they had no more ointment, and they had lost the power of doing so by being imprisoned. I have further noted that they were all scratched on the face and hands and legs; and that Pierre Gandillon was so much disfigured in this way that he bore hardly any resemblance to a man, and struck with horror those who looked at him. Finally, the clothes of the children which they have killed and eaten have been found in the fields quite whole and without a single tear; so that there was every appearance of the children having been undressed by human hands.

Who now can doubt but that these witches themselves ran about and committed the acts and murders of which we have spoken? For what was the cause of the fatigue which they experienced? If they had been sleeping behind some bush, how did they become fatigued? What caused the scratches on their persons, if it was not the thorns and bushes through which they ran in their pursuit of man and animals? Again, is it not the work of human hands to unclothe a child in the manner we have described? I say nothing of their confessions, which are all in agreement with one another.

I am well aware that there are those who cannot believe that witches eat human flesh. But such people ought to consider that from all time there have been tribes which use this practice, even if they were not were-wolves, and that they have therefore been called Anthropophagi; and that it is even said that there are still a great number of them in Brazil and the lands of the New World, whose chief boast is to have eaten many of their enemies. Witches go even further; for they take down the corpses from gibbets in order to eat their flesh. Lucan says:

> She gnaws the rope through with her witch's teeth,
> She drags the gibbet down, unhangs the corpse,
> And then in cruel banqueting tears out
> The stomach's entrails and the marrow bones.

Horace also gives us sufficient evidence that witches are hungry for human flesh:

Ars poet.

> From the bloated body of an aged witch
> They cut a child which was not yet quite dead.

And Apuleius in the "Golden Ass" says that there were witches in Thessaly who used to search everywhere for dead bodies, so that if a corpse was not carefully guarded it would be found all gnawed about the nose and cheeks and mouth and several other parts. Not long ago at Nancy in Lorraine the corpse of one who had been tortured was left in the road outside the town; and it was found that during the night a thigh and a leg had been cut off from the body. There were many various opinions concerning this event; but for my part I maintain that only a witch did this deed; for on the same night there was seen a spectre hovering about the body, which so frightened a passer-by that, although he put his hand to his sword, he was compelled to run away into the town.

Cf. Bodin, Demonom. IV. 5.

Fulgosus also mentions a villager who was

burned alive because she had killed several children and salted them to keep as food for herself.

I am only puzzled by the fact that our witches said that they could not eat the head or the right side of those whom they killed. Groz-Jacques stated that he could not touch the head, by reason of the Holy Chrism with which it is anointed; and Clauda Jamguillaume said that they did not touch the right side because the sign of the Cross is made with the right hand. But I do not know that these are sufficient reasons, although they are largely substantiated by the strength and power which lies in the Cross and the Holy Chrism, of which we shall hereafter speak more fully.

And if anyone ask with what instrument witches, when appearing to be wolves, effect the death of those whom they kill, I shall answer that they have only too many contrivances for this purpose. For sometimes they use knives and swords, as did Perrenette Gandillon, who killed Benoist Bidel with his own knife; and therefore he who painted the three were-wolves of Poligny represented them as each carrying a knife in its right paw. At other times they drag their victims through rocks and stones, and so kill them. Clauda Jamprost, Clauda Jamguillaume and Thievenne Paget confessed that they did this. I make no doubt also that, for the most part, they strangle them.

For the rest, Jacques Bocquet and Pierre Gandillon said that, when they wished to turn into wolves, they rubbed themselves with an ointment given them by the Devil. Michel Udon, Gros Pierre and others confessed the same.

They said also that, when they wished to resume their former shape, they rolled in the dew or washed themselves with water. This agrees with Sprenger's statement that a man who has been changed into a beast loses that shape when he is bathed in running water. Again, the man mentioned by Vincent of Beauvais, who was changed into an ass, resumed his human shape when he was dipped in the water. Apuleius gives another method for restoring a man from the shape of an ass, which is to eat fresh roses or else anise and laurel leaves together with spring water. Pierre Burgot similarly said that, to lose his wolf's shape, he rubbed himself with certain herbs. But since, as we have shown, the metamorphosis of a man into a beast is for countless reasons a very controversial subject, we must not pay much attention to these remedies. Moreover, I believe that most often witches who think that they are wolves neither wash nor anoint themselves in order to resume their natural shape. I had nearly omitted to say that were-wolves couple with natural wolves according to the confessions of Michel Udon and Gros Pierre, who said that they had as much pleasure in the act as if they had been embracing their wives.

So much have I thought good to set down concerning Lycanthropes or were-wolves. Yet I should be sorry to leave this subject without reprimanding those who would excuse them and cast the blame for all that they do upon Satan, as if they were entirely innocent. For it is apparent from what I have said that it is the witches themselves who run about and kill people; so that we may here apply the Proverb which says: "Man is a wolf to man." And even if they were guilty in nothing but their damnable intention, they should still be thought worthy of death, seeing that the law takes cognisance of the intention even in matters which are not very serious, although nothing has actually resulted from such intention. I may add that such people never have this intention, except those who have first renounced God and Heaven.

L. 1. de Siccar. cum similib.

Chapter XLVIII.

That Witches generally Consecrate their Children to Satan; and of the Pain Suffered by Groz-Jacques and Certain Other Sorcerers.

GROZ-JACQUES confessed also that Satan had demanded one of his daughters from him, but that he had been unwilling to surrender her. But I am of a contrary opinion; for it is the custom of witches to dedicate their children to Satan, as is proved by many examples.

Psal. 106. *II Kings* 23.

Pierre Vuillermoz, the son of Guillaume Vuillermoz, said that his father had twice taken him to the Sabbat near the village of Coirieres when he was only ten years old, and that he continually urged him to give himself to Satan. The brothers Claude, Charloz and Perrenette Mollard likewise said that Clauda Gindre, their maternal grandmother, had taken them to the Sabbat when they were of very tender age. It is probable that Guillaume Vuillermoz and Clauda Gindre had vowed their children to Satan: yet these children had only to be frightened at the sight and hearing of the Devil to cause them not to give themselves to him. I surmise that this was owing to the fact that they had not yet reached the age of puberty. For Satan pursues only those who have passed the age of twelve or fourteen; since in his cunning and guile he knows full well that an agreement made with those who are younger than this cannot be binding, seeing that such have no judgement or discretion.

Clauda Gindre was the mother of Guillaume Vuillermoz, so that it is probable that she had also debauched her son. Pierre Gandillon debauched his children George and Antoine Gandillon, and took them to the Sabbat.

From this it is apparent that the common saying is true, namely, that it needs but one witch to pollute a whole family. And so it happened that there were formerly whole families in Africa and Italy which could kill people by looking at them or complimenting them, and that the race of Antæus in Arcadia used to turn into wolves, and afterwards resume their human shape.

But an even stranger matter is that there are fathers who, to please the Devil, have murdered their own children, as Manasses, King of Judah, who sacrificed his children to Satan, who in return promised to make him powerful. Medea also sacrificed two of her own children in order to cause the death of Glauce, daughter of King Creon. This has apparently happened in many other instances; so that David in one place complains, saying: "They sacrificed their sons and their daughters unto devils." And again: "And shed innocent blood, even the blood of their sons and of their daughters, whom they sacrificed unto the idols of Canaan."

Psal. 106.

There are even those who have not spared them even in their mother's womb, as the Baron de Rays.

Therefore I am not much surprised that strangers should have done the like, as did Stadlin, who confessed that he had killed seven children in their mother's womb; and the Emperor Maxentius, who used to have mothers ripped open all alive and their offspring taken away to be sacrificed to Satan and to form the material for the making of his virgin parchments.

> He opened up the wombs of wretched mothers. *Baptis. Mantua.*
> To have their fruits to sacrifice to devils.

It is not without cause then, to return to my argument, that it is taken as a great presumption of guilt against the accused if his father and mother, or one of them, are witches. Some have *Bodin,* maintained that this is an infallible rule; and *Demonom. IV.* there seems much to be said for such a view, con- *4.* sidering the great number of instances of parents who have destroyed their children in this way, and the fact that Satan's one object is the ruin of the whole human race in order that he may thus increase his kingdom. And therefore he urges those witches who have no children to debauch their neighbours and bring them into his net, as we have seen in the cases of Groz-Jacques, Grosse Françoise, the husband of la Micholette and several others.

Groz-Jacques was in the end burned alive, and died contrite and penitent. Clauda Jamguillaume, Thievenne Paget and Clauda Gaillard accompanied him in death; but the last of these would never confess anything, and proved so obstinate that it was with difficulty that she was persuaded to call upon God for mercy. We have spoken of her already, and shall later treat of the reasons for her condemnation.

I must not forget the methods used to draw the truth from Thievenne Paget. After she had remained in prison for about three months without confessing at all, she was lodged in a cell next to that of Groz-Jacques, who was one of her accusers. But they spoke to Groz-Jacques first, and he promised to do his utmost to induce her to confess. And he fulfilled his promise; for after Thievenne had been but one night next to him she confessed, and stood so well to her confession that, by order of the Judge, a man was sent in to her the next day, and told her that he had been to the Sabbat with her, and told her particulars of it which he took from the confession of Groz-Jacques and that of the other witches who had accused her. This is a practice which I recommend Judges to follow sometimes, but not always for reasons which I have hinted elsewhere.

As for Clauda Jamprost, she was executed some time before the others, being burned alive. She repented, and died very bravely.

CHAPTER XLIX.

Of Guillaume Vuillermoz known as le Baillu. Of his Confrontation with Pierre his Son, and the Causes of his Condemnation.

THE next trial was that of Guillaume Vuillermoz known as le Baillu, who had been committed to prison on the accusation of Groz-Jacques, Françoise Secretain and Rollande du Vernois. Christofle of Aranthon also asserted that she had seen him at the Sabbat, and also his son Pierre Vuillermoz maintained that he had taken him to the witches' assembly. He would never, however, confess: yet we would not have failed to condemn him, if he had not anticipated his sentence by dying in prison. The following were the reasons upon which we based his conviction.

1. The accusation of five of his accomplices.
2. The common report, attested by twenty-three witnesses, that he was a witch.
3. The fact that Clauda Gindre, his mother, was also suspect. This was deposed by the same witnesses, and was not denied by himself, or by one of his brothers who has since undergone torture at Dôle.
4. The fact that he was never seen to shed a single tear, however much he endeavoured to weep before the Judge.
5. That he had himself volunteered to be examined, so that we might see whether he had any mark upon him.

6. The execrable imprecations which he commonly used in his answers.
7. His confrontations with his son Pierre Vuillermoz, which I will here set down in writing. Since this man remained stubborn in his replies, and when confronted with Groz-Jacques, Françoise Secretain, Rollande du Vernois and Christofle of Aranthon, it was decided to confront him with his son, who was only twelve years old. When the boy had changed his coat in the prison, he was brought before his father, and the father was asked if he knew him. The man answered that he did not; whereupon the boy was brought nearer and was directed to speak, and said to his father that he knew him well. The man continued to deny it, and told the boy that he had changed his clothes. The boy was then stripped, but the father still had difficulty in recognising him. He was then asked if it was long since he had seen his son, and he answered that it was only four months, and that he had seen him on the very day of his arrest. The boy was then made to speak to him again; and at last, after having considered with himself for a long time, the father recognised him and said that it was his son Pierre. After this the son was asked whether his father had ever taken him to the Sabbat near the village of Coirieres; and the boy answered that he had, adding that all that he had told us was true. At this the father began to rage and shout and utter such words as: "Ah, my son, you will ruin us both," and he suddenly threw himself face downward on to the ground, so that it was thought that he had killed himself. Yet he recovered, and declared that he had never been to the Sabbat, and still less had he taken his

son there; but his words were always mingled with certain execrable imprecations, and at times he made as if to tear his lips and face with his nails. The son persisted in his statements, and calmly gave particulars of the time, place and manner of his being taken to the Sabbat by his father, who, he added, had promised him that they would thereby become rich, although he himself knew well that this was false. So much for the first confrontation of le Baillu with his son.

Afterwards the son was questioned separately as to whether he had not been suborned to say what he had said in front of his father; and he was remonstrated with, and given to understand that he would be the cause of his father being burned alive; he was even threatened with the lash. But he remained absolutely unshaken, and never varied in his statement. Therefore, a few days later, he was again brought before his father, to whom he maintained, as before, that he had twice taken him to the Sabbat near the village of Coirieres. The father denied this with his customary oaths. The boy added that, when at the Sabbat, his father had urged him to give himself to the Devil, but that he had refused to do so.

It was a strange and harrowing experience to witness these confrontations. For the father was emaciated through his imprisonment, he had fetters on his hands and feet, he wailed and shouted and threw himself to the ground. I remember too that, when he became calmer, he sometimes spoke kindly to his son, saying that whatever he did he would always own him as his child. And all the time the son never trembled in any way, but seemed as one insensible, so that it appeared that Nature had furnished him with weapons against herself, seeing that his own blood was in a way to bring to an ignominious death the man who had given him life. But assuredly I believe that in this was manifested a just and secret judgement of God, who would not allow so detestable a crime as witchcraft to remain hidden and not be brought to light. Also it is reasonable to believe that the son was not at that time pierced by the pangs of Nature, because his father had openly leagued himself against God and Nature.

C. privilegium 11. q. 3. C. cum accessissent de constitut. etc.

From this I would conclude that, in a case of witchcraft, it is right to admit the evidence of a son against his father and of a father against his son; and still more that kindred may testify one against the other, although their evidence against other persons may rightly be inadmissible.

L. parentes de testib. C.

Another reason which I would add is that the father usually makes his son, and the mother her daughter, a witch; the brother so initiates his sister, and the aunt her niece or nephew. And they always commit their crimes and abominations in the night and in secret, so that it is only their own kindred who are able to give evidence against them. In such cases effect must be given to the law which admits the evidence of those who are otherwise inadmissible as witnesses, when the crime has been committed at night. And further, if, in a case of treason against man, a son may bear witness against his father, and a father against his son, why should not this be allowed also in the crime of witchcraft, which is treason against both God and man in the highest degree? In olden times God commanded the Levites to take up arms and kill, each his own

D.D. in d. L. parentes.

C. vergentis de hæret. L. fin. de malefic. C.

brother and his kindred, because they had worshipped the golden calf. In short, if this practice were not allowed, this crime would for the most part remain unpunished, than which no greater misfortune could happen to the world, since God has so expressly commanded us to put witches to death.

CHAPTER L.

Whether one Accused of Witchcraft and Dying in Prison may be Buried in Consecrated Soil.

SINCE le Baillu died in prison there was some argument concerning his burial; for it seemed that he ought not to be buried in consecrated ground in view of the crime with which he was charged. However, the contrary opinion was followed as being more humane and equitable. Also it is in conformity with the law, which holds that the accused shall not be considered as guilty until he has actually been sentenced and the sentence has been confirmed. This holds good to the extent that, if the accused has lodged an appeal to a higher Court, he shall not be considered as guilty during the hearing of his appeal. Therefore, if a man be convicted of larceny, or any other crime which involves disgrace, and has appealed against his conviction, he shall not be held to be guilty until his appeal has been disallowed and his sentence confirmed. Similarly, the law upholds the validity of the will of a man who has lodged an appeal against a capital sentence, if he dies during the hearing of the appeal.

L. furti in princip. de his qui notan. infam.

L. qui a latronibus, § fin de testan. D.

I go further, and say that this condition should hold good not only in the case of one who has been convicted by witnesses, but also in that of one who has been convicted by his own confession, provided that he is penitent in the manner set forth in the Canon Law. For if he had lived, he might have proved that his confession was falsely made. Furthermore, the law intends that the crime shall be nullified by the death of the criminal.

C. placuit, 23. q. 5.

L. defuncto de public. judic.

It is another matter if the accused wilfully and deliberately kills himself in prison; for then he must be entirely denied the rites of burial. In this country it is even the custom to drag such a man on a hurdle through the town to the place of execution, where his body is either burned or hanged according to the gravity of his crime. I have seen this done to a schoolmaster who had hanged himself in prison; for by order of the Court his body was dragged on a hurdle through the town to the Tartre and there hanged on a gibbet. The same practice is observed in several other places, although some hold that it is contrary to the law, seeing that, as they say, it is not permissible to carry out an execution upon a dead body. But I maintain that our practice is defensible, because it is found by experience that the fear of being disgraced after death has deterred many from committing a crime. There is a notable example of this in Plutarch, where he tells of the Milesian virgins who could not be prevented from strangling themselves until an edict was published to the effect that any who hanged themselves in the future would be stripped naked after their death in the sight of all. Certainly it cannot be but that this practice must strike terror

C. placuit, &c. 1. de tornea. ex.

Jul. Clar. lib. 5. § fin. q. 51. nu. 15; 17.

into the hearts of those who contemplate a similar crime.

I do not wish to enter here into the question whether the body of a witch who has been put to death may be demanded by his relatives or others for the purpose of burial; for the matter is of itself evident. There is no doubt that we must refuse such a request. For if it is not allowed in a case of high treason, why should it be allowed in a case of witchcraft? For witchcraft is treason against both God and man, and is the most execrable crime that can possibly be imagined. This request may certainly be granted in cases of lesser crimes; and in this country particularly it is so, where the Court is accustomed piously to grant the body, of one who has died penitent, to the Brothers of the Cross, whose zealous care it is to vie with each other in taking such corpses from the gallows and burying them in consecrated ground in the most honourable manner possible. And this is in accordance with the provisions of the Canon Law.

L. 1. de cadaver punitor.

C. quæsitum 13. q. 2. vide Clar. § fin. q. 100. nu. 1, & Navar. consil. 16. nu. 1. 4. 5. lib. 5.

Chapter LI.

The Causes and Reasons of the Sentence Condemning Claude Gaillard.

THE condemnation of Clauda Gaillard was founded on the same reasons as that of Le Baillu.

1. It was popularly rumoured that she was a witch.

2. She was never seen to shed a single tear, however much she tried to weep.

3. In her answers she commonly used execrable imprecations.

4. Like le Baillu, she convicted herself before she was accused. For when she was asked, among other things, whether Humbert Guichon was married, she replied that he was, and that his wife was named Marie Perrier; and she immediately added of her own accord that she had never harmed that woman; and all the time that was the woman whom she had made sick by breathing on her face.

5. She was convicted on being brought face to face with Christofle of Aranthon; for when she and another were brought into the room where the Officers were, Christofle recognised her and firmly declared that she had seen her, together with other women whom she named, at the Sabbat near the village of Coirieres.

Also there were many discrepancies in her answers.

Finally, she was charged with several acts of witchcraft, and with having caused Marie Perrier and Clauda Perrier to fall sick by breathing upon their faces; also with having caused the death of six goats belonging to Pierre Perrier, and with having made one of Jean Perrier's mares sick, and with having afterwards cured it; and also with having changed herself into a wolf. It is true that in the case of most of these charges there was only one witness against her; but as they were all agreed in accusing her of witchcraft, and were all either kindred or connexions of hers, their evidence was considered as sufficient.

Chapter LII.

Of Pierre Vuillermoz and of Christofle of the Village of Aranthon, and how they were Treated Leniently on Account of their Youth and for Certain Other Reasons.

I Come now to Pierre Vuillermoz, son of le Baillu, and Christofle of the village of Aranthon, whom I can only name so, because she never knew the name of her father and mother, except that her mother was called Jeanne. These two were both put into prison: Christofle on the accusation of Groz-Jacques, and because she had spread the report that she had been taken by Groz-Jacques and Françoise Secretain to the Sabbat near the village of Coirieres; and Pierre Vuillermoz on the accusation of Christofle, and because he also affirmed on all sides that he had been twice taken by his father to the Sabbat near the village of Coirieres. Pierre was twelve years old when he was put in prison, and Christofle fourteen; but it was two years since either of them had been to the Sabbat.

Further, Pierre Vuillermoz had never been dedicated to the Devil, and it did not appear that he had committed any act of witchcraft; and although he confessed that, the last time his father had taken him to the Sabbat, he had urged him to give himself to Satan, he said that he had never consented to do so; and he added that he had been so frightened at seeing the Evil One and at hearing him speak, that for that reason he had never consented to go to the Sabbat again.

As for Christofle, she admitted that she had been given to the Devil, and that she had killed a cow at Coirieres at the instigation of Groz-Jacques and Grosse Françoise, who had given her a certain ointment with which she had rubbed the cow on the behind.

Christofle made a full confession; but Pierre Vuillermoz was three days in prison without any statement being drawn from him. Yet he was in the end released, the procurator being ordered to approach his nearest of kin with a view to having him catechised and instructed in our Catholic Apostolic Roman faith, and on condition that they undertook to prove that they were carrying out their duty within the next three months. This boy was treated thus leniently because he seemed to be innocent. For although he had been to the Sabbat, he was not therefore guilty, since he did not know where he was going when he was being taken there; also he was taken by his father, whom he dared not disobey. But his innocence was even more clearly shown by the fact that, when his father urged him to give himself to Satan, he would not do so, and would not again go to the Sabbat.

Christofle of Aranthon was banished from the land of Saint Oyan; and she was further commanded to be present at the execution of Groz-Jacques, Clauda Jamguillaume, Clauda Gaillard and Thievenne Paget, so that she might be afraid to continue in the service of Satan, and that the gravity of the punishment which she saw them suffer might be the occasion of her changing her life. They gave her three weeks in which to leave the country, and ordered the procurator in the meantime to have her catechised and instructed.

I have no doubt that a stricter Judge would have condemned her to death. For besides her confession that she had been to the Sabbat and had given herself to the Devil, it also appeared that she had killed a cow by witchcraft, so that she was to be reckoned as a witch, and was therefore deserving of death. Another very pregnant reason is that, once a person has been entangled in Satan's coils, he can never escape from them; for this is proved by the fact that no witch has ever been known to change her life, so that it is but waste time to show any mercy to witches, and by doing so they are even given the chance to commit ten thousand atrocities which would not have happened if justice had been done to them. And although Christofle was of tender age, yet that is no excuse; for in cases of serious and atrocious crime little count is taken of the criminal's age, unless it be to mitigate the sentence in some degree. And consequently it has been known for children of not more than fifteen years to be punished with death in accordance with the law, which is strict in this matter.

Barth. de Spin. q. de Strigib. c. 10. Remy, Daemonol. II. 2. Cf. Art. 63.

Bodin, Demonom. IV. 5. L. excipiuntur ad Syllania. L. si arrogati de Tutel. D.

Yet for several reasons it was judged better to confine this girl's punishment to banishment. Chiefly because she, as it were, anticipated justice in that, when Groz-Jacques and Grosse Françoise were put in prison, she immediately spread the report that she had been taken by them to the Sabbat; and because she freely confessed as soon as she was in the hands of Justice, and accused her accomplices, and asked to be instructed in our Holy Faith. And under such circumstances a

Cf. Bodin, ibid.

witch's punishment should be mitigated, especially when she is of tender age, as was Christofle, who had not yet reached the age of puberty when she was at the Sabbat. For the law itself excuses those who are not at the age of puberty, provided that they are incapable of fraud. This is in agreement with the words of Lucan:

C. illud 15 q. 1. & ibi glos. L. illud relatum de jurejur. D.

Lib. 9.

But we forgive him for his tender age.

And the prompt confession of this girl, and the simplicity of her answers, clearly showed that there was no malice in her.

She might well have been sentenced to the lash. But it was considered that this would irritate her rather than induce her to mend her ways. For since witches never leave the service of Satan for any punishment that is given them, except that of death, it is certain that, when they are released, that mortal Enemy of the human race urges them to avenge themselves and to do worse than before. Of this we have many examples, but I will take only that of Jeanne Harvillier. This woman, while still very young, was given the lash at Verbery for witchcraft; but she did not desist for that, but always continued in her wickedness until, thirty years later, she was burned alive at Ribemond. But it need be no matter of surprise that witches are not corrected by being scourged, or by any such punishment; for the Devil torments them far more than this, and even beats them to death, without their being able to abandon him, as we read in Sprenger, who tells that he condemned several witches who were cruelly beaten by the Devil if they did not do his commandments, and that they had no rest until they did so. Also Antide Colas confessed that

Bodin, Demonom. Preface.

the Devil urged her, while she was in prison, to throw herself from a window, or to hang herself from it; and because she would not, he beat her cruelly on the body.

And this is why it seems that one should not compromise when dealing with a witch, but should either treat them leniently, or else condemn them to death. This agrees with the advice which, as Livy says, an old Samnite captain gave his soldiers as to how they should treat the Romans. *Lib.* 9.

For my part I shall always maintain that, on the least pretext, they should be put to death; even if there were no other reason for this than the one which I have often mentioned, namely, that they never change their manner of living. Nevertheless it is possible that there may be such grounds for excusing them that it would be wrong to proceed to a sentence of death against them. But that must be left to the discretion of the Judge.

Chapter LIII.

Of Rollande du Vernois and how she was Possessed of Demons in Prison, and of her Deliverance.

Let us come now to Rollande du Vernois, whom we have mentioned several times. This woman was from the village of Cheyserie in Savoy and lived at the place of the Croya in the country of Saint Oyan de Joux. She was about thirty-five years old, and was put in prison on the accusation of Jacques Bocquet and Françoise Secretain. I propose to write a full account of the proceedings taken against her; for they are worth recording, particularly because, whilst a prisoner, she was possessed of two demons, and was delivered of them in prison.

After she was placed in prison, the Judge at once had her brought up for examination; and she was first asked whether she knew Jacques Bocquet and Françoise Secretain, to which she replied in the affirmative, making, the while, as if to weep, and crying that she was not what she was accused of being, and that she had not been to the Sabbat; yet without shedding a single tear. She confessed also that she had said to the sergeants that she was not marked, but that Groz-Jacques and Françoise Secretain were, and that she had heard tell to that effect.

She was at once confronted with Groz-Jacques and Françoise Secretain, who affirmed to her that they had seen her three or four times at the Sabbat near Coirieres; and this she denied, using execrable imprecations and many threats, even to the Judge.

She was then narrowly confined in prison, but after one day and night she told the gaoler that she had resolved to tell the truth if they would take her from that cell and bring her where she could warm herself. The Judge, who had meantime arrived, promised to take her to the fire himself, if she would confess the truth. To this she agreed, and thereupon confessed that she had been to the Sabbat near Coirieres once.

While she was warming herself they asked her

if she had been to the Sabbat, and she answered that she had been there once near Coirieres. Afterwards, they asked her what she did there; but to this question she remained dumb and unable to give any other answer than that she was prevented from telling the truth by the evil spirit which was possessing her, and which she felt like a big lump in her stomach, showing with her hand the place where she felt the pain. She then fell to the ground and began to bark like a dog at the Judge, rolling her eyes in her head with a frightful and horrifying look. From this it was concluded that she was possessed; and this was confirmed by two priests who were fetched to her, to whom she declared with great difficulty that the evil spirit was preventing her from telling the truth. Soon afterwards she returned to her senses and, in reply to the questions put to her, confessed:

1. That it was about six months since she had been to the Sabbat.
2. That she had been taken there one Thursday evening by Groz-Jacques.
3. That the Devil at that time appeared at the Sabbat as a big black cat.
4. That all those who were at the Sabbat went and kissed this big black cat on the rump.

They went on to ask her who this big black cat was; and she answered that it was the Devil; and upon that the evil spirit again began to torment her more than before, so that it was a long time before she could with difficulty pronounce the Holy Name of Jesus.

In the morning the demon left her again, and she confessed:

1. That when she was at the Sabbat she had given herself to the Devil.
2. That she had first renounced God, the Chrism and Baptism.
3. That Satan had carnally known her twice in the place of the Croya; and she at once added that the Devil did not wish her to tell the truth.

She was again asked if it were a fact that the Devil had had carnal knowledge of her; and she answered that he had, and that his semen was cold. But no sooner had she made this answer than the evil spirit renewed his attacks and closed her mouth, so that not a single word could be got from her, and to certain questions which were repeated to her she made signs with her head and two fingers that Satan had twice known her carnally, and then began to yelp and yowl like a dog, upon which they let her be.
The next day she confessed and said:

1. That she had been present when they were making the ointment at the Sabbat, but that she had not helped to make it.
2. That she had seen Clauda Coirieres and several others at the Sabbat.
3. That Groz-Jacques had afflicted her with the demons by which she was possessed, and that they came from an apple that Groz-Jacques had given her to eat.
4. That she had never before been to the Sabbat.

That was all that could be got from her at that time, for the evil spirit again began to torment her with such violence that it was decided that it would be best to have her exorcised. And this was done on the following day.
The priest, then, being ready first gave the pos-

sessed woman the Holy Virgin Mary for her advocate, and then proceeded with his exorcisms. First he conjured the demon to tell him his name: the demon proved to be obstinate in answering this, but on being pressed said that he was called Cat. He was then asked if he was alone, to which he replied that he was not, but that there were two of them, and that his companion was called Devil, and that they had been sent into Rollande's body by Groz-Jacques. The priest continued his exorcisms, and commanded the demons to come out. The Devil answered that their hour was not yet come, and that they still had a long time. And here began a great struggle between the priest and Satan. The priest made use of prayers and conjurations, and the Devil defended himself with blasphemy and mockery, and pretended that he took no notice of the minister of God. It was strange to see how the Evil One made use of the body and limbs of the possessed woman; for sometimes she squinted at the priest frowningly, sometimes she shook her head at him, sometimes she made grimaces at him and twisted her mouth, mocking at him. But chiefly I wondered at the strength of the poor creature's arms and hands; for if they tried to get her to kiss the Cross, she held her hands out to prevent anyone from approaching her with such vigour that no one could come near her; and if they tried to get her to take the Cross in her hands to sign herself with it, she was at once deprived of all use in her arms and hands, so that she could not even take hold of it. From which it was judged that the Cross is indeed a flail of the Devil.

It was the same when they tried to sprinkle her

with Holy Water; for she put every conceivable obstacle in the way of her receiving a single drop of it, sometimes putting her hands in front of her, and sometimes bowing her face to the ground. But it was an extraordinary sight when she was made to drink some of it; for it took two or three men to get her mouth open, and as soon as she had swallowed one drop the demon barked like a dog and cried, "You are burning me, you are burning me." And he said that if they continued to make him drink it, he had already had more than enough; and he even threatened to torment the woman all the more, the more they sprinkled her or made her drink Holy Water. And so he did; for at times he made her so weary and worn out that she could hardly breathe, and at other times she was as one dead.

The priest repeated his exorcisms and conjurations, and commanded the demons to come out and to depart into the lowest Hell; but the Devil answered that he would not come out, for his hour was not come. The priest again pressed him; and the Devil at last said that he was very near, but that his companion was still very low, and at this the possessed woman put her hand on her belly, and with her hand followed some object up as far as her throat, which in the end appeared as a lump in her throat. The demon then said that he was very near, yet that his hour was not come. Meanwhile night was approaching, so that it was necessary to go away and leave the possessed in the protection of God.

Nevertheless, one of the demons, namely Devil, did not fail to leave her at about seven or eight o'clock in the evening and came out of her mouth like a black slug, which crept about the ground a little and then disappeared, as Rollande stated the next morning.

There remained the other demon, namely, Cat. This one caused the possessed woman to be dumb for three whole days, so that during that time there was no means of drawing any information from her. He was also much more troublesome than the other, and therefore more labour was required in his case. The priest began his conjurations with a good heart: he asked in the Latin tongue what was his name, but it was difficult to elicit an answer. He persisted, still in Latin; and at last he replied with the word "Cat." He was questioned concerning his companion, and became stubborn about answering; but on being pressed said that he had already come out and was gone to hell. He was told that he must follow him, but answered that his hour was not come. The priest redoubled his exorcisms, using the Cross and Holy Water against the miserable spirit; and the possessed woman behaved just as she had on the first day, looking terrible and twisting her mouth and making horrible grimaces, and shaking her head in mockery she threw herself to the ground, so that at times it took four or five men to hold her.

But it was terrible to hear the demon crying and barking when the priest came to pronounce the Holy Name of Jesus, or invoked the aid of the Blessed Virgin Mary, or brought the Cross near to the demoniac, or sprinkled her with Holy Water or made her drink it. For at times he said that they were burning him, and at times that they had given him enough Holy Water, and that if they sprinkled him with any more he would never come out, but would torment the body of Rollande all the more.

The priest then conjured him to come out, but he replied that he would not and that his hour was not come; and then he tormented the possessed more violently, at times using gloating words: "I have well tormented this body," or "I am very close." At these words Rollande's throat was seen to swell as before, so that it was thought that the demon was just about to come out. But he never did, saying that his hour was not come and that he would not come out.

Finding him so obstinate, the priest prepared a fire, upon which he cast certain perfumes, and then wrote his name on a paper which he immediately burned. At this the demon howled and barked furiously, so that our hair stood on end to hear him, and to see Rollande so exhausted that she could hardly draw her breath.

At this moment Rollande made a gesture with her hand and eyes in the direction of the room in which Groz-Jacques was confined, and then towards the windows which looked out on to the road. When she was asked what she meant by this sign, she could only answer, "Groz-Jacques." For the demon made her dumb. I saw at once that she wanted Groz-Jacques brought in, thinking that, since it was he who had sent the demons into her, he might, if he were brought near her, rid her of her demon. And when she was asked if that was not what she meant, she signed that it was. Nevertheless, she was warned that, for the reasons which I have shown elsewhere, it was not good to seek the help of Groz-Jacques.

Therefore the priest continued his exorcisms. Being pressed, the demon said that he would come out on condition that he was given something. He was asked what he wanted, and said that he wanted bread and cheese. The possessed was then given Blessed Bread, without having been told that it was Blessed. She put it in her mouth, but immediately spat it out again. All the time the demon clamoured to be given something, using the Savoyard words *quaque ran.* Yet he was given nothing, except Holy Water by force; and since night was approaching, we withdrew. Nevertheless, two or three hours after we had left the possessed woman, the demon came out of her in the same manner as the other one.

I must not omit to say that, once when I went to see this woman while she was possessed by the latter demon which made her dumb, she put her hand to her mouth in such a way that it was easily seen that she wanted something. And when I asked her what she wanted, she answered in her own language by this single word, *l'asse,* which means milk. I then asked if it was she herself who wanted the milk, and she signed that it was not she, but the demon. From this I recognised the cunning and astuteness of the Devil, who always tries to get us to give him something; and therefore he usually persuades the person he is possessing that he is hungry, as he did in the case we are speaking of, and in that of Loyse Maillat. All demoniacs bear witness to this fact.

Chapter LIV.

Against those who Mock at the Exorcisms and Conjurations of our Priests.

Cf. Richer, Discours des Miracles, c. 33.

HERE I cannot but marvel at those who mock at the exorcisms and conjurations used by our priests towards demoniacs. What reason can they have? Did not Jesus Christ cast out devils when He was upon earth? The New Testament gives us countless examples of it; but I will be content to quote the case of him who

Mark 5.

had a legion of devils, of whom St. Mark writes in his Gospel. Besides, do we not know that

Matth. 17.

Jesus Christ gave the same power to men? "Ye shall know them that believe on Me by this sign, that they shall cast out devils in My name." And again: "This sort goeth not out save by prayer and fasting."

Acts 16.

It was thus that St. Paul delivered a certain damsel possessed with a spirit of divination from the devil which tormented her; and in another

Acts 19.

place it is said that God wrought special miracles by the hands of St. Paul, so that from his body were brought unto the sick handkerchiefs or aprons, and the diseases departed from them, and

St. Gregor. 1. 1. Dial. c. 10. St. Jerome, in vita D. Hilario.

the evil spirits went out of them. After the Apostles, holy men did likewise. We read that St. Fortunatus and St. Hilarion used by their prayers to cast devils out of men, and that the latter cast out two hundred in the Isle of Cyprus. The like is told of St. Bernard, St. Martin, St. Gall and many other holy men. Then why should not our priests do the same? The hand of God is as powerful now as it was in days of old.

I say further that the devils themselves have made use of conjurations. For one of them, speaking to Jesus Christ, in the Gospel of St. *Mark* 5.
Mark, said: "I adjure Thee by the living God that Thou torment me not"; and in fact he obtained his request, which was that he and his companions should not be sent out of the country of the Gadarenes. But the countless examples of those who are daily delivered in the sight of all, and of whom I have elsewhere made mention, should suffice to shut the mouths of these atheists and heretics; to whom I would further point out that the ceremonies of our priests are holy and religious, and shall put before them a thing which happened not far from here some eight years ago, which should quite put them to confusion.

The son of a Huguenot gentleman was possessed of a devil, and they brought the local minister to conjure it. But this minister had no power against devils, as was at once recognised by the father; who, being more anxious for his son's health than strict in the observance of his own religion, secretly sent for a Catholic priest, who used the accustomed exorcisms of the Roman Church with such sincerity that the possessed was soon delivered. I would name the gentleman if I were not afraid of his being arrested by the Governors of the Canton to which he is subject. It is enough to say that I have this story from a most reliable source; and that I do not marvel that the minister of whom we have spoken could not cast out the devil from the body of the possessed, for no minister has ever had that power, any more than we read that any heretic has ever performed a miracle. I refer the reader to what I have said in Chapter 17.

But to resume the thread of our argument; is it not in the name of Jesus Christ that our priests conjure the evil spirits to depart? Did not St. Paul do the same? "I command thee," he said, "in the name of Jesus Christ to come out of her"; and he came out the same hour.

Acts 16.

And as for the Cross and the Holy Water which the priests use, are not these the flails of the Devil?

Chapter LV.

Of the Power and Virtue of the Cross against Demons and their Subjects.

As to the Cross, history tells us that a certain Gregory, Bishop of Langres, and one Albinus, Bishop of Anjou, used to drive devils from the bodies of the possessed by this sign. It was the same weapon that the hermits of times past and other Saints used to fight devils. So did St. Antony and St. Margaret; and with the sign of the Cross St. Justina drove away the two demons sent to her by St. Cyprian, when he was yet addicted to sorcery, to attempt her virginity. Similarly Epiphanius tells that a Christian lady at the Baths of Gadara in Judæa freed herself by means of this healing sign from the enchant-

Greg. Turo. in vit. patr. c. 7. Vincent, III. 243.

Lib. 1. To. 2. contr. hæres.

ments of those who were persecuting her. We read also of several who, when they have found themselves either by accident or out of curiosity at the Sabbat, have made the sign of the Cross, whereupon everything, devils, dishes and persons, has vanished.

But let us take the far stranger example of Julian the Apostate. This renegade met one day in a temple of idols with several devils who were conspiring for the ruin of the whole human race. He was frightened by the sight of such an assembly and, in imitation of the Christians, made the sign of the Cross; thereupon all the devils at once vanished, saying of Julian that he was an empty vessel, but that he was protected by the sign of the Cross with which he had armed himself.

A similar thing happened about forty years ago when the Bernese held the bailiwick of Gex under a certain Charcot, who was of the so-called reformed religion. This man was attacked one night in the Wood of Rat by a number of cats, against which he defended himself with a sword; but finding that his sword was no protection, he made the sign of the Cross, upon which all the cats vanished. The Bailiff, a Bernese named Augustin de Lutherno, hearing of this sent for Charcot, who confirmed the story which had been told to him; and the Bailiff then said to him that, if he found the sign of the Cross of such benefit, he ought always to make use of it in the future. I have this story from the Lord of Pongny, a gentleman of the land of Gex, and a man of honour.

Only nine months ago Antoine Gentil of the country of Vaux, also a Bernese subject and of the same religion as Charcot, in the same way drove off the Devil with the sign of the Cross. He was taking a large quantity of cheeses by water to Lyons, and they were submerged by a storm which suddenly arose. In despair over this loss, Gentil wandered about until, as he was passing a wood, he met a big black man who said that, if he would give himself to him he would recover his cheeses for him and make him rich again. Gentil asked him who he was, and he answered that he was the Devil. Thereupon Gentil made the sign of the Cross, and the big black man at once disappeared. Afterwards, when he was asked why he had made the sign of the Cross, seeing that he was a Huguenot and that there is nothing which the heretics more hate than the Cross, he answered that in a case of necessity it was good to use all possible means of protection. I know this from those who went with him to Lyons. There was also one Joseph who, although not a Christian, cast out devils from those who were possessed by means of the Cross; and this caused him to embrace Christianity.

In short demons can never bear the sign of the Cross without trembling all over. Besides those which I have just related, we have a good instance of this in Caron's "Antichrist Unmasked," which I shall here quote. "When the matter was thus confirmed" (he is speaking of a child who was found to be possessed), "I went one day into the house where the child was; and on my entry, there came up to me a Huguenot girl about eighteen years old holding a little silver Cross, who signed to me to take notice of what she would do. The child was all bunched up in bed, with his nose pressed against his knees, well covered up and with his back to us, so that it was impossible for him to see us; and the Huguenot girl began to apply the Cross to his shoulders. Upon this the child suddenly twisted and stretched himself out, grimacing and crying out against us. Then he put himself back into the bed as he was before. I then took the Cross; but I could never come within two fingers' breadth of the possessed but that he immediately rose up and twisted himself about as before. I tried several times on that and the following days." So says Caron; but this is no more strange than that which I saw happen in the case of Rollande du Vernois, which I have already related.

Chap. 53.

Further, witches never have a Cross on their rosaries, or if they have, it is defective; and, as I have before remarked, he who says the Mass at the Sabbat has no Cross on his cope. Witches always have great difficulty also in making the sign of the Cross; this was the case with Antide Colas, chiefly when she was in church. And if they are carefully watched when they sign themselves, it will be seen that they never make the complete sign of the Cross, and that they are hardly able to place their right hand in the position we are accustomed to use when we make the sign of the Cross. This need not appear strange, when we consider that the Devil makes them swear and vow very solemnly to put no faith in the Cross, but rather to trample it always underfoot, as we are told by Sprenger. By such behaviour they act in direct opposition to the Edicts of the Emperors Theodosius and Valentinian, which forbade under heavy penalty anyone even to carve or paint the Cross on the

Mall. malef. II. 1. 2.

L. unic. cum suo nigro nemin. licer. Sign. Salvato Christ.

hum. vel in silic. vel in marmor. aut insculp. aut ping.

ground, saying that it was the sign of the Saviour, so that no one should walk upon it or soil it.

It can therefore easily be understood that the Devil holds the Cross in great abhorrence. So true is this that the first artifice which he uses is to have the Crosses destroyed, as they have been in several places in the New World, and especially in the realm of Quabacondono, who forbade his subjects to wear the Cross on pain of death; and he was not even content to banish it from his land, but wished his Edicts to have effect on the sea also, so that the people were compelled to destroy the Crosses on the banderoles of their ships. Antichrist also brands his subjects with his mark upon the brow or the hand, so that none may make the sign of the Cross on his brow. A dog, seeing the stick with which it has been beaten, at once cries out and runs away: in the same fashion the Devil fears the power of the Cross, which he well felt when Jesus Christ felled him to the ground with it; so that, on seeing it, he quickly takes to flight. Further, it is obvious that the Cross has this power not only *ex opere operantis*, but also *ex opere operato*, as the Theologians say; since even when it is used by heretics, the Devil is put to flight by them.

And for this reason the Holy Fathers, knowing very well that this sign is one of the greatest flails of the Devil, exhort us to protect ourselves with it in all our actions so that Satan may never have any power against us. I shall quote the words of Tertullian, one of the most ancient of the Fathers. He says: "We sign ourselves with the Cross on the forehead at every step, at every coming in and going out, when we rise up, at the

St. Greg. lib. 1. Dial. c. 3. St. Jerome in Ep. ad Eustoch.

bath, at the table, in public, in our chamber, on sitting down, in short to whatever side we turn and wherever we go we shall sign ourselves with this sign." St. Gregory, St. Jerome, St. John Chrysostom, St. Cyril and Theodoret teach us the same. St. Athanasius also has written that at the sign of the Cross all magic arts vanish, and witchcraft is without virtue or power: "Let him who wishes to prove this hereafter make the sign of the Cross and invoke the name of Jesus Christ when the demons are doing their utmost to impose upon his belief with their impostures and deceits and magic miracles, and he will see how, merely through fear of this sign and this Name, the Demons will flee away, their magic answers will be silenced, and their sorceries numbed and dead." Origen says as much in one place.

Tertull. de Coron. milit. c. 3.

De Incarn. Dom. & salv. eius advers.

In Exod. c. 15. homil. 6.

Finally, Constantine the Great (for I wish to finish this chapter with him), having proved in warfare how great was the power and virtue of this Sign, had the following words inscribed on a Cross which he caused to be set up in Rome to the right of his statue: "This is the Sign of Salvation."

Euseb. in vita Constant.

Chapter LVI.

Of the Might and Virtue of Holy Water against Demons.

Can. aquam de consecr. dist. 3.

Holy Water was in part instituted for driving away evil spirits; and experience proves that it is effective in this. For why is it that demons whine and bark like dogs when we sprinkle the bodies of those whom they possess? Why do they so often cry out that "they are burning, they are burning," if it be not that they feel this Water to be one of the greatest scourges that is used against them?

Cf. Thyr. de loc. infest. Part I. c. 1. *num.* 19.

Again, why do they also flee away when we sprinkle the place which they have been haunting? This happened at Camon in Germany, where a spirit began to trouble the people without at all showing himself at first, by throwing stones at them and beating upon the doors of the houses. But soon after he showed himself in the form of a man and did ten thousand mischiefs. Yet, when the place was sprinkled with Holy Water by certain priests sent by the Archbishop of Mayence, the spirit at once disappeared and never returned. The same thing happened in another place mentioned in the Life of St. Gregory, where the Evil Spirit in the form of a bull ran after the herds and the shepherds; and the place could not be rid of him until it had in the same way been sprinkled with Holy Water.

Ioan. Diac. in vita D. Greg. IV. 93.

St. Martin also used Holy Water to cast a demon out of one who was possessed. What Caron relates in his "Antichrist Unmasked" makes it *Marg.* 1.
clear that the demons have no love for this Water. For he says that he himself made several demoniacs sit down at his table, and gave orders for their wine to be diluted with Holy Water. But they could never be taken off their guard or be induced to swallow a single drop, but shuddered when they carried the glass to their mouth: yet they had no difficulty in drinking wine diluted with ordinary water. We have sufficient proof in what we have already told concerning Rollande du Vernois. For what reason, then, is it that the Devil forbids witches to take Holy Water, as he did in the case of Pierre Burgot among others, if it is not because he knows that it has power to frustrate his designs and magical endeavours, and because he abhors it, since it turns to fire and burns him?

CHAPTER LVII.

Of the Perfumes Used by Priests in their Conjurations.

IT remains for us to show that it is not out of place for our priests to use perfumes in their exorcisms; and this will be very easy. I will readily admit that perfume has no direct virtue against the Evil Spirit, since he has no body and consequently no sense of smell: yet it must be granted me that this wicked Serpent is very glad to find in the bodies of men humours which the more dispose them to be tormented by him, the chief of these being the melancholy humour, which is of its nature apt to be heavy and sad; and therefore we find that those of a melancholy humour are more often possessed by a devil than are other men.

Card. de vareit. lib. 16. *Wier, de praestig. V.* 9.

Now it is certain that there are perfumes which consume and correct these humours, for even sulphur works in a very subtle manner to that effect; and therefore I conclude that the Devil will be more easily cast out of a demoniac's body if it be purged of the humours of which we have just spoken, than if it be still charged with them. I am strengthened in this belief by the fact that Holy Scripture teaches us that the Evil Spirit is more glad to be in one body than another, as we see in St. Mark, where the devils, being commanded by Jesus Christ to come out of a man's body, asked to be sent into some swine. It follows, therefore, that the perfumes of our priests must not be decried, since they are, in some manner, of use against devils. This is even better shown by the example of the youth Tobias, who drove away the Devil with a perfume which he composed from the heart and liver of a fish. It is true that he accompanied this with prayers and fasting; but do not our priests the same? There is no doubt, also, that perfumes which are hallowed by the Word of God are of greater virtue against the Devil than such as are used in their own natural state; and therefore Origen, speaking of perfumes and incense, says that the sanctification by the Word of God, with Holy Prayer

Mark 5.

Homil. 20 *in Jos.*

and the help of the Angels, is the reason for perfume and incense driving out demons.

But who will contradict me when I say that God endows these perfumes with a supernatural power against demons and their works, seeing that we have already mentioned certain stones and herbs which drive away all spells and enchantments? For that He may the more manifest His Majesty, God wishes to fight and overcome demons by means of these insignificant things, just as He put Pharaoh's magicians to shame when they tried to create flies; for although they, as well as Moses, had made frogs and serpents and dragons, yet they could not succeed in making these small and minute little creatures.

Chapter LVIII.

Against those who Assert that Satan Pretends merely to Fear the Cross, Holy Water and Exorcism; and that in Reality he Cares not.

Further, we may laugh at those who say that the Devil does not really fear Exorcisms or the Cross or Holy Water, but only pretends to fear them. For if it be true that this Enemy of the human race seeks nothing but our total ruin, how can we believe that he would willingly leave the body of a man whom he wishes to torment and lead to perdition? Why does he not remain always in him, to make him drown himself or hurl himself down? Why, again, when Jesus

Christ was about to cast him out of a man whom he was possessing, did he use these words:
Mark 1. "What have we to do with Thee, Thou Jesus of Nazareth? Art Thou come to destroy us? I know Thee who Thou art, the Holy One of God"? We must infer from these words that it sorely vexed the Evil One to leave the body which he was possessing.

Chap. 55. Again, we have seen how the devils fled at the sign of the Cross made by Julian the Apostate; and who can say that this flight was merely simulated? If it were, we could only conclude that the devils wished by this means to invite Julian to return to Christianity and again worship the Cross; and that they left men's bodies
Ibid. when Joseph made the sign of the Cross, in order to draw him to Christianity. It would follow also that the cats, which were no other than devils and witches, who fled when Charcot made the sign of the Cross, did so to persuade this member of the so-called reformed religion to range himself under the standard of the Roman Church, which has the Cross as its chief emblem of salvation. To argue similarly from the case of Antoine Gentil, of whom we spoke in the Chapter on the Cross, would be to draw an
Cf. Thyr. de loc. infest. par. 3. *c.* 68. *n.* 12. 13. absurd conclusion, as certain Theologians say. No, no; it is impiety to deny the might and virtue of the Cross and Holy Water and Exorcisms. For even the most irrational beasts obey them, as may be seen from St. Thomas, who holds that it is lawful to conjure them, since they are troubled by Satan in order to bring
In manual. c. 27. *n.* 13. harm to men. This view is upheld also by Navarro.

It should not be a matter of wonder that we

have said that the throat of Rollande du Vernois was seen to swell before the departure of her demons, and that the demons came out of her mouth in the form of slugs; for there is nothing abnormal in either of these points. As to the first, the Devil usually gives some sign of his departure from a person's body, and it has been noted that the commonest of these signs is for the place by which he means to come out to become swollen and big beyond measure. This happened to the demoniac whom St. Catherine of Siena delivered, when the demon raised horrible tumours in the sufferer's throat.

Thyr. de Dæmon. par. 4. c. 52. num. 13.

Raim. in vita Cath.

And as to the second point, demons have often been seen to leave the bodies of possessed persons in the form of some animal, such as flies, spiders, ants, lizards and other such beasts. Palladius even tells that he saw a devil once come out of a young man in the shape of a dragon seven cubits long.

Thyr. de Dæmon. p. 3. c. 44. nu. 5. & p. 4. c. 52. nu. 8.

Sect. 25 in uita Paul simpl.

But let us return to the history of Rollande.

CHAPTER LIX.

Continuation of the Replies of Rollande du Vernois; and of her Condemnation.

WHEN this woman was delivered of her demons, and was again examined, she gave the following answers:

1. She confirmed her first and second confessions, except in the matter of having been car-

nally known by the Devil; for this she retracted.
2. She added that, when she was at the Sabbat, she had offered candles to the Devil, and together with the rest had kissed him on the hinder parts.
3. That she had helped to cause the last hailstorm which fell in the district of Moussieres.
4. That, besides Groz-Jacques and Françoise Secretain, she had also seen at the Sabbat Clauda Coirieres, Guillaume Vuillermoz known as le Baillu, and a brother of his.
5. That she had been to the Sabbat only three weeks before she was put in prison.

She was again examined on the 3rd of November; and after having repeated her first, second and third statements, confessed further:

1. That the Devil, in the form of a black cat with horns, appeared to her at the place of the Croya on the same night that she went to the Sabbat, which was about six months before she was put in prison.
2. That after a long struggle she gave herself to Satan, and renounced God, Chrism and Baptism.
3. That she then at once went on foot to the Sabbat near the village of Coirieres, with Groz-Jacques and Françoise Secretain.
4. That when she went to the Sabbat she was already possessed.
5. That she had only been there once.

Upon this it was pointed out to her that she was mistaken in saying that she had only once been to the Sabbat, since it was apparent from her answers that she had been there twice. For first she had confessed that she had been there three weeks before her imprisonment, and then that about six months before she was put in prison the Devil had appeared to her at the place of the Croya in the form of a cat, and that she had been to the Sabbat the same night. She answered that she had not properly understood the question on this last point, and that she thought she had been asked whether she had long been possessed before she was put in prison. Yet the question had been put to her very clearly.

Some days later she was again examined; and after repeating her first, second, third and fourth statements, said:

1. That she knew Pierre Vuillermoz, le Baillu's son, and Christofle of Aranthon, but that she had never seen them at the Sabbat.
2. That she had several times quarrelled with Perrenette, the wife of Claude Panisset; and that in the course of these Perrenette had reproached her with a rumour that she was a Vaudoise; saying that if she were certain of this she would have nothing to do with her, but that she could not believe it.
3. That more than three years before her imprisonment all the villagers of Prel had reproached her with being a Vaudoise and a witch, but that she did not know the reason for this.
4. That she had several times helped Clauda Coirieres to gather her hemp.
5. That when the Devil appeared to her in the form of a black cat at the place of the Croya, she had been of perfectly sound mind, and not at all troubled.
6. That before her imprisonment she did not know that she was possessed; but only felt that there was something which moved in her belly,

and that her sight troubled her at times, and that she sometimes had words with her sister Jeanne; but that this only happened intermittently, and not continuously.

7. That she went to the Sabbat with Groz-Jacques and Françoise Secretain, and that she met them near the place where the Sabbat was held.

8. That, when he appeared to her, the Devil told her where the Sabbat was held.

9. That she did not know by what means she went there.

After these confessions, she was confronted with Pierre Vuillermoz and Christofle of Aranthon, who stoutly maintained that they had seen her at the Sabbat near Coirieres twice, and two years before her imprisonment. But she denied all this.

Upon this the Judge ordered her to undergo torture in order to draw the truth from her concerning certain points. She then lodged an appeal; but the Court declared this null and void, together with the order for her torture; and by a fresh and just sentence condemned the appellant to be led by the executor of High Justice to the Tartre, and there to be tied to a stake and burned. This was carried out on the seventh of September in the year 1600.

But as they took her from the prison, the air at once became darkened by very dense clouds, which burst into such abundant and furious rain that it was with great difficulty that the fire could be lit to burn her. It is probable that this sudden rain was caused by Satan, who may have given Rollande an assurance that she would not be burned, or at least that she would not feel the flames and the heat of the fire. For he usually makes this promise to witches, so as to keep them in the coils of his net, and that they may lose the opportunity to repent. So it happened to this witch, for she died obstinate; and when she was exhorted to repent and turn to the immense mercy of God, she only answered that she had a good master.

In my opinion the principal reasons for her condemnation were these:

1. That it was evident, both from her replies and from her confrontation with Françoise Secretain and Pierre Vuillermoz and Christofle of Aranthon, that she had given herself to the Devil, and had been to the Sabbat long before she was possessed. Moreover, this was also affirmed by Groz-Jacques, in whose word the more faith was put because, dying contrite and repentant, he had prayed the Officers to do justice upon her, saying that if they let her escape she would spoil all.
2. Her consorting and familiarity with Groz-Jacques and Clauda Coirieres, who had been burned a few days before for the crime of witchcraft.
3. The discrepancies found in her answers.
4. The common rumour which had long been against her, which she herself admitted, saying that all the people of Prel had accused her three years before her imprisonment of being a Vaudoise and a witch.
5. That she had never shed any tears, although she had often tried her hardest to weep.
6. That those whom she had accused of having been to the Sabbat with her were all suspected

of the crime of witchcraft, so that some of them had been burned, some tortured, and others had died in prison.

7. Finally, many things were noticed about her which could not be simply attributed to a demoniac. Namely, that she shed no tears; that she had been carnally known by the Devil; and lastly, that she had been to the Sabbat and had there caused it to hail. All these are deeds that cannot be attributed to mere possession by a devil.

For these reasons little notice was taken of her plea as an excuse that she was possessed when she went to the Sabbat, and that if she had confessed anything which told against her, it was not she who confessed, but the demons which possessed her, speaking through her mouth. For this was clearly proved to be false by what we have just said.

And although she retracted certain points, that could not be held to be of any consequence; for, as we have shown elsewhere, not too much reliance is to be set upon a witch's first confession. Moreover, she did not make it apparent that there was any mistake in her confessions.

One thing I shall add concerning this woman. It has been a matter of wonder that she should have been possessed when she was already a witch ; for there are those who have held that witches are not easily possessed by demons. This point is fully argued by Thyraeus in his "Treatise upon Demoniacs."

CHAPTER LX.

Whether the Eucharist may be Administered to One Accused of Witchcraft.

I HAVE thought good to add here two questions very useful and necessary for the subject of which we are treating. First, whether the Eucharist may be administered to one accused of witchcraft. Second, whether, when the person accused of witchcraft be but found guilty of having been at the Sabbat, without being charged with any act of witchcraft, the Judge may pass sentence of death upon him. These two questions I shall briefly discuss in two chapters.

As for the first question, I will admit that it applies equally in the case of those who are charged with any crime, other than witchcraft, which involves a sentence of death.

Although the difficulty seems to be resolved by *C. queasitum*
the Canon, which provides that, when the con- 13. *q.* 2.
demned has confessed his sins and is contrite and penitent, the Eucharist should be given to him, nevertheless we read in Gaguin that the contrary was observed in the year 1475, in the time of King Louis the Eleventh, in the case of Louis of Luxemburg, Constable of France, to whom the Eucharist was denied after his sentence had been pronounced.

Also it is the custom in Spain and France not to administer the Eucharist to the condemned on the same day of their sentence, but to do so on

Consil. 16 de penitent. & remiss. lib. 5. d. consil. 16. nu. 2. 12. the foregoing days. Navarro testifies to this custom; and he also is of opinion that the Eucharist may be administered in the morning, one hour before the sentence is passed.

But whatever may be advanced in respect of other crimes, I for my part maintain that, in the crime of witchcraft, the Eucharist should never be given to the accused, for fear lest he should abuse it. For it is noted that witches normally *Lib. 5.* abuse the Eucharist, as did those of whom Pontanus speaks, who, to help the French besieged by the Spaniards in the town of Sessa Aurunca in the Kingdom of Naples, dragged the Cross through the streets with a thousand insults and blasphemies, and threw it into the sea, and afterwards gave a consecrated Host to an ass, which they buried alive under the church door. Froissart also tells in his History of a certain man of Soissons who had a toad baptised, and afterwards made it eat a consecrated Host. The Inquisitors likewise relate that a witch confessed to having received the consecrated Host in her handkerchief instead of swallowing It, and that she shut It up in a pot where she was feeding a toad, and mixed all with other powders which the Devil gave her, and then put this mixture under the threshold of a sheep pen after saying certain words, in order to cause the sheep to die. Even a certain great King of Christendom abused It formerly through the agency of a necromancer. For he cut off the head of a first-born child of ten years, and placed the head upon a consecrated Host to know his future fate; and the head answered in these words; *Vim patior*. The King died mad.

And within recent memory Antide Colas of

Betoncourt in the County of Burgundy, who was burned at Dôle on the twentieth of February, 1599, confessed that the Devil had commanded her to bring him the Host when It was administered to her, and that at the previous Easter she had with great difficulty received It, being unable to swallow It without great pain; for a voice said to her in the form of a vision that she might not swallow It, and that she must take great care not to swallow It.

In short this cursed vermin ordinarily make use of the Host in their acts of witchcraft, as was also admitted by several of those who were accused at Paris by the Blind Man of the Fifteen-twenties, named Honorat, in the time of King Charles IX.

I cannot omit mention of President Gentil, who was found in possession of the Host by the executioner who hanged him at Montfaucon, as Bodin tells in his "Demonomania." *IV. 5.*

Another reason why the Eucharist must be refused to one who is accused of witchcraft is that this Sacrament is of such reverence, so holy and so deeply august, that, according to Navarro, so *de Consil. 16.* high a mystery must not be communicated to one who is going to execution for his sins. And why should It be given to a witch, who tramples It underfoot and never speaks of It except in mockery and derision; seeing that such a one renders himself unworthy of the benefit of the law, which acts justly towards him, according to the Jurisconsult.

Besides, consideration should be given to the disadvantages which might follow. For it is possible that, at the instigation of Satan, the witch may spue It on to the ground, or behave in some such way with It; and this, I think, is the reason why in the primitive Church the Holy and Sacred Communion was never administered to demoniacs, as we learn from St. Denis and St. Theodore.

S. Denis, Hier.: Theod. de sacr. Synax.

I am well aware that no one will oppose me in my contention when the accused has not yet confessed. But I make no doubt that there are some who will hold the contrary view in a case where the accused has confessed, even after the sentence has been pronounced and some hours before it has been confirmed, basing their opinion on the Canon above quoted. Yet I maintain that in neither case must the Host be administered. For the reasons already adduced, this is clearly just in the first case. As to the second, Judges know well enough how witches usually behave at their examination; for sometimes they confess and sometimes deny, now they say one thing and now another, and they generally contradict themselves two or three times in one day. They have even been known to retract when going to the fire, although they have repeated their confession countless times, and have previously shown every mark of repentance. This was so a few days ago in the case of Clauda Paget, known as la Foulet.

And indeed I do not find this very strange, seeing that the Devil is ever about them to prevent them from confessing. And therefore it is very difficult to place any reliance upon a witch's penitence, having regard also to the fact that it has been noted that they seldom or never leave the service of Satan, as we have said elsewhere. It is sufficiently clear, therefore, that the Sacred Host must not be given to witches, either before or after their condemnation or confession, in order to avoid the danger spoken of by St. Paul, who says that he who receives and eats the Body of Jesus Christ unworthily, eateth his own damnation.

And if it be objected that a witch's confession may sometimes be sincere, I answer that it is necessary to follow the safest and more usual course; and that in such a case the good-will and intentions of the accused will suffice for him, just as the Theologians assure us that it does in the case of those who die at sea or elsewhere where the Sacrament cannot be obtained. *L. nam. ad ea de legib.*

As for the Canon above quoted, I say that it does not apply to witches, but to those guilty of other crimes, where there is no fear of the Eucharist being abused, and where none of the calamities of which we have spoken can ensue.

Chapter LXI.

If One Accused of Witchcraft be but Found Guilty of Assisting at the Sabbat, even though he has done no other Ill, the Secular Judge may Pass Sentence of Death upon Him.

THE second question is this: whether, when he who is accused of witchcraft is found guilty only of having been to the Sabbat, without being charged with any act of witchcraft, the Secular Judge may pass sentence of death upon him. I discussed the former question because once, in my absence, the Holy Communion had been given to some who were detained in our prisons for this crime, so that I supposed that the same may have been done elsewhere. And now I deal with this second question because I know of Judges and Advocates so scrupulous that, when it appears that the accused has only been to the Sabbat, without having worked any witchcraft, they would send him back to the Ecclesiastical Court without sentencing him to death.

Abbas, c. 1. nu. 3. 4. de Sortileg. sul. Clarus referens Nunium de communi attestantem lib. 5. § hæresis num. 25.

But I am of quite another mind. For since, as all the Doctors, both Canonical and legal, are agreed, the crime of witchcraft is equally the concern of the Ecclesiastical and the Secular Courts, it follows that the trials of witches can be conducted by the Secular Judge even in the first place, as Julius Clarus says. This procedure is observed in France just as it is in this country, as I have noted in my Instruction.

Art. 1.

Moreover, it cannot be denied that he who is present at the Sabbat, and dances there, and makes the customary offerings, is a witch, even though there is no evidence that he has practised witchcraft; for he could not be at the Sabbat but for his pact and intimacy with the Devil.

It remains, therefore, to discuss whether such a witch ought to be punished with death. I maintain that he should, and it is easy for me to support this view with several particular reasons, without delaying over the general provisions in this matter made by the Law of God and the Constitutions of the Emperors. But I speak of those who have confessed that they have formed a pact with the Devil, and have afterwards been

Deut. 18. Tototit. de malefic. et mathematic. C.

to the Sabbat, even if it is only once; or of those who, without confessing to the pact, admit that they have been twice or oftener to the witches' assembly. There are also those who have at times found themselves accidentally, or out of curiosity, at the Sabbat: such must be judged quite differently. For some are free from guilt or deceit, and some are quite innocent: yet I think that even these last are deserving of some punishment, or at least some fine, seeing that their curiosity has evil consequences or, as the Jurisconsult says, is an evil example. It must always be understood that what I have said concerning such persons is conditional upon their having in no way acquiesced in the deeds of Satan or his subjects. But as for those who have confessed that they have formed a pact with Satan and have been to the Sabbat afterwards, or those who have been to the Sabbat twice, without confessing to the pact, there is no doubt that they all deserve death. I see no distinction between these last. For it is certain that those who go more than once to the Sabbat must have entered into some agreement with Satan, whether it be expressed or tacit, and that they conduct themselves in the same way as the other witches; for the Devil compels them to do so, even if they do not at once do it of their own volition. This is quite clearly apparent from the daily trials of witches. Furthermore, the repetition of such acts is a clear proof of consent on the part of those who commit them.

Covar. c. quam vis part 3. § si. nu. 6. Pinel. 1. 2. de rescind. venditio. Part 3. c. 1. nu. 36.

Passing, then, to my reasons, I say in the first place that the pact of which we have just spoken is enough to condemn a witch to death, if it be

Levit. 20. *Deut.* 18. considered that God expressly forbids us on pain of death to hold any communication with Satan or his subjects. But let us see of what this pact consists. The witch renounces God, Chrism, Baptism, and his part in Paradise: he gives himself to Satan and takes him for his sole master, and swears to him never to speak of God or the Virgin Mary or the Saints of Heaven, except in mockery and derision. What does all this prove but his Idolatry, his Apostasy, his Paganism, and his Atheism? And these are all crimes worthy of death, even in the case of one who, at his Baptism and for long after, has made a profession of Christianity. I say that the first pact of the witch with Satan shows his Idolatry, because he turns from the Creator to the creature; his Apostasy, because he bankrupts himself of his first and true religion and his first Baptism to hurl himself into a sea of superstitions; his Paganism, because he undertakes to serve and worship devils as true Gods; his Atheism, because the first three crimes easily lead to Atheism, especially the last, which is to serve and worship many devils as gods, since Polytheism is the same thing as Atheism.

Let us again set forth more particularly how a witch who makes this pact with Satan is worthy of death.

He renounces and deserts God, to turn to the Devil: a crime which God punishes with death,
Deut. 13 & 18. so that He commands us not to spare the false prophets who turn the people from Him.

The witch further promises not to speak of God save in mockery and derision. And yet God
Levit. 24. wills that he who has pronounced His Name in mockery or has blasphemed It shall be stoned;

and the constitutions of the Emperors likewise punish this crime with death.

Again, let us consider what happens after the formation of this pact. Satan, binding those who have thus leagued with him, makes them go to the Sabbat where they worship the Devil, who sometimes appears as a man, sometimes as a goat; and they offer him candles, and kiss him, some on the shoulder, some on the shameful parts. Now who does not know that this crime is altogether abominable and worthy of death in the sight of God? For in Jeremiah He swears that He will punish with fire and the sword the town which has sacrificed to Baal and other strange gods. And in another place He commands that he who worships any other God but Him shall be put to death. This was indeed put into practice against the children of Israel; for at one time there died about twenty-three thousand who had worshipped the Golden Calf, and at another time twenty-four thousand who had sacrificed to Baal-phegor.

In auth. ut non luxur. contr. natur. sub. fin.

c. 32.

Exod. 20.
Deut. 13. 27.

Exod. 32.

Num. 25.

Again, when at the Sabbat, witches eat and feast with Satan. This is another crime worthy of death, since it is a capital crime merely to associate with Satan, as we have shown already. This may be more clearly proved by the example of the prophet spoken of in the Book of Kings, who was slain by a lion for having eaten and drunk in Samaria against the commandment of God.

I Kings 13.

Finally, witches couple with Satan, who becomes a man for the women, and a woman for the men; and he usually couples with the women in the form of some beast, such as a goat or some such animal. This is a third crime no less worthy of death than the other two; seeing that *Exod. 34. Deut. 7.* God so abhors the copulation of the faithful with an infidel that He put to death twenty-four thousand Israelites because they had fornicated *Num. 25.* with the daughters of Moab; and greatly praised Phinees and rewarded him. But what are we to think when the Devil, in the form of a goat or some other beast, couples with witches, as there is no doubt that he does at the Sabbat? Is not *Levit. 20. Deut. 23. Can. mulier 15. q. 1.* this act worthy of death? The Law of God is very clear, which says that not only the man, but the beast too shall be put to death. This is *Pap. tit. 7. arrest. 1. lib. 22.* also in accordance with what Boere and Papon say on the subject.

These, therefore, are my reasons for maintaining that those whom we have described in this chapter are worthy of death, and that they can be so punished by the Secular Judge without any need to refer them back to their Ecclesiastical Judge.

And if it is objected that, when the accused does not confess to the pact or the adoration or the banquets and couplings, he cannot be condemned for these actions, provided that there is no accomplice who accuses him of them: I answer that I have already said all that need be said with reference to the pact; and as for the adorations and banquets and couplings, we must admit them as soon as we have admitted the fact that the accused has been to the Sabbat two or three times.

Further, in all trials of witches it is made clear that, at their first, or at least their second, visit to the Sabbat they worship Satan and feast and couple with him. This is amply proved by what I have already written in several chapters. For the Evil One most often has carnal relations with the women the first time he approaches them; as it happened to Thievenne Paget, Antide Colas and others whom we have mentioned.

It stands to reason that, in such trials, we are chiefly faced with matters done secretly and at night, which are not capable of proof save through the mouths of those who have been present at the Sabbat. And therefore, according to common law, in the case of such a horrible and secret crime a less absolute proof is sufficient. Moreover, it is necessary to assume that the usual crime has been committed, and to act accordingly.

Qua de re per Mascard. de probatio coclus. 1313. *num.* 2, *etc., vol.* 3.

Further, I dare to say that it is probable that those of whom we are speaking have beaten the water together with the others at the Sabbat in order to cause it to hail, and have like them taken the powder and the ointment which Satan gives them to use for causing the death of persons and cattle, or for making them ill; and I cannot doubt that they do so. For it is certain that Satan, who only seeks their ruin and that of the whole human race, continually urges and incites them to do evil; and this the witches all unanimously confess.

L. Nam ad ea de legib.

THE MANNER OF PROCEDURE OF A JUDGE IN A CASE OF WITCHCRAFT

By HENRY BOGUET of Dôle, Chief Judge in the District of Saint Oyan de Joux

To Monsieur Daniel Romanet, Advocate to the See of Salins

ARTICLE I.

THE Judge in this country can by himself conduct the trial of witches when there is definite evidence of the fact: this was decreed by the Court on the 28th September, 1598. This is also the practice to-day in France.

Pap. arrest. lib. 22. tit. 3. art. 1. 2. Cf. Imbert. lib. Instit. Forens. 3. c. 6. Clar. § hæresis nu. 25. Bodin, Demonom. IV. 4.

ARTICLE II.

Witchcraft is a crime apart, both on account of its enormity, and because it is usually committed at night and always secretly. Therefore the trial of this crime must be conducted in an extraordinary manner; and the usual legalities and ordinary procedure cannot be strictly observed.

Article III.

Jacob. de Bel. vis. in sua pract. tit. de Inquisitio. nu. 52. Clar. lib. V. q. 40. nu. 1.

The Judge must decide whether the presumptions and conjectures are enough to warrant his committing the accused to prison; for we can give no certain rule as to this. Yet I shall always maintain that a person should always be imprisoned on the accusation of even only a single accomplice. For it has been noted that witches who have confessed have as a rule never laid information against any who were not of their brotherhood, or at least were not deeply suspected. In fact Binsfeld, Suffragan of Trèves, wrote that of a hundred witches he hardly found one who made a false accusation against another.

De confess. malefic. membr. 2. conclus. 1.

Bodin, Demonom. IV. 4.

The same applies when the person is accused by common rumour; for this is almost infallible in the matter of witchcraft.

Article IV.

Cf. chaps. 23, 24, & Art. 31.

Those whose duty it is to arrest the accused must make careful search lest he have any ointments or powders about him; for they use such drugs in their witchcraft.

They must also take particular notice of the prisoner's countenance, and especially of what he shall say. For when he is surprised, many words may escape from him which are direct evidence against him; as "may he die but he is not one of those people," that "he is not marked," that he "wishes to be re-baptised," etc. And the prudent Judge will base his examination upon this.

Article V.

There are some who, when they seize a witch, are accustomed to prevent him from touching the ground, thinking that thus it will be easier to draw the truth from him. But I do not like this manner of acting, holding that it is superstitious. Yet Sprenger defends it, but on such grounds that there is no need to reply to him.

Remy, Demonol. III. 9.

III. 8.

Article VI.

The same author warns the Judge to take care that the witch does not touch him on the bare hands or arms or look at him before he looks at the witch; so that the witch may not by this means corrupt him. But I hold that this also is full of superstition; for neither the hand nor the look of a witch has in itself any virtue to cause such an effect; and further, it is certain that such people have no power to harm the Officers of Justice, as I have shown elsewhere.

III. 15. Cf. chaps. 27, 28.

Chap. 37.

Article VII.

The Judge should bring the accused up for examination as soon as he is made prisoner. For when a witch is arrested, Satan, momentarily

Bodin, Demonom. IV. 1.

at least, forsakes him, and he is so surprised that he is altogether confused; so that it is easier at such time to draw the truth from him than if he is left for some days in his prison without being seen; for in that case his master will not fail to advise him. None knows this better than

Cf. chap. 41.

do the Judges. For all witches confess that Satan assists them even when they are being questioned. Further, it has been noted that they always bend their eyes upon the ground and mutter I know not what, when the Judge is speaking to them; and this leads us to believe that they are then consulting with the Devil that he may advise them how to answer.

Article VIII.

Sprenger, III. 6 *& sequ. Bodin, Demonom. IV.* 4.

Sprenger and Bodin have given instructions as to what questions the Judge should put, and reference may be made to their works. But I would add that the Judge must question the accused without interruption and strongly press him, always with gentle words: that if the accused refuses to answer one question, he must

Psal. 95. *II Kings* 23. *Jerem.* 32. *Levit.* 18. *Cf. chap.* 48.

pass on to another, and afterwards go back to the former one, and must repeat the same questions again and again. The accused will then, if he be guilty, be very easily trapped into contradicting himself.

Article IX.

The Judge must also ask the accused whether he has any children, whether they are dead, and if so of what sickness they died. For it has been noted that witches ordinarily dedicate their children to the Devil, or else kill them in their mother's womb or as soon as they are born.

ARTICLE X.

The Judge must take careful note of the accused's countenance during his examination, and whether he sheds any tears, or looks down at the ground, or mutters to himself, or uses blasphemy and imprecations. For all these are presumptive indications against him, as we shall say later.

Cf. Arts. 35, 36, *etc.*

ARTICLE XI.

And because the witch is generally ashamed to confess his abominations before many people, and because also he is frightened when he sees his answers being set down in writing; therefore it is best for the Judge to remain alone with the accused, concealing his Clerk and other Assessors.

Bodin, Demonom. IV. 1.

ARTICLE XII.

If the prisoner is accused by his accomplices, they should at once be brought face to face. The reason for this is that there is nothing which so confounds a witch as to see before his eyes one who has been his companion at the Sabbat, even if the accomplice remains constant and loyal to him. Sometimes it has even been found effective to employ a stranger who is not a witch for this confrontation.

Cf. chap. 48, *& Arts.* 18, 19.

Article XIII.

The accused must be repeatedly brought up for examination.

Article XIV.

Some Judges, finding that they can get no confession from the accused, cause him to be stripped and shaved all over. This custom is not impertinent, by reason of the spells for maintaining silence which they conceal about them. I have treated of this more fully elsewhere.

Chap. 43.

Article XV.

There are others who make use of the ducking stool. But I doubt whether this practice does not serve rather to tempt God than to prove anything against the witch who is ducked. For Satan may let a guilty one sink to the bottom, or an innocent one float on the water, so that he may cause an innocent man to be put to death wrongfully and so protect the guilty. Also, the ducking stool is condemned by the Canons; as is also the ordeal by red-hot iron, so that the Suffragan of Trèves even says that it is sin to practise it.

C. Mennam. C. consuluisti 2. *q.* 5. *C. fin. de purg. canon. Binsfeld, de confess. Malefic.* 2. *sub* 3. *dub. princip. Thyr. de Dæmon. I.* 19.

Article XVI.

It is quite another matter to examine the accused all over his body to see if there is any mark upon him. For this is permitted and lawful, since all witches are ordinarily marked. But it is necessary to have a very expert chirurgeon, for these marks are difficult to find. *Cf. chap.* 44.

ARTICLE XVII.

If the Judge can draw no confession from the accused, he must confine him in a very narrow and dark cell; for it has been proved that the hardship of prison very often impels witches to confess, especially when they are young.

ARTICLE XVIII.

It is good also to bring in someone who shall say that he is imprisoned for the same crime, so that every lawful means may be used to induce the witch to confess the truth. *Bodin, Demonom. IV.* 4.

ARTICLE XIX.

For it has sometimes even proved profitable to lodge the witch near him who has accused him, as was done in the case of Thievenne Paget. But I shall never advise the Judge to adopt this course except as a last resource, and when he is very sure of the accomplices; for witches have often been known to corrupt their accusers and to cause them to retract their confessions. *Cf. chap* 48.

ARTICLE XX.

Judges have been known to extract the truth from witches by means of a promise of impunity, yet have not failed to put them to death afterwards. This practice is used by many to-day, and it seems to be approved by the common opinion of the Doctors of Civil Law. Yet I feel great doubt as to the morality of this; for it is unlawful for us to deceive our neighbour in any way by a lie; neither ought we ever to do evil that good may come of it, as St. Paul says. This practice is also condemned by the Theologians, and fully refuted by Binsfeld where he replies to Bodin.

Clar. lib. 5. § fin. q. 55. num. 7. 8, etc.

Psal. 14. Prov. 6. Sap. 1. Eccl. 7.

De confess. malef. 3. dub. princip. post prælud.

Article XXI.

But above all the Advocate of the accused must particularly beware against doing as one did whom I know. This man cunningly got the truth from a witch, and then revealed it to the Judge: the Judge then confronted the witch with the Advocate, and the witch confessed. It is beyond doubt that it is unlawful for the Advocate to reveal matters which are prejudicial to his client. This is so incontestably true that the Theologians hold that he who acts in such a way is guilty of mortal sin if his revelation is notably prejudicial to his client. The Advocate may certainly decline to continue the defence; but, according to the opinion of St. Thomas, approved by Navarro, he must not discover anything which might injure his client.

Navarre in manua. c. 25. num. 29.

D. Thom. 2. 2. q. 71. art. 3. Navarr. d.c. 25. num. 28.

Article XXII.

The Judge must avoid torture as much as possible; for, besides the spells for maintaining silence which witches bear about them, they have other charms which prevent them from feeling any pain. This secret is known also to nearly all other criminals, so that to-day torture has become almost without effect. And with particular reference to witches, Sprenger writes that it is as difficult to apply torture to a witch as it is to exorcise a demoniac.

Cf. chap. 43.

III. 13. *sub fin.*

Article XXIII.

I have said that witches and other criminals use certain charms against torture; but I do not mean to include with these the passages and verses of Holy Scripture which they for the most part use. For it is impious to believe that such passages help them to endure the pain of torture, seeing that God cannot be made responsible for their impunity for their witchcraft.

Cf. chap. 43.

Article XXIV.

Moreover, the Judge must reject as superstitious the practice used by some in the hope of extracting the truth from those who are exposed to torture. For they whisper certain words in their ear. Marsilius speaks of this, and, as he says, has practised it.

In pract. crim. § *nunc. videndum num.* 52.

Article XXV.

In this crime it is lawful to expose the accused to torture on a Holy Day, even if the day be Sacred in honour of God.

L. nemo C. de Episcop. audi. L. provincia um C. de fer. Clar. § *fin. q.* 64.

Article XXVI.

Bins. de confess. malefic. 2. memb. sub conclus. 1.

If the Judge is forced to have recourse to torture, he must consider well whether there are grounds enough for doing so, having regard to the indications, conjectures and presumptions against the accused. For no sure rule can be given for this matter because of the variety of deeds and persons involved in this sort of charge. Yet I shall set down some of the commonest of these.

Article XXVII.

Glos. 1. cap. 5. de adulter. Menoch. de presump. lib. 1. q. 89. num. 14.

In the first place, a confession made out of Court is a sufficient reason for resorting to torture against one accused of witchcraft. This rule is observed with regard to other crimes also.

Bins. ad 1. 4. C. de malef. Mascard. de probat. conclus. 349. num. 6. vol. 1. Cair. in practic. in 7. indic. Clar. § fin. q. 21. num. 31. Boer. decisio 90. num. 4. Clar. d. q. 21. num. 30. 33. L. non fatetur de confess. Late per Jacob. de Bell. vis. tit. d. q. num 58.

We must even go further, according to the opinion of Julius Clarus, in the case of a prisoner who has recanted his confession made out of Court, for otherwise no confession made out of Court would be of any effect.

But this has particular reference to the crime of witchcraft, seeing that it is a crime in a class by itself, which is very difficult to bring home against the accused.

The same must be said of a case where the accused has confessed before an incompetent Judge.

Yet, if the confession has been made in error, and the accused offers to rectify the error, the torture should be postponed, and the accused granted a hearing: *Ob id quod fateri non videatur, qui errat.*

Article XXVIII.

Secondly, a witch's confession is warrant enough for the employment of torture against his accomplice, if such confession is substantiated by some other presumption or indication.

Clar. § fin. q. 21. num. 8. Boss. tit. de Indic. num. 149.

And although the common opinion of the Doctors is that in this case the accomplice is not to be accredited, if he should not abide by his confession under torture; yet this rule is not observed in this country, any more than it is in many other places. And this seems to me to be very reasonable; for what need is there again to extort by torture a confession which has been voluntarily made without it, seeing that a voluntary confession is always of greater weight than one which is forced by torture? *Quæ etiam dicitur probatio minus legitima.*

Cairer. pract. in 8. Indic.

Bins. de confess. malefic. memb. 2. conclus. 3. 4. 5. Clar. d. q. 21. num. 11.

Navarr. Consi. 1. de Jud. lib. 2.

Article XXIX.

Thirdly, the familiarity and association of the accused with a witch is enough to warrant the same procedure, if it is substantiated by some other evidence or indication. This rule is founded upon Holy Scripture, which declares that Good brings good, and Evil evil.

Carr. in pract. in 25. Indic. monoch. lib. 1. de præsump. q. 8. num. 125. Mascar. de probat. conclus. 451. num. 4. Psal. 17. Prov. 13.

Article XXX.

Fourthly, the afore-mentioned threats, if they are followed by any effect, are enough to justify the resort to torture.

Clar. § fin. q. 21. num. 37. Menoch. d. q. 8. num. 59. 60. Cairer. in pract. in 12. Indic.

Article XXXI.

Bins. ad 1. *si de malefic. C.*

Cf. chaps. 23, 24, *& Art.* 4.

Fifthly, if the accused be found in possession of certain powders or unguents, it warrants his torture; especially if he can give no satisfactory account of such powders or unguents. For it is notorious that witches ordinarily use such drugs in their witchcraft.

Article XXXII.

Clar. § fin. q. 21. *num.* 1. *Cairer. in pract. in* 2. *Indic. Menoch. de præsumpt. lib.* 1. *q.* 89. *num.* 28. *Bodin, Demonom. IV.* 4.

Sixthly, common rumour, combined with other indications, is also sufficient. It does not seem to me necessary in this case to particularise the circumstances requisite for the verification of a common rumour with regard to other crimes; for the crime of witchcraft is one which is called exceptional, and one which is very difficult of proof. Else common rumour would never be of any account; for it is so difficult to prove that even lawyers themselves, when produced as witnesses, have found themselves at a loss to give reasonable evidence, as Clarus has said.

§ fin. q. 6. *nu.* 18.

And therefore we require some indications in support of the common rumour, to supply the want of such circumstances; for otherwise only a common rumour duly verified would be enough to warrant torture, as some have thought.

Marsi. in pract. § diligenter num. 19. *Gandi. de malef. tit. de queast. num.* 39. *August ad Ang. in verb. fama publica num.* 41. *Marsil in d. § Diligenter nu.* 74.

Article XXXIII.

Seventhly, lying and discrepancies at the examination, supported by other evidence and indications, serve also as grounds enough for torture.

ARTICLE XXXIV.

Finally, when there are a mass of indications such as the Doctors call "light indications," that provides sufficient warrant for proceeding to the torture: *Nam quæ non prosunt singula multa juvant.*

Lancel. de offic. præto. c. de neg. crim. nu. 29. Bins. memb. 2. Glos. 1. 2. sub si. C. de eden. g o. 1. Instrumenta de probat. C.

ARTICLE XXXV.

These light indications are:

1. If the accused generally turns his eyes to the ground during his examination.
There are some who would count it the same if the accused has a frightened look, basing their opinion on those who hold that it is possible to draw from the repulsiveness of a man's face an indication against him sufficient to expose him to the torture.

Bodin, Demonom. IV. 4. Cf. Cap. 41. Marsil. in pract. § expediata num. 53. Menoch. de præsump. I. q. 89. nu. 130. Cairer. in 29. indic.

ARTICLE XXXVI.

2. If the parents of the accused were witches. For I hold this to be only a light indication; although Bodin considers it as an infallible rule that the son must be a witch if his father or mother was one. But it has often been known that a bad father may have good children, and that conversely a good father may have bad children. And therefore Homer has said in his "Odyssey" that "Few sons are like their fathers."

Cf. chap. 48.
IV. 4.
Lib. 2.

Article XXXVII.

Dan. point 4. *Bod. IV.* 4. *Bins. ad* 1. 7. *de malefic. C. Cf. chap.* 44. *Sim. in com. cath. instit.* 8. *de Blasph. facit Menoch. de præsump. I. q.* 19. *nu.* 71.

3. If the accused has a mark upon him.

Article XXXVIII.

4. If the accused is prone uneasily to fall into a mad and trembling rage and blaspheme and use other execrations: *Cum sit enim timida nequitia dat testimonium condemnationis*, as Aristotle says. And Cicero says on this subject: *Magna est vis conscientiæ, ut nec timeant, qui nihil commiserunt, et pœnam semper ante oculos versari putent, qui peccaverunt.*

Sap. 17. *Cic. pro Milo.*

Article XXXIX.

Cf. chap. 44. *IV.* 4.

5. If the accused makes as though to weep, and yet sheds no tears; or even if he only sheds a very few. Yet Bodin again writes that this is one of the strongest presumptive indications that the Inquisitors and Paul Grilland have noted against witches.

Article XL.

Cf. chap. 39.

6. If the accused has no Cross on his rosary; or if the Cross is defective in some particular.

Article XLI.

7. If the accused has at times been reproached with being a witch, and has let the reproach pass unanswered, without seeking redress by law or otherwise.

Marsil. in pract. § diligenter num. 137. Menoch. de præsump. I. q. 19. nu. 129.

Article XLII.

8. If he asks to be re-baptised. For since the Devil requires witches to renounce their baptism, and causes them to be baptised in his name, therefore when they fall into the hands of Justice they ask to be re-baptised. We have remarked upon this in another place.

Bins. ad l. fin. de malefic. C.

Article XLIII.

If the accused confesses under torture, he must be made to repeat his confessions some time later, say twenty-four hours, and in another place than that of torture. But it is very necessary to take care that one of his accomplices does not speak to him in the meanwhile, lest he should corrupt him. Also it is well not to leave him alone, for fear lest the Devil may likewise come to advise him.

Clar. § fin. q. 64. num. 40. 41 Marsil. in l. 1. § Divus Severus num. 6. de quæst.

Bod. IV. 4.

Bart. l. unius § reve. de q. Blanc. de Indic. num. 219. Boss. tit. de Tortura num. 34.

Article XLIV.

If he recants, he must be again exposed to the torture. This the Judge may do three times, but no more.

Clar. § fin. q. 21. num. 36.

ARTICLE XLV.

And then if the accused continues to persist in his denials, he must be released. But there is great doubt whether he may be fully and absolutely released, or only subject to being again called for trial.

Boer. decisio. 163. num. 15. Cf. Clar. d. q. 21. nu. 35 & q. 62. nu. 2. & q. 64. nu. 38.

The common opinion of the Doctors on this question as it affects other crimes is that if all the indications against the accused are entirely purged, then he must be fully and absolutely discharged; but if they are not, his discharge must be conditional upon his being liable for recall.

Cf. chap. 52.

But I shall always hold that one accused of witchcraft must never be unconditionally discharged, whatever torture he may have suffered, if there remains the slightest indication against him. For, as we have seen, he who has once given himself to the Devil cannot easily withdraw from his clutches: so that, after having been detained by Justice, he will be even busier in evil-doing.

ARTICLE XLVI.

Clar. d. q. 64. nu. 38. Pap. lib. 24. tit. 9.

In any case, if the indications were very strong and almost beyond doubt, the Judge could proceed to sentence the accused notwithstanding the fact that he had suffered torture; but he should not then sentence him to the usual punishment of witches, but to something extraordinary, such as banishment, etc. This practice is observed in some countries in the case of other crimes.

ARTICLE XLVII.

Further, if the accused ratifies outside the place of torture the confession which he has made there, the Judge shall at once discharge him, not so much as a reproach to the witnesses who may have testified against him as because he may recant his confession. For he may prove that his confession is false, and in that case he must be freely and absolutely discharged. This is a practice followed in many Provinces, not only in respect of confessions made under torture, but also of those made voluntarily without torture, as we have said elsewhere.

Clar. § fin. q. 64. nu. 44. & q. 66. nu. 1.

ARTICLE XLVIII.

But if the accused cannot prove that his confession was false, then the Judge must proceed to pass sentence upon him, even if he afterwards commutes it.

I am speaking of a confession made under torture or at least in Court, for a confession made out of Court can only be confirmed by torture. Yet Bodin maintains that both sorts of confession are equally sufficient ground for passing to a condemnation for this crime; but such an opinion is too harsh, for we are very apt at times to say things against ourselves out of Court which are not true. Also neither the civil nor the criminal law reckons such a confession as a complete proof.

L. certum confessus § si quis absente. Clar. De Confess. § fin. q. 55. nu. 1. L. qui sententiam de pœn. C. Clar. § fin. q. 65. nu. 1.

Article XLIX.

With regard to a confession made in Court but not under torture, it is certain that according to precedent it must be considered as sufficient proof for proceeding to condemnation, such being the common opinion of our Doctors.

Notwithstanding, the Judge must not fail to discharge the prisoner for the reasons already mentioned. *Art. 47.*

But the confession must be supported by some other indications; for a confession is not by itself enough. *Si quis ultro fateatur, non semper ei fides habenda est, nonnunquam enim aut metu aut aliqua de causa in se confitentur*, says the law; and in another place it says, *volens mori non auditur.* *L. si quis ultro de quæst. D. L. non tantum de appellatiu.*

I have said that the confession must be supported by other indications; but I do not mean that there must be a clear case of the death of some person or animal, or of the prisoner having been to the Sabbat; for, as we have several times shown, witches work only at night and in secret, and a clear proof of such deeds is, as the Jurisconsult somewhere says, impossible. *Bod. IV. 5.*

The following are examples of the kind of indications which I mean: if the accused is presumed or suspected or generally believed to be a witch; and it seems to me that the indications we have mentioned before are more than sufficient in such a case. *Arts. 27, 28, etc.*

Quid Pap. q. 339. Iacob. de Bell. vis. in practic. tit. de quæst. nu. 97. Clar. § fin. q. 65. nu. 2.

Article L.

Also it is not necessary for the prisoner's confession to be made spontaneously in Court, or to be repeated or reiterated.

ARTICLE LI.

When the accused retracts his first confession this must always be regarded with suspicion; for it is known that the Devil instructs witches in prison and very often causes them to recant their first confessions. This has been well pointed out by Bodin; and I have had several experiences of it.

Cf. Art. 7.

IV. 3.

ARTICLE LII.

Similarly the accused must be condemned when he is lawfully convicted by a sufficient number of witnesses. And in this crime all sorts of people are admitted as witnesses, even accomplices. There is reason in this, since it is an exceptional crime, in which equally guilty accomplices provide the proof of each other's guilt. Besides, the crime of witchcraft is for the most part committed at night and always in secret. Therefore who is better fitted than the witches themselves to give evidence concerning the Sabbats and nocturnal assemblies of witches? For it is certain that men of good life never attend the Sabbat, except by accident.

Bod. IV. 2. *Bins. de confess.* 2. *memb. conclus.* 1. *Glos. l. fin. de accus. C. DD. in C. quoniam de testibus.*

ARTICLE LIII.

In consequence of this a son is admitted as witness against his father, and the father against the son, in this crime; and similarly other relatives and connexions may testify against each other: yet all such witnesses are disallowed by the law in cases of other crimes, except that of high treason.

Bod. IV. 2. *Bins. de confess.* 2. *b. conclus.* 1. *Cf. cap.* 49. *L. parentes de testibus. C. DD. in d. l. parentes & in l. quisque ad l. Jul. majest. C.*

Article LIV.

C. in fidei. C. accusatus § vero de heret. in 6. Mal. malef. III. 4.

For the same reason infamous and notorious characters may legally give evidence in a case of witchcraft.

Article LV.

Mal. malef. III. 5. Bod. IV. 2.

Even personal enemies are admitted, unless there is mortal hatred between them and the accused.

Article LVI.

Cf. chap. 48.

In this crime the Judge must not even reject the evidence of children who have not yet reached the age of puberty. For it is known that witches usually take their children to the Sabbat, however young they may be, as well as their neighbours' children; and they have been known to take them for the very reason that they are too young. But how can they avoid doing so, since they vow and dedicate them to the Devil while they are yet in their mother's womb? Therefore these children must be heard in evidence, seeing that the crime is hidden and secret, and that there is no one who can better witness to it than those who have been at the Sabbat.

Bod. IV. 2. Innoc. C. qualiter de accus. Glos. l. ob carmen § fin. de testib. D.

Article LVII.

For the same reasons witnesses to this crime are admissible, even if there is only one witness as to each particular point in the accusation, provided that all the witnesses agree as to the general charge of witchcraft. This applies also to other excepted crimes.

ARTICLE LVIII.

We have said that accomplices may give evidence against each other which may lead to a conviction. This is true provided that two other conditions are fulfilled. The first of these is, that the accomplice who brings the accusation must die in contrition and penitence: for it is unlikely that, dying so, they will bring a false accusation against another and so damn themselves miserably. This is the argument used by Hyppolitus de Marsilius in his 109th Counsel, where he says: "Those on the point of death are then more than at any other time afraid to lie and offend the Divine Majesty." In this connexion the famous jurist Barthole also says: "A witness who would not otherwise be believed, may be believed when he is near to death." Binsfeld also has words very pertinent to this matter, namely, that not one witch in a hundred will bring a false accusation against another. This I know also from my own experience.

Arg. l. fin. ad l. Jul. repetund. C. incip. audito. & intellecto nu. 33. 39. in l. admovendi nu. 41. sub. fin. de jurejur.

De confess. malef. membr. 2. conclus. 1.

The second condition is that there should be a sufficient number of accomplices as witnesses. For since, because of their crimes, they are not entirely unexceptionable witnesses, it follows that this defect must be supplied by a number greater than the usual, which is only two. But Bodin, who agrees with this view, does not define the number of witnesses, but seems to leave it to the discretion of the Judge. This is a reasonable

IV. 2.

l. ubi numerus de testibus.

l. 3. § quæ argumenta de testib.

attitude to take, and is based upon the teaching of the Roman jurist Callistratus. Yet I would always stipulate for four witnesses in these cases, that two may count as one, and four as two, in conformity with the statutes of Venice and of those that prevail throughout all the East, which provide that the evidence of two women shall be equivalent to that of one man, and that of four women to that of two men.

Article LIX.

And when there is not this sufficient number of accomplices to give evidence, then the Judge cannot proceed to a condemnatory sentence unless there is also some very strong presumption against the prisoner, such as those which are sufficient to warrant application of torture, which we have already enumerated.

Article LX.

The other proofs which are sufficient to lead to the condemnation of one accused of witchcraft may be seen in Book IV, chaper 2, of Bodin's "Demonomania," and in Binsfeld.

Article LXI.

There are times when the only course is to release the accused from prison. Such is the case when he has been detained for a very long time, and there is not enough evidence to justify either an acquittal or a sentence of death; for there may be evidence of great weight, yet not such as can lead to a conviction. Meanwhile further inquiries must be made into the question of the guilt of the accused; and in this matter much is left to the discretion of the Judge.

ARTICLE LXII.

Now the usual penalty for witches is that they shall be burned, but there is some doubt as to whether they should be burned alive, or whether they should first be strangled. Both these views are upheld by various Doctors. *Bod. IV. 5.*

The second seems to be the more reasonable course to take, so that the criminal need not be brought to despair because of the harshness of his punishment. This is approved by Diego Covarruvias and several others, who say that such is the custom throughout all Christendom. *Lib. 2. varia. c. 10. nu. 9. Clar. § fin. q. 99. nu. 7.*

Nevertheless I know that the practice in this country is not so with regard to those who turn themselves into wolves and in that shape kill people; for such are burned alive, and the Court has many times passed this sentence.

ARTICLE LXIII.

Yet the usual penalty for witches is not always put into execution. For in the case of a child who has not reached the age of puberty it should, according to Bodin, only be sentenced to the lash. Binsfeld goes further, and says that sentence of *Bod. IV. 53. perl. auxilium de minorib.*

death should never be passed upon a child of less than sixteen years of age.

Bins. ad l. 5. q. 1. sub. 5. objectio. de malefic. C. confert. auth. si captivi cum glos. de episcop. aud. C.

But I am entirely of the contrary opinion; for I maintain that not only a child witch who has reached the age of puberty, but even one who has not, should be sentenced to death, if it is proved that he has acted out of malice. Yet I would not in such a case employ the usual penalty for witches, but some gentler means, such as hanging, etc. My reasons for this view are, first the enormity of the crime, which is the most abominable of all crimes that can be imagined. For the atrocity of this crime is the reason why the ordinary provisions of the law are not applicable to it; and therefore in the case of atrocious crimes children are often put to death for their fathers, without any regard being had to their ignorance; and sometimes even brute beasts are put to death, just as if they were rational creatures. I need not mention the usual practice with regard to the children of those who are convicted of high treason.

Tiraq. de pœn. can. 40. nu. 17 et seq. 16. c. parvulos 1. q. 4.

Qua de re in l. quisquis ad. l. Jul. majest. C.

Secondly, we have seen that he who has once been caught in Satan's net can never, except with the greatest difficulty, escape from it. And therefore I conclude that it is better to condemn child witches to death than to let them continue to live in contempt of God and to the danger of the public. I am quite aware that Binsfeld does not support this view, saying that God always holds out His arms to receive a criminal in mercy. But what we have already said about witches has been proved by experience, and comes about, I believe, through a secret Judgement of God.

Cf. chap. 52.

De confess. malefic. in princip. 5. præլud. ad Rom. 5. Spin. q. de Strigib. c. 2. Remy, Demonol. III. 3.

Thirdly, I base my opinion on the law *Excipiuntur*, which punishes with death a child below the

ad Syllamia. D.

age of puberty for not having cried when its master was killed. In accordance with this law many children of less than twelve years of age have been sentenced to death. *Bod. IV. 5*

Finally, I have the memorable authority of Holy Scripture; for forty-two children of the city of Bethel were devoured by two bears because they mocked Elisha. *II Kings 2.* For if God was so angered by the insult to His prophet, how must His wrath be kindled when He is Himself despised and outraged and denied, seeing that He is jealous of His honour! I much misdoubt that He does not visit it upon the Judges whom He appoints to avenge the wrongs done to Him here below.

Article LXIV.

But if the father has compelled his young son to go to the Sabbat and to give himself to the Devil, then I should judge the son worthy of the lash or of banishment. For when a person is compelled to obey in the commission of an atrocious crime, the penalty may excusably be mitigated. *l. sed & si unius § usi. juss. de injur. l. ad ea de reg. jur late Tiraq. de pœn. caus. 34. nu. 1, 2, 3.*

I am unwilling to say that, in such case, they deserve the usual penalty for witchcraft, because, since they were compelled to go to the Sabbat and to renounce God, there was no free will on their part; and this excuses them from the usual penalty for witchcraft.

But it must not therefore be concluded that they must not suffer some other extraordinary penalty; for we must consider that it is forbidden to renounce God under any coercion whatever. *Matth. 10. l. 3. § sed ex S.* Also the matter involves evil consequences and, as Callistratus says, *mali exempli*. And in such

C. de Siccar. l. si quis aliquid qui abortionis de pœn. D.

cases the law punishes the guilty party not only with banishment and confiscation of his goods, but even sometimes with death, although there may have been no malice on his part.

Article LXV.

Arg. l. Balista ad S. C. Trebell. & l. si mulier ad S. C. Velleian. Jas. in l. cunctos populos nu. 21. se summ. Trin. & fide. Cathol. C.

What I have said in the last Article is applicable only if the child has been to the Sabbat but once or twice at the most. But if he has been there repeatedly, then he is worthy of being punished with death; for such repetition shows a consent and evil intent on the part of the child, even if he is not yet capable of ill-doing.

Article LXVI.

l. Illud ad l. aquil. D. Everard in loco a simile.

A daughter must be judged in the same way as a son, as also must a servant who in this case obeys his master's order. For the same reasons apply in all these cases.

Article LXVII.

Brun. de Indic. part. 1. q. 4. nu 7. Clar. § fin. q. 20. num. 5. 6.

It is well to note again that, in the crime of witchcraft, it is lawful at times to proceed to a condemnation on the strength of those indubitable indications and conjectures, neither more or less, which are applicable to other atrocious crimes committed in secret.

Bins. de confess. malefic. 3. dub. princip. post prælud. Conclus. 7.

And although there are some who hold that, in such case, the penalty should be an extraordinary one, such as the lash or banishment, yet I should not scruple to sentence the accused to death; not the usual death of witches, but some milder form; for such is the practice in cases of murder and heresy, which are less horrible crimes than witchcraft.

Clar. § *assasinium nu.* 6. *&* § *hæres. nu.* 29. *& iterum* § *fin. q.* 20. *nu.* 7.

Article LXVIII.

The Judge ought of right to be present with the Clerk at a witch's execution, that he may know whether he recants anything of what he has before said concerning his accomplices, and whether he accuses any fresh ones, and also whether he dies contrite and penitent. For an accusation or confession made in such circumstances is of great moment, as we have shown elsewhere.

Art. 54.

For witches do not lightly accuse their accomplices, since, as we have already said, the Devil makes them swear a solemn oath to that effect at the Sabbat; and therefore it is well that the Judge should, when questioning them, refer frequently to this oath during the trial; for by this means he will more easily bring them to reason.

Chap. 21.

Article LXIX.

A puisne Judge may not grant to anybody at all the body of a witch who has been executed, that it may be buried in consecrated soil. Neither do I think that the Supreme Court would ever grant this, considering the enormity of the crime. And even in the case of other atrocious crimes it is customary to expose to view the bodies of

l. 1. *de Cadav. puintor. D.*

Clar. lib. 5. § *fin. b.* 100. *nu.* 1.

those who have been executed, to serve as an example and warning to others. Yet this seems to be contrary to the law of Moses in Deuteronomy. *Deut. 21.*

Article LXX.

But if the witch dies in prison before sentence has been pronounced upon him, he should be buried in consecrated soil even if he has confessed, provided always that he died penitent and contrite and gave clear proof of such a state of mind. We have dealt more fully with this point in another place *Chap. 50.*

NOTES

NOTES

S. Oyan or Oyand is S. Eugendus (Augendus). *Title-page.*
S. Eugendus was born *circa* 449 at Izernore, *Saint Oyan*
Ain, Franche-Comté, and died 1 January, 510, *de Joux.*
at Condat. At the age of seven he was entrusted by his father, who had become a priest, to the care of S. Romanus and S. Lupicinus of the monastery of Condat in the French Jura, and thenceforth he never left the enclosure. He led a life of great sanctity and austerity. About 496 he was elected to follow Minausius as Abbot. Immediately after his death his eminent holiness was attested by miracles, and his successor, S. Viventiolus, built a church over his tomb, which soon became a celebrated place of pilgrimage. A town arose and was named after the Saint, S. Oyan de Joux. But when S. Claude, Bishop of Besançon, resigned his diocese and retiring to Condat died in 694 (or 696) as Abbot of the monastery, the number of pilgrims who visited his shrine became so great, particularly after the solemn translation of the body of the Saint, which having been concealed from the Saracen invaders in 1260 was brought back to Condat with great pomp twelve years later, that the abbey and the town began to be more generally known as Saint-Claude, and this name has to-day quite superseded the other. However, the old Saint Oyan de Joux lingered until the seventeenth century

Title-page. The procedure. This procedure or "Instruction," which was for many decades the authoritative code used in the prosecution of witches, first appears in the Second Edition, Rouen, 1603; the Second Edition, Lyons, 1603; and Second Edition, Paris, 1603. It will be noticed that all three issues from the several cities are in each case described as "Seconde édition."

Page xii. Ferdinand de Rye. This prelate, who was born of a distinguished house in 1556, was in 1585 preconized by Sixtus V to succeed Bishop Antoine II in the see of Besançon. Unfortunately François de Grammont had been elected by the Chapter, and although their choice was at once nullified, it was not until 13 November, 1587, that Ferdinand de Rye was enthroned in his Cathedral. The following year, on 24 September, being the feast of Our Lady of Ransom, the King of Spain appointed him titular Abbot of S. Claude. This was solemnly ratified by Clement VIII. Bishop Ferdinand died at Fraisans 20 August, 1636, at the age of eighty.

Page xiii. François de Rye. The nephew of Bishop Ferdinand, and since 1618 Bishop-Coadjutor with right of succession. He held the see barely eight months, dying 17 April, 1637, aged seventy-one.

Page xiii. Oddo. "One *Oddo*, a *Dane*, a mighty Pirat, was so well learned in Magick, that he would wander at Sea without a Ship, and oft-times drowned his Enemies ships, by raising Tempests with his Charms. Wherefore, that he might not fight at Sea with Pirats, he was wont, by Witchcraft, to raise and exasperate the Winds and Waves to destroy them." Olaus Magnus, *A Compendious History of the Goths*. Translated by J. Streater. London. 1658. Book III, c. 17 (p. 49).

"Filimer, rex Gothorum . . . qui et terras Scythicas cum sua gente introisse superius a nobis dictus est, reperit in populo suo quasdam magas mulieres, quas patrio sermone Haliurunas is ipse cognominat, easque habens suspectas, de medio sui proturbat, longeque ab exercitu suo fugatas in solitudinem, coegit errare. Quas spiritus immundi per eremum uagantes dum uidissent, et earum in complexibus in coitu miscuissent, genus hoc ferocissimum edidere. . . . Tali ergo Hunni stirpe creati, Gothorum finibus aduenere. Jordanes, *De Getarum siue Gothorum origine*, xxiv, ed. C. A. Closs, Stuttgart, 1861 (pp. 93–94). *Page xiii. Huns.*

Olaus Magnus, Book III, c. 18 (London, 1658, p. 49). "*Haguinus*, King of *Norway*, when he was to fight against the *Danes*, he raised a storm by Witchcraft, and so beat upon the Enemies heads, with Hail-stones of an unusual greatness, that their Eyes were hurt as with arrows from the Clouds, and they could not see, the Elements fighting more against them, than the Enemy." *Page xiii. Haakon.*

The land forces of Xerxes, says Herodotus (vii, 61, *sqq.*), contained forty-six nations. Upon his march he received further accessions of strength, and when he reached Thermopylae the land and sea forces amounted to 2,641,610 fighting men. This does not include the attendants, the slaves, the crews of the provision ships, and others, which according to the reckoning of Herodotus *Page xiii. Xerxes.*

exceeded in numbers the actual warriors. Even if it be supposed that the tally was equal, the total figure of the army of Xerxes at Thermopylae is 5,283,220. It must be remembered that his forces were the result of a maximum of effort throughout a vast empire, and that provisions had been stored for three years before all along the line of march.

Page xiii. Trois-eschelles. See *The Geography of Witchcraft* by Montague Summers, c. v, pp. 398–9 and 426. Bodin, *Démonomanie*, IV, 5 (ed. Lyons, 1593, p. 509), has: "Trois-eschelles dist au Roy Charles IX, qu'il y en alloit plus de trois cens mille [Sorciers] en ce Royaume." Charles IX reigned 1560–74.

Page xiv. Saul. *I Kings* (*A.V.*, *I Samuel*), xv, 22–23: "And Samuel said: Doth the Lord desire holocausts and victims, and not rather that the voice of the Lord should be obeyed? For obedience is better than sacrifices: and to hearken rather than to offer the fat of rams. Because it is like the sin of witchcraft, to rebel: and like the crime of idolatry, to refuse to obey."

Page xiv. God . . . threatened. *E.g. Leviticus*, xx, 6: "The soul that shall go aside after magicians, and soothsayers, and shall commit fornication with them, I will set my face against that soul, and destroy it out of the midst of its people." *Ibid.* xx, 27: "A man, or woman, in whom there is a pythonical or divining spirit, dying let them die: they shall stone them: their blood be upon them." *Malachias*, iii, 5: "And I will come to you in judgement, and will be a speedy witness against sorcerers, and adulterers, and false swearers." *II Paralipomenon* (*A.V., II Chronicles*), xxxiii, 6, of Manasses: " And he made his sons to pass through the fire in the valley of Benennom: he observed dreams, followed divinations, gave himself up to magic arts, had with him magicians and enchanters: and he wrought many evils before the Lord, to provoke him to anger."

Page xv. Emperor.

Suetonius, *Caligula*, xxx: "Insensus turbae fauenti aduersus studium suum exclamauit: Utinam populus Romanus unam ceruicem haberet." The phrase is often said to be Nero's, but Seneca and Dio Cassius agree with Suetonius in attributing it to Caligula, Dio, lix: *Καὶ ποτὲ παντὶ τῷ δήμῳ ἀπειλῶν εἶπεν: εἴθε ἕνα αὐχένα εἴχετε.* Seneca, *De Ira*, iii. 19: "Qui optabat, ut populus Romanus unam ceruicem haberet, ut scelera sua tot locis, ac temporibus diducta, in unum ictum, et unum diem cogeret."

Preface, xvii. People who do not believe that there are witches.

The authority of the *Malleus Maleficarum* distinctly proves that a "belief that there are such beings as witches is so essential a part of the Catholic faith that obstinately to maintain the opposite opinion savours of heresy." Part I, Question 1.

Preface, xviii. Grilland.

Pauli Grillandi Castellionis, *Tractatus duo de Sortilegiis et Lamiis.* Lyons, 1533; 1536; Frankfort, 1590; and other editions.

Preface, xviii. The Psalmist.

Psalm lxxxv, 9: Quoniam magnus es tu, et faciens mirabilia: tu es Deus solus.

Preface, xix. The Inquisition. I.e. *Malleus Maleficarum.*

Preface, xix. Bodin. Jean Bodin, 1530–96. The famous *De la Démonomanie des Sorciers*, first issued in 1580, Paris, was several times reprinted, the last edition being Rouen, 1604. There are Latin (1590), German (1581), and Italian (1587) translations. Of Bodin's *Le fleau des démons et sorciers* there are editions 1616 and 1626.

Preface, xix. Remy. Nicolas Remy, 1554–*c.* 1600. His *Dæmonolatreia* appeared in 1595 (Lyons), and was very frequently reprinted. One of the latest, if not the last, edition is Hamburg, 1698. There is a German translation of 1598. Another translation was printed at Hamburg in 1693. For a full account of Remy see the Introduction to the English translation of *Dæmonolatreia* in the present series.

Preface, xix. Binsfeld. Peter Binsfeld, one of the most important names in the history of witchcraft, was born *c.* 1540, and died 1603. His *Tractatus de Confessionibus Maleficorum*, Trèves, 1589, which ran into many editions, is regarded as of high authority. For fuller details see the Introduction to the translation of the *Tractatus* in this series.

Page 8. Royal Prophet. *Psalm* viii, 3: "Ex ore infantium et lactentium perfecisti laudem propter inimicos tuos, ut destruas inimicum et ultorem." Quoted by Our Lord, *S. Matthew*, xxi, 16.

Page 8. Pope Paul IV. Giovanni Pietro Caraffa, born 28 June, 1476: elected 23 May, 1555; died 18 August, 1559.

I Corinthians, v, 1–5. "Omnino auditur inter uos fornicatio, et talis fornicatio qualis nec inter gentes, ita ut uxorem patris sui aliquis habeat. Et uos inflati estis: et non magis luctum habuistis ut tollatur de medio uestrum qui hoc opus fecit. Ego quidem absens corpore, praesens autem spiritu, iam iudicaui ut praesens, eum, qui sic operatus est. In nomine Domini nostri IESU CHRISTI, congregatis uobis et meo spiritu, cum uirtute Domini nostri IESU, Tradere huiusmodi satanae in interitum carnis, ut spiritus saluus sit in die Domini nostri IESU CHRISTI." And I *Timothy*, i, 20: "Hymenaeus, et Alexander: quos tradidi satanae, ut discant non blasphemare." *Page* 9. *S. Paul.*

lxxvii. (A.V. 78) 49: "Misit in eos iram indignationis suae: indignationem et iram, et tribulationem: immissiones per angelos malos." *Page* 9. *Psalm.*

Jean Benedicti, the celebrated Franciscan theologian of the sixteenth century, belonged to the Observantine Province of Tours and Poitiers. He arose to high office, being commissary-general of the French and visitor of many Italian provinces. His *Somme des pechez et le remède d'iceux*, first published at Lyons in 1584, was many times reprinted. *La triomphante victoire de la Vierge Marie sur sept Esprits malins, finalment chassés du corps d'une femme dan l'Eglise des Cordeliers de Lyon*, Lyons, 1611, relates the case of Perrenette Pinay, who was exorcized and freed from a most grievous demoniac possession. *Page* 9. *Benedicti.*

Peter Thyræus, S.J., of Neuss, was Professor of Theology at Mainz. The important work to *Page* 9. *Thyræus.*

which reference is here made is his *Daemoniaci, hoc est de obsessis a spiritibus Daemoniorum hominibus*, Cologne, 1594. There are reprints, Lyons, 1603; Cologne, 1604; and Lyons, 1626.

Page 9. *Simon Magus.* Peter Thyræus, *Daemoniaci*, Pars I, c. xvi, 199, writes: "Refert Anastasius Nicaenus, quaestione 23, Simonem Magum eos, qui ipsum praestigiatorem dicerent, Daemonibus subiecisse."

Page 9. *Eighty girls and women.* This affair, which caused a great sensation, commenced in the reign of Julius III, continued during the short pontificate of Marcellus II (9–30 April, 1555), and was prolonged until the days of Paul IV. The possessed were exorcized by a Benedictine monk belonging to the household of Cardinal Pierre de Gondi, Bishop of Paris, and it is recorded that the demons proved particularly stubborn and obstinate, so powerful were the Hebrew sorcerers at work.

Page 9. *Cook.* The woman's name was Elsa Kamer. Both she and her mother, a notorious witch of long continuance, were executed.

Page 9. *Caron.* Loys Charondas Le Caron, born at Paris 1530; died 1617.

Page 10. *Fernel.* Jean Fernel, "le Galien moderne," born at Clermont-en-Beauvoisis (or at Montdidier) in 1497. He was the Chief Physician to Henry II and Diane de Poitiers. Dr. Sauecrotte thus describes Fernel: "Il était professeur éloquent, écrivain non moins élégant que disert, artiste en l'art d'éxposer et d'enchaîner avec lucidité les doctrines qu'il conciliait."

The shrine of St. Claude was visited by many pilgrims of the highest rank, such as Philip the Bold, Duke of Burgundy, who went there in 1369, 1376 and 1382: Philip the Good in 1422, 1442 and 1443; Charles the Rash in 1461; Louis XI in 1456 and 1482; Blessed Amadeus, Duke of Savoy, in 1471. In 1500 Anne of Brittany, wife of Louis XII, made a pilgrimage of thanksgiving to the shrine in gratitude for the birth of her daughter Claude. Unhappily in March, 1794, the sacred body of St. Claude was burned by order of the revolutionaries. *Page 10. St. Claude.*

Dialogues, I. iv. *Page 12. S. Gregory.*

Daemoniaci, II, c. 32: "In huius Capitis ingressu B. Hieronymi, superiori Capite allatam constituimus sententiam. Quae causa est, inquit, ut saepe bimuli trimuliue, et ubera materna lactantes a daemonio corripiantur? Inuisibilia haec inscrutabili altissimi Dei iudicio sunt relinquenda." *Page 13. Thyræus.*

S. Gregory the Great (Hom. xxxiv. in Euangel.) says: "We know on the authority of Scripture that there are nine Choirs of Angels: Angels, Archangels, Virtues, Powers, Principalities, Dominations, Thrones, Cherubim and Seraphim." S. Thomas (*Summa*, I, Q. cviii), following S. Dionysius, *De Caelesti Hierarchia*, vi and vii, divides the Angels into three hierarchies, each of which comprises three orders. *Page 14. Hierarchy.*

κακαρχία. *Page 15. Cacarchy.*

The "Master of the Sentences," *c.* 1100–*c.* 1160–64. His famous *Book of Sentences* was *Page 15. Peter Lombard.*

written 1145–51. In a long series of questions the author covers practically the whole body of theological doctrine, writing it in one systematized whole.

Page 15. *Thyræus.* *Daemoniaci*, I, 12, says: "Cum igitur ex bonorum Angelorum numero et classibus spiritus nequam deciderint, etiam inter ipsos aliquis erit ordo, et procul dubio is ipsus, qui antequam ad suas miserias prolapsi sunt, fuit."

Page 15. *Behemoth.* Bodin in his *Démonomanie*, I, 1, says: "Il semble que Dieu a creé ce grand Satan au commencement du monde, que l'escripture appelle Behemoth, et Leviathan; car l'escripture saincte dit, Is prima rerum origine a Deo conditus est." *Job*, xl and xli.

Page 15. *Flagellum Daemonum.* This famous work is by Girolamo Menghi, a Capuchin of Valmontone. It first appeared Venice, 1599, and was reprinted as late as 1708. *Flagellum Daemonum, exorcismos terribiles, potentissimos et efficaces . . . in malignos spiritus . . . complectens . . . Accessit postremo pars secunda quae Fustis daemonum inscribitur.*

Page 15. *Binsfeld.* *De Confessionibus Maleficorum.* III. Decima Conclusio. "Magi uirtute diabolica possunt aliquando Daemones cogere, et e suis sedibus expellere."

Page 15. *Nider.* John Nider, O.P., born in Swabia, 1380; died at Colmar, 13 August, 1438. As a theologian he adheres closely to S. Thomas. His *Formicarius*, an encyclopædic treatise, which may be dated 1435–37, was first printed about 1500.

There are many subsequent editions. Strassburg, 1517; Paris, 1519; Douai, 1602; Helmstadt, 1692. The last Book, V, deals with witchcraft and sorcery, and is continually cited by the demonologists as of the first authority.

Page 16. *Ezekiel.* Chapter vii. The prophet writes: "The spirit lifted me up between the earth and the heaven, and brought me in the vision of God into Jerusalem." Here he beheld the secret sorceries of the seventy men of the ancients of the house of Israel who were worshipping with incense the frescoed animals and creeping things *more Aegyptiano.* He was also shown the women who wept and wailed for Adonis in the north porch of the temple. The rites of Adonis, moreover, were intimately connected with the practices of the *Kedeshim.* Boguet is mistaken in saying that Ezechiel was transported to Azotus (Ashdod), and he is perhaps thinking of S. Philip diaconus, who was carried away to Azotus after the baptism of the Ethiopian eunuch. Acts viii, 26–40.

Page 17. *Tobias.* Tobias was accompanied by the Archangel S. Raphael.

Page 17. *Two Angels who visited Lot.* The appearances of Angels in the Old Testament often present points of some complexity with reference to the personality of the Being who was manifested. The earlier Fathers tell us that on certain occasions Almighty God Himself appeared, as in the bush to Moses, and on Mt. Sinai, whilst Tertullian saw some foreshadowing—as it were—of the Incarnation, and many of the Eastern Fathers follow the same line of thought. It would seem that the three Angels who visited Abraham were an actual Theophany, for the narrative implies that the Supreme Being remained when the two departed. Yet it is probable that two Angels visited Lot. The whole incident is one of extraordinary difficulty. Vandenbroeck, *Dissertatio Theologica de Theophaniis sub Ueteri Testamento*, Louvain, 1851, may be consulted with profit.

Page 17. *Augustus Cæsar.* An account of the many and very early legends that make Augustus Cæsar one of the "prophets of Christ" may be found in Graf, *Roma nella memoria e nelle immaginazioni del Medio Evo*, Turin, 1882, I, ix. 308, 331.

Page 17. *Pope Leo.* Pope S. Leo I, 440–61.

Page 18. *Spina.* Bartolomeo Spina, O.P., whose *Quaestio de strigibus et lamiis*, Venice, 1523, was widely esteemed and often reprinted. This celebrated theologian was born at Pisa about 1475, and rose to high honours in his Order. In July 1542 he was made Master of the Sacred Palace by Paul III. He died at Rome in 1546.

Page 18. *Pliny.* Lib. VII. Ep. 27: "Ego ut esse credam, in primis eo ducor, quod audio accidisse Curtio Rufo. Tenuis adhuc et obscurus obtinenti Africam comes haeserat: inclinato die spatiabatur in porticu : offertur ei mulieris figura humana grandior pulchriorque: perterrito, *Africam se, futurorum praenuntiam,* dixit: ***iturum enim Romam, honoresque gesturum, atque etiam cum summo imperio in eandem prouinciam*** *reuersurum, ibique moriturum.* Facta sunt omnia. Praeterea accidenti Carthaginem, egredientique nauem, eadem figura in litore occurrisse narratur."

Hector Boece, chronicler, and one of the founders of Aberdeen University, 1465–1536. The impetus he gave to historical studies at Aberdeen was of lasting effect. His works are highly esteemed. *Page* 18. *Boethius.*

Scotorum Historiae, VIII.—I have used the first edition, 1526, where this story and other similar adventures may be read, folios cliv–v. "In Gareotha regione, uico quatuordeum uix passuū millibus ab Aberdonia, adolescēs multa formositate, coram Aberdonen̄ antistite questus est palam, sese a dęmone Succuba (vt dicunt) gratissima omniū quę uidisset forma, multo antea menses infestatum eandē occlusis foribus noctu ad si ingredi blanditiis, in sui amplexus cōpellere. Dubia luce abiri sine strepitu poene, nullo se posse modo quū plures attentasset a tāta, actā turpi uesania liberari. Iubet cōtinus optimus episcopus adolescētē, alio se cōferre, & vt christiana religiōe magis laudatis, ieiuniis & oronibus plus solito accōmodaret uim: fore vt piis operibus incēto, uictus cacodęmon tādē terga esset daturus. Euenit adolescēti salubre cōsiliū religiose exequuto, paucos post dies vti uenerādus antistes erat p̄fatus."

The story is found in Paulus Jovius, *Elogia Doctorum Uirorum*, c. 101. See my *History of Witchcraft*, p. 103. Weyer, *De Magis Infamibus*, V. 11 and 12, relates the circumstance. *Opera omnia*, 1670, pp. 110–11: "Silentio inuolui *Page* 19. *Agrippa.*

diutius . . . non patiar quod in diuersis aliquot scriptoribus legerim, diabolum forma canis ad extremum Agrippae halitum comitem ipsi fuisse, et postea nescio quibus modis euanuisse. . . . Canem hunc nigrum mediocris staturae, Gallico nomine Monsieur (quod Dominum sonat) nuncupatum noui ego . . . at uere naturalis erat canis masculus . . . causam autem huic falsae opinioni dedisse opinor, partim quod canem hunc pueriliter nimis amaret (ut sunt quorundam hominum mores) oscularetur plerumque, aliquando et a latere hunc sibi admoueret in mensa."

Page 19. *Abdias.* A collection of "Acts of the Apostles" which was formed, probably by a monk, in the Frankish Church in the sixth century by a mistake concerning the authorship was under the title *Historia Certaminis Apostolorum* ascribed to Abdias, who is said to have been a disciple of the Apostles and first Bishop of Babylon. The nucleus of this collection was formed by the Latin *Passiones* of those Apostles concerning whom there were no Gnostic or semi-Gnostic *legenda*, that is, SS. James Major and Minor, Philip, Bartholomew, Simon, and Jude. Amongst many accretions there is a very early tradition to be found, and it is believed historical truth.

Page 19. *Agnan.* "Ou *Agnian*, démon qui tourmente les Américains par des apparitions et des méchancetés. Il se montre surtout au Brésil et chez les Topinamboux. Il parait sous toutes sortes de formes, de façon que ceux qui veulent le voir peuvent le rencontrer partout." Collin de Plancy, *Dictionnaire Infernal* (6me ed.), Paris, 1863.

It is very commonly held that this colour, especially in certain circumstances, is unlucky. Cf. Heywood, *The Fair Maid of the West*, 4to, 1631. Part I, Act IV, scene 2: *Page* 20. *Black.*

Besse. Then first, you said your ship was trim
and gay:
Ile have her pitcht all ore, no spot of white,
No colour to be seene, no saile but blacke,
No flag but sable.
Goodlache. Twill be ominous,
And bode disaster fortune.
Besse. Ile ha' it so.
Goodlache. Why then she shall be pitcht blacke
as the devil.
Besse. She shall be call'd *The Negro.*

"Daemones . . . impetum in animalia nonnulla faciunt . . . quia mirum in modum animali calore capiantur. Nam cum in profundissimis locis uersentur, quae frigida extreme siccaque sunt, sit ut multum frigiditatis sibi contrahant, qua quidem contracti atque afflicti, humidum at animalem calorem appetunt, quo ut potiantur, in bruta quoque animalia insiliunt, et in balnea concauaque loca penetrant. Ignis enim solisque calorem, quia urit et exsiccat, auersantur: animalem uero, tanquam humiditati temperatum, libenter amplexantur, maximeque hominum, congruum quidem illum et temperatum." Michaelis Pselli, *De Operatione daemonum Dialogus*, Latin translation by Petus Morellus, Paris, 1615, pp. 52 and 55. *Page* 20. *Psellus.*

Sorcerers could often be distinguished by their foul and fetid odour. In the patois of the Pyrenees wizards were commonly known as *Page* 21. *Cardan.*

poudouès and witches *poudouèros*, both words being derived from *putere*, which signifies to have an evil smell. See my *History of Witchcraft*, pp. 44–45.

Page 24. *Renunciation.* For this abjuration of the Catholic Faith as noted by Francesco-Maria Guazzo in his authoritative *Compendium Maleficarum*, see my *History of Witchcraft*, c. iii, pp. 81–82.

Page 24. *Bodin.* In his *Démonomanie*, II, c. iv, Bodin says: "Les plus detestables Sorciers, sont ceux, qui renoncent à Dieu, et à son service." Lambert Daneau (English translation, *A Dialogue of Witches*) writes: "He commaundeth them to forswere God theyr creator and all his power, promising perpetually to obey and worship him, who then standeth in their presence." De Lancre, *Tableau de l'Inconstance des Mauvais Anges*, Livre II, Discours 1 (ed. Paris, 1612, p. 74), tells us that a neophyte was told it was necessary "qu'il renonce & renie son Sauueur, la Vierge Marie, les saincts & sainctes de Paradis, son baptesme, le sainct chresme, le ciel & la Terre, & particulierement son pere confesseur, ses pere & mere, parrain & marraine, & autres parens."

Page 25. *Rebaptised.* Remy, *Dæmonolatreia*, III, vi: "Non desunt & qui se iterum sacramento initiali expiari postulent, rati se ea ratione in Christi familiam rursus cooptari posse." It may be worth remarking that the Sacrament of Baptism cannot, of course, be repeated. The Sacrament validly administered impresses an ineffaceable character on the soul, which the Tridentine Fathers call a spiritual and indelible mark—S. Thomas treats of the nature of this indelible seal in the *Summa*, III. Q. lxiii, a. 2.

Page 25. Chrism. This is actually a mixture of oil of olives and balsam, blessed by a bishop in an especial manner, and used in the administration of certain Sacraments, particularly Confirmation (as also Baptism and Holy Orders).

Page 25. St. Cyril. S. Cyril of Jerusalem, *c.* 315–86.

Page 25. Jesus Christ. It is held by great theologians such as S. Thomas, *Summa*, III. Q. lxxii, a. 4, and Suarez, *De Confessione*, D. xxxiii, and is indeed humanly certain that chrism was immediately instituted by Our Lord Himself.

Page 25. Fabian. Pope S. Fabian, 236–50.

Page 26. Cold. A Belgian witch, Digna Robert, in 1565, said that the devil "était froid dans tous ses membres." At the North Berwick Sabbat in 1590, "he caused all the company to com and kiss his ers quhilk they said was cauld lyk yce." In 1661 a Forfar witch "Katheren Porter confesseth that the divill tooke hir by the hand, that his hand was cold." In 1662 Isabel Rutherford "confesst that ye was at ane meeting at Turfhills, where Sathan took you by the hand and said 'welcome Isabel,' and said that his hand was cold." Margaret Litster of the same coven spoke of "Sattan having grey clothes and his hand cold." In 1697 Thomas Lindsay, a boy, gave witness that "Jean Fulton his Grand-Mother awaked him one Night out of his Bed, and caused him to take a Black Grimm Gentleman (as she called him) by the Hand; which he felt to be cold."

Page 26. *Of the voice of demons.* The demon who presided at the meetings or synagogues of the Vaudois spoke "uoce rauca." J. Friedrich, *La Vauderye*, Munich, 1898, p. 188. Remy, *Dæmonolatreia*, I, viii, says of demons: "nec adeo feliciter humanam uocem imitantur, quin ficta, ementitaque audientibus facile appareat. Nicolaea Ganatia, Eua Hesoletia, Iana Nigra Armacuriana, ac pluraque aliae uocem illis esse aiunt, qualem emittunt, qui os in dolium, aut testam rimosam insertum habent."

Page 27. *Black ram.* In the case of Guillaume Edeline, who was condemned in 1453, "Confessa ledit sire Guillaume, de sa bonne et franche voulenté, avoir fait hommage audit ennemy en l'espéce et semblance d'ung mouton, en le baisant par le fondement au signe de révérence et d'hommage." De Lancre tells us that the witch Silvain Nevillon, when on his trial at Orleans, in 1614, "dit qu'il a veu le Diable en plusieurs façons, tantost comme vn bouc, ores comme vn gros mouton."

Page 28. *Fulgosus.* Baptista Fregoso, an Italian writer of the fifteenth century.

Page 28. *Rook.* This is from Suetonius, *Domitian*, xxiii: "Ante paucos quam occideretur menses, cornix in Capitolio locuta est, ἔσται πάντα καλῶς. Nec defuit qui ostentum sic interpretaretur:

Nuper Tarpeio quae sedit culmine cornix,
Est bene, *non potuit dicere: dixit*, Erit.

Page 28. *Cœlius Rhodiginus.* Lodovico Ricchieri, the famous Italian philologist, surnamed Rhodiginus from Rovigo (*Rhodigium*), where he was born about 1450, and where he died in 1525. His *Antiquarum lectionum*, lib. xvi, was published at Venice, folio, 1516; Paris, folio, 1517. A more complete edition, comprising thirty books, was issued under the care of Camillo Ricchieri and Goretti at Bale, folio, 1550. I have used the folio Geneva edition of 1620.

Page 28. *Vair.*

Leonardo Vairo (or Vair), born at Benevento, of Spanish descent, *c.* 1540; Bishop of Pozzuoli, where he died in 1603. His *De Fascino*, Libri III, Paris, 1583; Venetiis apud Aldum, 1589, is a work of singular erudition.

Page 29. *Of the copulation of the Devil.*

A phallic orgy was an essential part of the Sabbat. At the nocturnal synagogues of the Vaudois the presiding demon—or he who filled the devil's office—took aside the neophyte, "trahit ad partem in nemore receptam, ut eam suo modo amplexetur et cognoscat carnaliter, cui ex malicia dicit, quod iaceat super terram in facie ad duas manus et pedes, et quod ei aliter non potest copulari, et in quacumque forma fruitur presidens, tacto primo per receptam membro presidentis, quod sepius frigidum et molle indicat, ut sepius totum corpus. Primo immittit in portam naturalem et relinquit sperma corruptum et croceum susceptum in pollucione nocturna aut alias, secundo in locum egestionis, et ita inordinate abutitur." Upon her return to the company, " recepta transit ante refectionem in copulam carnalem alicuius hominis." After a banquet the torches are extinguished and "quisque suam ad partem trahit et carnaliter cognoscit. Nonnunquam uero excessus indicibiles commictuntur in commutacionibus mulierum, iussu presidentis, de transitu de muliere in mulierem et de uiro in uirum; de abusu contra naturam mulierum inuicem, et similiter uirorum inter se; aut mulieris cum uiro extra uas debitum et ad partem aliam. . . . Uir uero cum dyabola aut mulier cum daemone nullam experitur delectacionem, sed ex timore et obediencia consentit in copulam. . . . In secunda autem congregacione ipsa mulier recepta cognoscitur carnaliter a demone familiari ac sollicitatore, modo quo prius a presidente, et non amplius a demone in aliis congregacionibus sequentibus, nisi cum propter paucitatem uirorum ad complendum copulas (quum ut plurimum plures sunt ibi mulieres, quam uiri) demones in copulis supplent uices uirorum, sicuti interdum, sed raro, uti pauciores sunt mulieres, supplecio fit per dyabolas, et ita sepius in aliis congregacionibus, preter duas primas congregaciones, in quorum prima in reditu a presidente, post receptionem ad congregacionem, cognoscitur a dyabola: est tamen reperire, sed raro, quod uir aliquis semper habet dyabolam in copula, et est signum maxime nequicia in eo, et similiter aliqua mulier semper in omnibus congregacionibus habet uirum uel demonem." J. Friedrich, *La Vauderye*, Munich, 1898, pp. 188–89. De Lancre, *Tableau de l'Inconstance*, III, Discours V, says: "Or cette operation de luxure n'est commise ou pratiquee par eux pour plaisir qu'ils y prēnent, parce que comme simples Esprits, ils ne peuuent prendre aucune joye ny plaisir des choses sensibles. Mais ils le font seulement pour faire choir l'homme dans le precipice dans lequel ils sont, qui est la disgrace de Dieu tres-haut & tres-puissant." He also records definite confessions: "Iohannes d'Aguerre, dict que le Diable en forme de bouc auoit son membre au derriere & cognoissoit les femmes en agitent & poussant auec iceluy contre leur deuant. Marie de Marigrane aagee de quinze ans habitante de Biarrix dict, Qu'elle a veu souuent le Diable s'accoupler auec vne infinité de femmes qu'elle nomme par nom & surnom: & que sa coutume est de cognoistre les belles pardeuant & les laides tout au rebours." It is certain from the detailed and overwhelming evidence of all countries that the copulation of the Devil or the Grand-Master of the Sabbat with the witches was no morbid hallucination but an actual and achieved fact. As the Platonist Dr. Henry More says: "*Witches* confessing, so frequently as they do, that the Devil *lies with them*, and withal complaining of his tedious and offensive *coldness*, it is a shrewd presumption that he doth lie with them *indeed*, and that it is not a meer *Dream*." The Salmanticenses in the authoritative *Theologia Moralis*, Tr. xxi. c. 11, p. 10, nn. 180, 181, lay down: "Some deny this, believing it impossible that demons should perform the carnal act with human beings. None the less the opposite opinion is most certain, and must be followed."

Page 31. *Cold.*

The coldness of the Devil and the repeated assertion at the trials that his semen was nipping and gelid would seem to point to the use upon occasion of an artificial penis. "In many of the cases of debauchery at Sabbats so freely and fully confessed by the witches, their partners were undoubtedly the males who were present; the Grand Master, Officer, or President of the Assembly, exercising the right to select first for his own pleasures such women as he chose. . . .

Yet when we sift the evidence, detailed and exact, of the trials, we find there foul and hideous mysteries of lust which neither human intercourse nor the employ of a mechanical property can explain. Howbeit, the theologians and the inquisitors are fully aware what unspeakable horror lurks in the blackness beyond." See my *History of Witchcraft*, c. iii, pp. 97—101. Mother Bush of Barton in 1649 said that the Devil who visited her as a young black man "was colder than man, and heavier, and could not performe nature as man." In 1662 Isobel Gowdie and Janet Breadheid of Auldearne described the Devil as "a meikle, blak, roch man, werie cold; and I fand his nature als cold within me as spring-well-water." "He is abler for us that way than any man can be," said Isobel, "onlie he was heavie lyk a malt-sek; a hudg nature, verie cold, as yce."

Page 31. A good finger's length. "Margueritte fille de Sare aagee de seize à dixsept ans, depose que le Diable, soit qu'il ayt la forme d'homme, ou qu'il soit en forme de Bouc, a tousiours vn membre de mulet, ayant chosy en imitation celuy de cet animal comme le mieux pourueu: Qu'il l'a long & gros comme le bras: que quand il veut cognoistre quelque fille on femme au sabbat comme il faict presque â chasque assemblee, il faict paroistre quelque forme de lict de foye, sur lequel il faict semblant de les coucher, qu'elles n'y prenent poinct de desplaisir, comme ont dict ces premieres: Et que iamais il ne paroist au sabbat en quelque action que ce soit, qu'il n'ait tousiours son instrumēt dehors, de cette belle forme & mesure: Tout à rebours de ce que dict Boguet, que celles de son pais ne luy ont veu guiere plus long que le doigt & gros simplement à proportion: Si bien que les sorcieres de Labourt sont mieux seruies de Satan que celles de la Franche Comité." De Lancre, *Tableau de l'Inconstance*, III, Discours v.

Page 31. *Woman in travail.*

"Marie de Marigrane fille de Biarrix aagee de quinze ans dict, Qu'il semble que ce Mauveais Demon ayt son membre my-party, moitié de fer, moitié de chair tout de son long, & de mesme les genitoires, & depose l'auoir veu en cette forme plusieurs fois au sabbat: & outre ce l'auoir ouy dire à des femmes que Satan auoit cognues: Qu'il faict crier comme des femmes qui sont en mal d'enfant: & qu'il tient tousiours son membre dehors.

"Petry de Linarse dict, Que le Diable a le membre faict de corne, ou pour le moins il en a l'apparence: c'est pourquoy il faict tant crier les femmes." *Ibid.* Francis Hutchinson in his *Historical Essay Concerning Witchcraft*, Second edition, London, 1720 (pp. 42–43), tells us that in 1594 Jeanne Bosdeau, a witch of Bordeaux, confessed that on the Eve of S. John (23 June) she accompanied an Italian necromancer who had debauched her long before to a field, where, after he had conjured from a black book, "there appeared a great *Black Goat* with a Candle between his Horns. . . . He had carnal Knowledge of her, which was with great Pain."

Page 32. *A dog or a cat.*

A Scotch witch confessed that "the Devil gaive hir his markis; and went away from her in the liknes of ane blak doug." (Pitcairn, III, p. 601.) Also: "He wold haw carnall dealing with us in the shap of a deir, or in any vther shap, now and then. Somtym he vold be lyk a stirk, a bull, a deir, a rae, or a dowg, etc. and haw dealling with us" (*Ibid.*, III, pp. 611, 613). Margaret Hamilton was thus indicted: "Yow . . . had carnall cowpulatiown with the devil in the lyknes of ane man, bot he removed from yow in the lyknes of ane black dowg." Bodin, *Démonomanie*, III, 6, relates, "il aduint au Monastere du Mont de Hesse en Allemaigne, que les Religieuses furent daemoniaques: & voiot on sur leurs licts des chiens qui attendoient impudiquement celles qui estoient suspectes d'en auoir abusé, & commis le peché qu'ils appellent le peché muet." Peccatum Mutum is the name given by Gregorio Lopez, O.P., Bishop of Basilia, to sodomy, because he says it is so shocking to honest ears that it is wrong to speak of it. And Ludovico Maria Sinistrari is of opinion that sodomia perfecta may be committed between women, not in all cases, but in some. He is inclined to believe that Philaenis first practised this lewdness. And in the work commonly attributed to Aloisia Sigaea, Colloquium II, may be read: "Philaenis uero, quod huic uoluptati indulgeret perditissime, inuenisse credita est; et usu suo, quae scilicet magni nominis erat, inauditae ad suam aetatem, uoluptati usum feminis puellisque apud suos suasisse."

Page 32. A natural dog. Dr. Havelock Ellis, *Studies in the Psychology of Sex*, Vol. V, *Erotic Symbolism*, iv, speaking of congress between women and animals says, "When among women in civilisation animal perversions appear, the animals is nearly always a pet dog." Several cases are discussed, and there is reference to other authorities (Bloch, *Beiträge zur Aetiologie der Psychopathia Sexualis;* Maschka; Irving Rosse) who state that these conjunctions are not an infrequent exhibition given by prostitutes in certain brothels. Mantegazza, *Gli Amori degli Uomini,* V. may be further consulted on the subject.

Page 32. *Pasiphaë.*

Ovid, *De Arte Amandi,* I, 280–96, 323–26:

Forte sub umbrosis nemorosae uallibus Idae
Candidus armenti gloria taurus erat;
Signatus tenui media inter cornua nigro.
Una fuit labes; cetera lactis erant.
Illum Gnosiadesque Cydoneaeque iuuencae
Optarunt tergo sustinuisse suo.
Pasiphae fieri gaudebat adultera tauri:
Inuida formosas oderat illa boues. . . .
Et modo se Europen fieri, modo postulat Io:
Altera quod bos est; altera uecta boue.
Hanc tamen impleuit uacca deceptus acerna
Dux gregis: et partu proditus auctor erat.

Page 33. *Fauns.*

See Sinistrari, *Demoniality* (Fortune Press, 1927) where these questions are most learnedly discussed in detail.

Page 33. *Vair.*

There is a French translation of Vair's *De incantationibus, Trois livres des charmes, sorcelages, ou enchantemens. . . . Faits en latin par Leonard Vair et mis en François par* Iulian Bardon, *Angeuin.* Paris, 1583, 8vo.

Page 33. *Satyrs.*

Called by Pliny, *Historia Naturalis,* vii, 2, "pernicissimum animal."

Page 34 *Egeria.*

Ovid, *Fasti*, III, 275–6 has:

Egeria est, quae praebet aquas, Dea grata Camoenis.
Illa Numae coniunx consiliumque fuit.

And Juvenal, III, 12–13, writes:

Hic, ubi nocturnae Numa constituebat amicae
Nunc sacri fontis nemus . . .

Upon this Grangaeus glosses: "Numa Pompilius, maximus ille Romanorum idololatra, nocturnum connubium et colloquium se habere simulabat cum Ægeria nympha, religionis causa." Upon *constituebat* Dorleans has a note: "Legendum puto, *nocturna Numa constertebat amica.* Id est, ubi cum amica Egeria simul dormiebat."

Page 35. *Pregnant by him.*

In 1652, during their trial at Maidstone, "Anne Ashby, Anne Martyn, and one other of their Associates, pleaded that they were with child pregnant, but confessed it was not by any man, but by the Divell."
A Prodigious and Tragicall History of the Arraignment, Tryall, Confession, and Condemnation of six Witches at Maidstone in Kent, at the Assizes there held in July, Fryday 30, *this present year,* 1652. London, 1652.

Page 35. *Merlin.*

Boece, *Scotorum Historiae*, folio 1526, VIII, says: "Constans tum fama erat, Merlinū incubi, ac nobilis Britānici sanguinis foeminae cōcubitu, p̄gnatū, magicis carminibus malos dęmones ad colloquia excire: & ex his quę futura essent cognoscere."
There is an old romance of Merlin: *Sensuyt le p̄mier volume de Merlin. Qui est le premier liure de la Table ronde. Avec plusiers choses*

moult recreatiue. P. le Noir, Paris, 1528. Here the demons, alarmed at the number of men who have escaped them since the Birth of Our Lord, hold a council of war and resolve to send to the world one of their company to engender upon some virgin a child. He shall be their vicegerent upon earth, and (*salua reuerentia*) according to their schemes endeavour to counteract the Redemption. The fiend deputed to this work obtains admittance into the house of a wealthy Briton, and true to his nature slays his host, seducing two of the three daughters. The youngest resists, but whilst in an enchanted sleep is swived by the devil. Witless of what has occurred she confesses to a holy hermit, Blaise, who protects her. She gives birth to Merlin, who is instantly baptized by Blaise, and thus the devil's designs are frustrated. Cf. James Huneker's tale, *Antichrist; Visionaries*, 1905. One may compare Machiavelli's *Belphegor*, and the Oriental Saga of the angels Harut and Marut, in the commentators on (*Sura*, 11, 96) the Qu'ran. In the Chronicle of Philippe Moustres, Bishop of Tournai, a diabolical origin is attributed to Eleonora of Aquitaine, who espoused Louis-le-Jeune, King of France, and afterwards was wedded to Henry II of England. J. Brompton (*Hist. Franc.*, XIII, 215) has preserved a similar legend, and in the *Livre de Badouin* (p. 13) Comtesse Jeanne de Flandre is supposed to be a daughter of the evil spirit. See Reiffenberg, Introduction to the *Chronicle of Philippe de Moustres*, p. lxviii.

With regard to Merlin one may consult *Die Sagen von Merlin* . . . by San Marte (A. Schulz), Halle, 8vo. 1853; and *Slavianskia Shazania o*

Solomenye i Kitrovrase i Zapadnya legendy o Morolfe i Merline, by A. Vesselovsky, S. Petersburg, 1872.

William Rowley's *The Birth of Merlin, or the Childe hath found his Father*, not printed until 1662, and once ascribed to Shakespeare, is a curious medley of farce and romance, awkward, but not wholly destitute of poetry. Herein the Devil appears as Merlin's father. He has got Joan Go-Too't, the Clown's sister, with child, and Merlin is born amid thunder and lightning. But Merlin, rebuking his father, who dubs him "Traitor to hell!" as

> "an inferior lustful Incubus,
> Taking advantage of the wanton Flesh,"

encloses him in a rock, and conveys his mother to a secure retreat.

An ancient authority is the *Chronica* of John Nauclerus, volumen secundum, generatio xv. "Inuentus est tum adolescens dictus Merlinus, cuius mater confessa est se a spiritu in specie hominis concepisse, hoc est, per incubum. hic Merlinus Ambrosius est dictus natus ex filia regis Demetae, quae monada erat." The marginal note has "Merlinus ab incubo daemone conceptus," p. 559, folio, Cologne, 1579.

Page 35. *Luther*. Luther's mother was Margaret, a peasant woman of Eisleben. The story of his alleged generation is related by Malvenda in c. vi of his *De Antichristo* with title, *Martinus Lutherus creditus a quibusdam uerus Antichristus*.

"Ex incubo daemonio genitum haud leuibus futilibusque coniecturis deprehensum est a plerisque, vt Coclaeus refert" (p. 71). See the

Historia Ioannis Cochlaei de Actis et Scriptis Martini Lutheri, Paris, 1565.
Johann Cochlaeus, properly Dobeneck, and named Cochlaeus from his native place, Wendelstein, near Schwabach, was born 1479; and died 11 January, 1552, at Breslau. After a brilliant career as a student and professor of theology, he was ordained at Rome in 1518, and was shortly to make his mark as an active opponent of the Lutheran movement. With indomitable ardour he poured forth pamphlet after pamphlet, and although it is hardly to be expected that everything from his pen has the same value, the bulk of his work is an excellent refutation of the contemporary anarchy and looseness of thought. His editions of ecclesiastical writers, and such historical studies as *Historiae Hussitarum*, XII *Libri* (1549), are of permanent value, as also is his sound criticism of Luther and the new tenets.

Page 35. *Plato.*

Diogenes Laertius has the following: *Plato* 11: *Σπεύσιππος δ' ἐν τῷ ἐπιγραφομένῳ Πλάτωνος περιδείπνῳ καὶ Κλέαρχος ἐν τῷ Πλάτωνος ἐγκωμίῳ καὶ Ἀναξιλαίδης ἐν τῷ δευτέρῳ περὶ φιλοσόφων φασὶν ὡς Ἀφήνησιν ἦν λόγος, ὡραίαν οὖσαν τὴν Περικτιόνην βιάζεσθαι τὸν Ἀρίστωνα καὶ μὴ ἐπιτυγχάνειν· παυόμενόν τε τῆς βίας ἰδεῖν τὴν τοῦ Ἀπόλλωνος ὄψιν, ὅθεν καθαρὰν γάμου φυλάξαι ἕως τῆς ἀποκυήσεως. Καὶ γίνεται Πλάτων, ὥς φησιν Ἀπολλόδωρος ἐν χρονικοῖς, ὀγδόῃ καὶ ὀγδοηκοστῇ Ὀλυμπιάδι, Θαργηλιῶνος ἑβδόμῃ· καθ' ἣν Δήλιοι τὸν Ἀπόλλωνα γενέσθαι φασί.* S. Jerome says: *Aduersus Iouinianum*, I, 42: "Speusippus quoque sororis Platonis filius, et Clearchus in laude Platonis, et Anaxilides in secundo libro Philosophiae,

Perictionem matrem Platonis, phantasmate Apollinis oppressam ferunt, et sapientiae principem non aliter arbitrabantur nisi de partu uirginis editum." Migne, *Patres Latini*, Vol. XXIII, c. 273.

Page 35. Servius Tullius. Of whose miraculous begetting Dionysius of Halicarnassus, *Antiquitatum* IV, 2, writes at length: Φέρεται δέ τις ἐν ταῖς ἐπιχωρίοις ἀναγραφαῖς καὶ ἕτερος ὑπὲρ τῆς γενέσεως αὐτοῦ λόγος, ἐπὶ τὸ μυθῶδες ἐξαίρων τὰ περὶ αὐτόν, ὃν ἐν πολλαῖς Ῥωμαικαῖς ἱστορίαις εὕρομεν, εἰ θεοῖς τε καὶ δαίμοσι λέγεσθαι φίλον, τοιοῦτός τις, ἀπὸ τῆς ἑστίας τῶν βασιλείων, ἐφ᾽ ἧς ἄλλας τε Ῥωμαῖοι συντελοῦσιν ἱερουργίας, καὶ τὰς ἀπὸ τῶν δείπνων ἀπαρχὰς ἁγίζουσιν, ὑπὲρ τοῦ πυρὸς ἀνασχεῖν λέγουσιν αἰδοῖον ἀνδρός. Τοῦτο δὲ θεάσασθαι τὴν Ὀκρισίαν πρώτην φέρουσαν τοὺς εἰωθότας πελάνους ἐπὶ τὸ πῦρ, καὶ αὐτίκα πρὸς τοὺς βασιλεῖς ἐλθοῦσαν εἰπεῖν, τὸν μὲν οὖν ταρχύνιον ἀκούσαντά τε καὶ μετὰ ταῦτα ἰδόντα τὸ τέρας ἐν θαύματι γενέσθαι, τὴν δὲ Τανακυλίδα τά τ᾽ ἄλλα σοφὴν οὖσαν καὶ δὴ καὶ τὰ μαντικὰ οὐδενὸς χεῖρον Τυῤῥηνῶν ἐπισταμένην εἰπεῖν πρὸς αὐτόν, ὅτι γένυς ἀπὸ τῆς ἑστίας τῆς βασιλείου πέπρωται γενέσθαι κρείττον ἢ κατὰ τὴν ἀνθρωπείαν φύσιν, ἐκ τῆς μιχθείσης τῷ φάσματι γυναικός. Τὰ δ᾽ αὐτὰ καὶ τῶν ἄλλων τερατοσκόπων ἀποφηναμένων, δόξαι τῷ βασιλεῖ τὴν Ὀκρισίαν, ᾗ πρώτῃ ἐφάνη τὸ τέρας, εἰς ὁμιλίαν αὐτῷ συνελθεῖν καὶ μετὰ τοῦτο τὴν γυναῖκα κοσμησαμένην, οἷς ἔθος ἐστὶ κοσμεῖσθαι τὰς γαμουμένας, κατακλεισθῆναι μόνην εἰς τὸν οἶκον, ἐν ᾧ τὸ τέρας ὤφθη. Μιχθέντος δή τινος αὐτῇ θεῶν ἢ δαιμόνων, καὶ μετὰ τὴν μίξιν ἀφανισθέντος, εἴτε Ἡφαίστου, καθάπερ οἴονταί τινες, εἴτε τοῦ κατ' οἰκίαν ἥρωος, ἐγκύμονα γενέσθαι καὶ τεχεῖν τὸν Τύλλιον ἐν τοῖς καθήκουσι χρόνοις. Pliny, xxxvi, 27, has: "Tradunt . . . ita Seruium Tullium natum, qui regno successit. Inde et in regia cubanti puero caput arsisse uisum, creditumque Laris familiaris filium."

Page 36. Terrible monsters. Vaisette, *Histoire de Languedoc* (p. 39), records that in 1275 the Inquisitor Hugues de Baniols condemned to death a witch of many years' continuance, Angele de la Barthe, who confessed to having had connexion with a demon from which intercourse she brought forth a monster whom she nourished with the flesh of infants, slain by her or dug up from their graves in lonely churchyards.

Page 36. Semen. This detail is discussed at some length by Sinistrari in his *Demoniality*.

Page 36. Binsfeld. *De Confessionibus Maleficorum*, Prior quaestionis pars; 5 Conclusio: *Malefici uel maleficae rem ueneream habent cum Daemone*. This learned author holds that there is actually copulation between witches and demons, as indeed is proved by what S. Augustine says, *De Ciuitate Dei*, V, 23. This is further maintained by a vast number of Popes, doctors and theologians; by S. Isidore; S. Thomas; S. Bonaventura; Dionysius the Carthusian; William of Paris; Martin of Arles; Alphonso de Castro; the authors of the *Malleus Maleficarum;* Innocent VIII; Cardinal Cajetan; Bartolomeo de Spina; Bartolomeo de Medina; Nider; Molitor; Grilland; Thomas Erastus; Bodin; and very many more.

Page 37. *Bodin.* *Démonomanie*, III, 6: "Il se trouua en vn monastere vn chien qu'on disoit estre un Daemon, qui leuoit les robbes des Religieuses pour en abuser. Ce n'estoit point vn Daemon, comme ie croy; mais vn chien naturel. Il se trouua a Toulouse vne femme qui en abusoit en ceste sorte: Et le chien deuant tout le monde la vouloit forcer. Elle confessa la verité, & fut bruslee. Il y en eut vne autre qui fut amenee prisonniere à Paris l'an mil cinq cens quarante, conuaincue de mesme cas."

Page 39. *Olympias.* Alexander was said to be the son of Jupiter Hammon (Quintus Curtius, IV, 7), who visited his mother Olympias, so Plutarch tells us (*Alexander*, II), as a snake or dragon. When Boguet writes of a swan he is thinking rather of Leda.

Page 40. *The Sons of God.* This passage has been much discussed by the exegetes, and one may profitably consult the commentary *in loco* of the learned Sinistrari, who in his *Demoniality*, XXXII–XXXIV (translation by the present writer, Fortune Press, 1927) says: "We also read in the Bible, *Genesis*, chap. 6, verse 4, that giants were born when the sons of God went in to the daughters of men: this is the actual text. Now, those giants were men of *great stature*, says *Baruch*, chap. 3, verse 26, and far superior to other men. Not only were they distinguished by their huge size, but also by their physical power, their rapine and their tyranny. Through their misdeeds the giants, according to Cornelius a Lapide, in his *Commentary on Genesis*, were the primary and principal cause of the Flood. Some contend that by Sons of God are meant the sons of Seth, and by daughters of men the daughters of Cain, because the former practised piety, religion and every other virtue, whilst the descendants of Cain were quite the reverse; but, with all due deference to S. John Chrysostom, S. Cyril, S. Theodore of Studium, Abbot Rupert of Deutz, S. Hilary and others who are of that opinion, it must be conceded that it hardly agrees with the obvious meaning of the text. Scripture says, in fact, that of the conjunction of the Sons of God and the daughters of men were born men of huge bodily size: consequently, those giants were not previously in existence, and if their birth was the result of that conjunction, it cannot be ascribed to the intercourse of the sons of Seth with the daughters of Cain, who, being themselves of ordinary stature, could but procreate children of ordinary stature. Therefore, if the intercourse in question gave birth to beings of huge stature, the reason is that it was not the common connexion between man and woman, but the operation of Incubi who, from their nature, may very well be styled Sons of God. Such is the opinion of the Platonist Philosophers and of Francesco Giorgio the Venetian; nor is it discrepant from that of Josephus the Historian, Philo Judæus, S. Justin Martyr, Clement of Alexandria, Tertullian, and Hugh of S. Victor, who look upon Incubi as corporeal Angels who have fallen into the sin of lewdness with women. Indeed, as shall be shown hereafter, though seemingly distinct, those two opinions are but one and the same.

"If, therefore, these Incubi, as is so commonly held, have begotten giants by means of sperm taken from man, it is impossible, as aforesaid, that of that sperm should have been born any but men of approximately the same size as he from whom it came; for it would be in vain for the Demon, when acting the part of a Succubus, to draw from man an unwonted quantity of prolific liquor in order to procreate therefrom children of higher stature; quantity is irrelevant since all depends, as we have said, upon the vitality of that liquor, not upon its quantity. We are bound, therefore, to infer that giants are born of another sperm than man's, and that, consequently, the Incubus, for the purpose of generation, uses a semen which is not man's. But what, then, are we to say with regard to this?

"Subject to correction by our Holy Mother Church, and as a mere expression of private opinion, I say that the Incubus, when having intercourse with women, begets the human foetus from his own seed."

Page 40. Council of Aquileia. "Some wicked women, reverting to Satan and seduced by the illusions and phantasms of demons, believe and profess that they ride at night with Diana on certain beasts with an innumerable multitude of women, passing over immense distances. It were well if they alone perished in their infidelity and did not draw so many along with them. For innumerable multitudes, deceived by this false opinion, believe all this to be true, and thus relapse into pagan errors. . . . It is to be taught to all that he who believes such things has lost his faith, and he who is not of the true faith is not of God, but of the devil." This early proclamation came to be attributed to the

Council of Ancyra, 314, but this is an error. It is, however, found in the work of Regino of Prüm, who died 917, and it was embodied in the canonical collections of Burchard, Ivo, and Gratian. It must be emphasized that it has no force, and it remains merely as an unauthoritative expression of opinion.

Page 40. *Ulrich Molitor.*

A Doctor of Roman and Canon law, who, at the instance of the Archduke Sigismund of the Tyrol, wrote his *De Lamiis et phitonicis (pythonicis) mulieribus* in some sort as an answer to, or a commentary upon, the *Malleus Maleficarum.* The first edition of the *De Lamiis* is Cologne, 1489. Molitor teaches that there are witches who make a pact with Satan, and that death is the penalty for this abomination, but he is sceptical as to the possibility of witches travelling many miles at night, and he attributes their transport by the devil to imagination wrought upon by the evil one. Weyer, *De Lamiis,* III, 12, explicitly says: "Falsum arte magica homines deferri per aerem," and he quotes with approval (11) the conclusion of Ponzibius, that these aerial transvections are fantasy. The matter, none the less, cannot be so easily settled and the weight of authority is against Molitor, Ponzibius, Weyer, and their followers.

Page 41. *Malleus.*

The authors of the *Malleus Maleficarum* conclude "that it is found that some witches are transported only in imagination, but that it is also found in the writings of the Doctors that many have been bodily transported." (Part II, Qn. 1, Ch. 3, *ad finem;* translation by present writer; John Rodker, 1928). This is the orthodox view and cannot be disbelieved without great rashness, for, as S. Augustine says, to deny so general a consensus of Fathers and Doctors were the height of impudence. This view is maintained by Bodin; Remy; Grilland; Vincenzo Dodo of Pavia (who very aptly rebukes Samuel de Cassinis of Milan); Bernard of Como, O.P.; Francesco Maria Guazzo; Silvester Prierias, O.P; Bartolomeo de Spino, O.P.; Arnaldus Albertini, Bishop of Patti; Francesco di Vittoria, Professor of Theology at Salamanca; the great Binsfeld; Crespet; Anania; Sisto of Siena; Bernard Basin; Martin Delrio, S.J. (*Disquisitionum Magicarum*, II, xvi, *De nocturnis sagarum conuentibus & an uera sit earum translatio de loco ad locum?*); even by the Calvinist Lambert Daneau, and many more. We cannot gainsay the common opinion of theologians that witches may fly through the air at night to their Sabbats, and it has been ratified by the famous jurist of the Roman Curia, Francesco Pegna, who in his Commentaries lays down that this opinion is "most certainly true, that it is indeed proven by many sound reasons and most apparent signs, by actual fact and experiment." *Opinio uerissima, multis quidem rationibus et euidentibus signis atque experimentis comprobata.* (*Directorium Inquisitorum F. Nicolai Eymerici, Ordinis Praedicatorum Cum Commendariis Francisci Peniae,* Venice, 1595. Quaestio XLIII: Comment. XLIII, 343.)

Page 44. *How . . . witches are conveyed to the Sabbat.*

For a full discussion of this point see my *History of Witchcraft*, c. iv, "The Sabbat," pp. 118–33.

Weyer, *De Lamiis*, III, xvii, treats at length of these flying ointments under the rubric: *De naturalibus pharmacis somniferis, quibus interdum illuduntur Lamiae, de earum item unguentis, & quibusdam plantis soporiferis, mentemque impense turbantibus*. He gives these formulae for the preparation of these unguents. (1) Hemlock, water of aconite, poplar leaves, and soot. (2) Cowbane, sweet flag, cinquefoil, bat's blood, deadly nightshade, and oil. (3) Fat of babes, juices of cowbane, aconite, cinquefoil, deadly nightshade, and soot. *Page* 44. *Ointment.*

Debrio, *Disquisitionum Magicarum*, II, xvi, says that the chief ingredient of the ointment is the fat of children whom the witches slay for this purpose. The ointment is actually of no effect *per se*, and the devil can (and often will) transport the witches to the Sabbat without any use of unguent or potions. But he will have them anoint themselves for various reasons, namely, in order that any of his followers who are fearful may pluck up courage and rely on this empty thing; that often their senses are addled by the potency of the drugs, and therefore they can the better endure his horrible embraces and connexions; and again, they use this ointment to mock the holy Chrism which is employed in the Sacraments. *Page* 44. *Neither ointment nor words . . . of any use.*

The authors of the *Malleus Maleficarum* have given particular attention to this point. Part II, Qn. 1, Ch. 3: "And since the public report of this sort of transvection is continually being spread even among the common people, it is unnecessary to add further proofs of it here. But *Page* 46. *As Dead.*

we hope that this will suffice to refute those who either deny altogether that there are such transvections, or try to maintain that they are only imaginary or phantastical. And, indeed, it would be a matter of small importance if such men were left in their error, were it not that this error tends to the damage of the Faith. For notice that, not content with that error, they do not fear to maintain and publish others also, to the increase of witches and the detriment of the Faith. For they assert that all the witchcraft which is truly and actually ascribed to witches as instruments of the devil, is only so ascribed in imagination and illusion, as if they were really harmless, just as their transvection is only phantastic. And for this reason many witches remain unpunished, to the great dispraise of the Creator, and to their own most heavy increase.

"The arguments on which they base their fallacy cannot be conceded. For first they advance the chapter of the Canon (*Episcopi*, 26, q. 5) where it is said that witches are only transported in imagination; but who is so foolish as to conclude from this that they cannot also be bodily transported? Similarly at the end of that chapter it is set down that whoever believes that a man can be changed for the better or the worse, or can be transformed into another shape, is to be thought worse than an infidel or a pagan; but who could conclude from this that men cannot be transformed into beasts by a glamour, or that they cannot be changed from health to sickness and from better to worse? They who so scratch at the surface of the words of the Canon hold an opinion which is contrary to that of all the

Holy Doctors, and, indeed, against the teaching of Holy Scripture.

"For the contrary opinion is abundantly proved by what has been written in various places in the First Part of this treatise; and it is necessary to study the inner meaning of the words of the Canon. And this was examined in the First Question of the First Part of the treatise, in refuting the second of three errors which are there condemned, and where it is said that four things are to be preached to the people. For they are transported both bodily and phantastically, as is proved by their own confessions, not only of those who have been burned, but also of others who have returned to penitence and the Faith.

"Among such there was the woman in the town of Brisac, whom we asked whether they could be transported only in imagination, or actually in the body; and she answered that it was possible in both ways. For if they do not wish to be bodily transferred, but want to know all that is being done in a meeting of their companions, then they observe the following procedure. In the name of all the devils they lie down to sleep on their left side; and then a sort of bluish vapour comes from their mouth, through which they can clearly see what is happening. But if they wish to be bodily transported, they must observe the method which has been told.

"Besides, even if that Canon be understood in its bare meaning without any explanation, who is so dense as to maintain on that account that all their witchcraft and injuries are phantastic and imaginary, when the contrary is evident to the senses of everybody? Especially since there are many species of superstition, namely, fourteen;

among which the species of witches holds the highest degree in spells and injuries, and the species of Pythonesses, to which they can be reduced, which is only able to be transported in imagination, holds the lowest degree.

"And we do not concede that their error can be substantiated by the Legends of S. Germain and certain others. For it was possible for the devils to lie down themselves by the side of the sleeping husbands, during the time when a watch was being kept on the wives, just as if they were sleeping with their husbands. And we do not say that this was done for any reverence felt for the Saint; but the case is put, that the opposite of what is set down in the Legend may not be believed to be impossible."

Page 47. *One Thursday.* There is an accumulation of evidence to show that the Sabbat was held every night of the week save Saturday and Sunday. Leger Rivasseau confessed that the Sabbat commenced at midnight, that the assembly generally met at crossroads, "le plus souuent la nuict du Mercredy ou du Vendredy. Que le Diable chercoit la nuict la plus orageuse qu'il pouuoit, affin que les vens & les orages portasset plus loing & plus impetueusement leurs poudres." De Lancre, *L'Inconstance* . . ., Livre II, Discours iv. In England it was stated that the "Solemn appointments, and meetings . . . are ordinarily on Tuesday or Wednesday night"; *A Pleasant Treatise of Witches*, London, 1673. Matthew Hopkins, *The Discovery of Witches*, 1647, says that the witches of Manningtree and the local covens "every six weeks in the night (being always on the Friday night) had their meeting close by his house, and had their severall solemne sacrifices there offered to the Devill." In certain districts of the Basses-Pyrénées, Monday, Wednesday, and Friday were chosen. (De Lancre, *Tableau de l'Inconstance des Mauvais anges*, Paris, 1612, p. 62). Saturday was always and everywhere particularly avoided as being the day sacred to the Immaculate Mother of God.

Page 48 *When the cock crew.*

De Lancre, *Tableau de l'Inconstance*, Livre II, Discours v, writes at length: "Du Coq, & s'il est vray ce qu'on dict, que tout aussi tost qu'il est entendu au Sabbat, il dissipe par son chant, & faict esuanouir toute l'assemblee." "Le Coq se oyt par foisés sabbats sonnant la retraicte aux sorciers, & fait qu'à vn instant tout disparoist." But Satan can teach the sorcerers a secret which will prevent the cock from crowing, or at any rate will retard his clarion. "Les sorciers sçauent coniurer les Coqs, & leur interdise le chāt." This, however, can only last for a little while, as the charm is an affair of half-an-hour at most.

Page 49. *No power to raise the dead.*

Neither the Devil nor the witches his servants can raise the dead. Delrio, *Disquisitiones Magicae*, II, Q. xxix, Sect. 1, discusses "An diabolus possit facere ut homo vere resurgat," and decides "Non potest facere ut homo a mortuis resurgat." But a demon may enter the corpse of some notoriously evil person and energize the dead body so that it will walk and have the appearance of life. The ethnic fables of Plato, Pliny, Apuleius, Philostratus and others concerning the raising of the dead are dealt with very fully by Delrio.

Page 49. *One of the poets.* Lucan, *Pharsalia,* VI, 570–830.

Page 49. *Saul.* For a full commentary upon the Witch of Endor, see my *History of Witchcraft,* Ch. v. "The Witch in Holy Writ," particularly pp. 176–81. That Samuel did actually appear is the opinion of S. Ambrose and S. Augustine, which should be maintained. This is also favoured by S. Jerome, who, however, has not definitely pronounced.

Page 49. *Apollonius.* Philostratus, *De Uita Apollonii,* IV, 45, relates that Apollonius raised a girl of consular family to life when she was being carried on the bier through the streets of Rome to her grave. But even the writer suggests that life was not really extinct and obviously doubts the seeming miracle.

Page 49. *Simon Magus.* A relation of the pseudo-miracles of Simon Magus will be found in the *Clementines,* particularly *Homilies,* II, 32, and *Recognitions,* II, 9.

Page 50. *Jerome Bolsecque.* Jérôme-Hermès Bolsec died at Lyons, *circa* 1584. Originally a Catholic, he separated from the Church about 1545, but even from a Protestant point of view he did not appear sufficiently orthodox, and he led an unquiet migratory life. Eventually, however, he recanted his errors and was reconciled. He then published a life of Calvin, *Histoire de la vie, des mœurs . . . de Jean Calvin,* Lyons and Paris, 1577; Latin translation, Cologne, 1580; German translation, 1581; edited by L. F. Chastel, 1875.

According to a doubtful tradition he failed to cure the daughter of Bahram I. It is certain that in 276–77 this monarch caused Mani to be crucified, had the corpse flayed, the skin stuffed and hung up at the city gates of Babylon in order to terrify the followers of this Persian dualist, whose sect he harried with relentless severities. *Page 50 Mani.*

Dæmonolatreia II, c. iv, has as rubric: *Perdifficiliter uitari posse quas ueneficae hominibus struunt insidias: quod de nocte in obseratas, clausasque domos ignota specie, ac forma illabantur: arctissimo somno decumbentes diris suis artibus obruant. . .* *Page 50: Remy.*

At the Lemuria: *Page 52. Ovid.*

Terque manus puras fontana proluit unda;
  Uertitur, et nigras accipit ore fabas.
Auersusque iacit: sed dum iacit, Haec ego mitto;
  His, inquit, redimo meque meosque fabis.
Hoc nouies dicit, nec respicit. Umbra putatur
  Colligere, et nullo terga uidente sequi.

De Legibus, II, 18: "Color autem albus praecipue decorus deo est." *Page 52. Cicero.*

The back to back dance was a favourite piece of choreography at the Sabbat, and there are very many references to this. De Lancre, *Tableau de l'Inconstance*, III, Discours iii, in describing the witches' dances, says: "La troisieme est aussi le dos tourné, mais se tenant tous en long, & sans se deprendre des mains, ils s'approchent de si près qu'ils se touchent, & se rencontrent dos à dos, un homme avec une femme: & à certaine *Page 52. Back to back.*

cadance ils se choquent & frapent impudēment cul contre cul." Hutchinson, *A Historical Essay Concerning Witchcraft*, Second edition, 1720 (p. 43), gives a confession of Jeanne Bosdeau (1594): "The black Goat carried a lighted Candle in his Fundament, and all the Witches had Candles which they lighted at his, and danced in a Circle Back to Back." There are in the trials many allusions to the masks which were worn at these assemblies. Thus in 1613 Barbe de Moyemont said that at the Sabbat "elle a veu dancer les assistans en nombre de sept à huict personnes, partie desquelles elle ne cognoissoit a cause des masques hideux qu'elles auoient de noire."

Page 52. Sword. This was the sword wrought of unalloyed steel with a copper handle fashioned like a crucifix. Mystical signs were engraved thereon, and it was consecrated at noon on a Sunday in the full rays of the hottest sun. It was heated in a fire of cypress and laurel, cooled with the blood of a snake, polished and then swathed in silk and bound with garlands of vervain, laid aside for use in the magic rites. The sword was often used in necromantic ceremonials.

Page 53. Of the day. De Lancre, *Tableau de l'Inconstance*, Livre II, Discours i, points out that in earlier times the Devil appointed a Monday on which to hold the Sabbat, but that later he preferred the night between Wednesday and Thursday, or that between Friday and Saturday. It became common also to hold a general Sabbat about the time of the high Christian festivals in evil mockery of these holy solemnities. So the

Scotch witches of Kinross (1662) met on S. Andrew's Day, 30 November; and in many parts of Europe when the Feast of S. George is solemnized with high honour and holiday, Satan held an assembly on the night of the 22–23 April.

Page 54. Of the Place.

For a full discussion of the locality of various Sabbats see my *History of Witchcraft*, ch. iv, pp. 113–17. The ordinary Sabbat was generally held in some remote and ill-omened spot near the town or village where the witches dwelt, sometimes in a house belonging to one of that crew. Dr. Fian and his associates (1591) were wont to forgather at the haunted church of North Berwick. In some countries certain spots acquired an infamous repute, as, for example, the Blocksburg or Brocken in the Hartz Mountains; Benevento in Italy; Malking Tower in Lancashire; Mohra and Elfdale where the Swedish witches met (1670); and many more of lesser note.

Page 55. First worship.

The congruity and similarity of the accounts given by witches in all countries of the Sabbat demand the most careful consideration. As might be expected, certain details differ in several localities, but the end of the ritual, the worship of Satan, is the same. The account of the Sabbat given by the witches who confessed to Boguet may be compared with the accounts gleaned by Sprenger and Kramer, De Lancre, Guazzo, Bodin, Remy, Binsfeld, and all demonologists. In Guernsey, 1617, Isabel Becquet went to Rocquaine Castle, "the usual place where the Devil kept his Sabbath . . . then immediately the Devil made her kneel down

. . . he then made her express detestation of the Eternal in these words: *I renounce God the Father, God the Son, and God the Holy Ghost;* and then caused her to worship and invoke himself." To the witches the Fiend was god incarnate manifesting himself for the worship of his followers. As Lambert Daneau says in his *A Dialogue of Witches*, English translation, 1575: "The Diuell comaundeth them that they shall acknowledge him for their god, cal vpō him, pray to him, and trust in him. Then doe they all repeate the othe which they haue geuen vnto him; in acknowledging him to be their God."

Page 55. *Goat.* This appearance was one of the most usual forms in France at the Sabbat, and there are very many examples to be found. Thus Guazzo, *Compendium Maleficarum*, I, 13, says: "Ibi Daemon est conuentus praeses, in solio sedet forma terrifica ut plurimum Hirci." And Elich in his *Daemonomagia*, Quaest. 10, has: "Solent ad conuentum Lamiae adorare Daemonem, Synagogae praesidem & rectorem in solio considentem, immutatum in Hircum horridum."

Page 56. *Candles.* The lighting of candles was not only to illuminate the orgy held under cover of darkness, but also a ritual observance in parody of the candles at Holy Mass. De Lancre, *Tableau de l'Inconstance*. II, Discours 1, says that the Devil appeared as a black goat, "qu'il a seulement trois cornes, & qu'il a quelque espece de lumiere en celle du milieu, de laquelle il a accoustumé au sabbat d'esclairer & donner du feu & de la lumiere, mesme à ces Sorcieres qui tiennent quelques chandelles alumees aux ceremonies de la Messe qu'ils veulent contrefaire."

There are continual references to the *osculum obscaenum*, or *osculum infame*, which formed one of the chief acts of homage of the witch. Guazzo notes: "As a sign of homage witches kiss the devil's fundament." Ludwig Elich, in his *Daemonomagia*, Quaestio 10, writes: "Then as a token of their homage—with reverence be it spoken—they kiss the fundament of the devil." One of the charges brought against Walter Langton, Bishop of Lichfield and Coventry (1296–1322), was that he had paid "homage to the Devil by kissing his posterior." Guillaume Edeline, a doctor of the Sorbonne, who was executed for sorcery in 1453, "had done homage to the aforesaid Satan, who appeared in the shape of a ram, by kissing his buttocks in token of reverence and homage." In Shadwell's play, *The Lancashire Witches*, produced at Dorset Garden, London, in the autumn (probably September) of 1681, 4to, 1682, at the end of the Second Act we have: "The Scaene Sir *Edward's* Cellar: *Enter all the Witches, and the Devil in the form of a Buck-Goat after.*

Page 56. Kiss.

Demdike. Lo here our little Master's come.
Let each of us salute his Bum. *All kiss the Devil's Arse.*

Shadwell, in his "Notes upon the Second Act," quotes several demonologists for this circumstance.

One of the charges repeatedly brought against the Knights Templars during the lengthy process of their examinations and trials, 1307–14, was that of the kissing the posteriors of the preceptors by the juniors, but this has nothing to do with sorcery, since it is to be connected with the homosexual practices of the Order.

Page 56. Pipes. Various musical instruments to accompany the dances were played at the Sabbats. De Lancre, *De l'Inconstance*, III, 3, says of the witches: "Elles dancent au son du petit tabourin & de la fluste & par fois auec ce long instrument qu'ils posent sur le sol, puis l'allongeant iusqu' aupres de la ceinture, ils le batent auec vn petit baston: parfois auec vn violon. Mais ce ne sont les seuls instruments du sabbat, car nous avons apprins de plusieurs qu'on y oyt toute sorte d'instrumens." Gellis Duncan of the North Berwick coven, who attempted the life of King James VI and I, was famous for her performances "on ane trump," whilst the witches danced "endlang" round the haunted old kirk-yard "to the number of sevin scoir of persounes." Elizabeth Styles (or Style) of Stoke Tryster in Somerset, when examined in January and February 1664 by the justice, confessed that the gang met on a lonely common where appeared a man in black to whom they did obeisance. "The Man in black sometimes playes on a Pipe or Cittern and the company dance." *Sadducismus Triumphatus*, 1681, Pt. II, p. 141.

Page 57. Catullus. XC. Nascatur magus ex Gelli matrisque nefando
Coniugio, et discat Persicum aruspicium.
Nam magus ex matre et gnato nascatur oportet
Si uera est Persarum impia religio.
Gnatus ut accepto ueneretur carmine diuos,
Omentum in flamma pingue liquefaciens.

Strabo (735) writes: *Τοὺς δὲ Μάγους οὐ θάπτουσιν, ἀλλ' οἰωνοβρώτους ἐῶσι· Τούτοις δὲ καὶ μητράσι συνέρχεσθαι πάτριον νενόμισται.*

These heretics were known under various names: Messalians, Adelphians, Lampetians, Enthusiasts. They arose about 360, and in 431 the third General Council of Ephesus utterly banned the *Asceticus*, "that filthy book of this heresy." In Armenia they were condemned for their lewdness in the fifth century, and their very name signified obscenity. After they had actually ceased to exist as Euchites or Messalians they revived under the name of Bogomiles. One of their tenets was that divine honours must be paid to the Devil, who is further to be propitiated by means of every outrage against the Saviour of mankind. This is, of course, modern Satanism.

Page 57. Euchites.

De Lancre says that sometimes the banquets at the Sabbat are of rare dainties, sometimes the witches are served with orts and offal. The wine, Guazzo tells us, is usually like black and clotted blood poured out in some foul and filthy vessel. But he continues that sometimes there is no lack of cheer at the tables, "save that they furnish neither bread nor salt." Remy agrees with this, *Daemonolatreia*, I, 16, for the witches confessed that at their revels "Nullarum fere rerum copiam illic deesse, praeterquam salis & panis." These details, however, differed widely. See my *History of Witchcraft*, ch. iv, "The Sabbat," pp. 143–45.

Page 58. Feasting.

"Sometimes, at their solemn assemblies, the Devil commands that each tell what wickedness he hath committed, and according to the heinousness and detestableness of it, he is honoured and respected with a general applause. Those, on

Page 59. Render. an account.

the contrary, that have done no evil are beaten and punished."—*A Pleasant Treatise of Witches.*

Page 60. *Mass.* The "Black Mass" of the witches and the Satanists has many variants; the hellish ritual, the vestments, the very shape of the host widely differ at several times and in several countries. See my *History of Witchcraft*, ch. v, "The Sabbat," pp. 145–57. Joanny Bricaud's *La Messe Noire ancienne et moderne* (1924) may also be consulted. The celebrant is stated by Boguet to have worn a black cope. The abbé Guibourg was arrayed in an ample cope or a chasuble of white silk embroidered with silver and black fir cones; Gaufridi (1611) confessed that the priest who said the Devil's mass at the Sabbat donned a violet planeta; at Orleans in the seventeenth century a phainolion of murky red, dark and ominous, was often assumed; to-day at the liturgy of Satanists the vestments are generally those of the ordinary ecclesiastical shape or form, but the chasuble though rich is of some garish and unusual colour and embroidered with malefic or obscene emblems.

Page 60. *A round.* Madeleine Bavent saw the ordinary wafers used, only coloured red; sometimes they were black and triangular, stamped with a hideous design. It may be noted that very often by the grace of God the Mass of the Satanists is irrite and vain, since there are defectus materiae, et panis et uini.

Page 60. *Goat . . . burns to ashes.* This Satanic illusion was largely effected to encourage the witches not to fear the flames of execution. Accordingly we find this glamour mentioned in France and Germany, where the stake was the penalty of witchcraft, but not in England, where the punishment was the gallows. Bodin, *Démonomanie*, II, iv, gives details of a trial at Poitiers in 1574 where the witches confessed they have been at the Sabbat, "et là se trouuoit vn grand bouc noir, qui parloit comme vne personne aux assistans, & dansoient à l'entour du Bouc: puis vn chacun luy baisoit le derriere auec vne chandelle ardente: & cela faict, le bouc se consommoit en feu, & de la cèdre chacun en prenoit pour faire mourir le boeuf ou vache," etc. In 1603 a Belgian witch, Claire Goessen, was at a Sabbat when "elle a, comme tous les assistans, baisé un bouc à l'endroit de sa queue, lequel bouc fut ensuite brûlé et ses cendres distribuies et emportées par les convives." The ashes were utilized in various potent charms, especially to harm herds and blast crops. Miss Murray, *The Witch-Cult in Western Europe*, in connexion with this burning of the goat, has idly advanced a ridiculous theory to link it with the "Sacrifice of the God," a divine victim, but this preposterous nonsense cannot be for a moment maintained.

Page 62. *Hail.*

Upon this point, which is dealt with in detail by nearly all demonologists, consult the *Malleus Maleficarum*, Part II, Qu. 1, Ch. 15 (translation, John Rodker, 1928, p. 147), of witches: *How they Raise and Stir up Hailstorms and Tempests, and cause Lightning to Blast both Men and Beasts.*

Page 69. *Ointments.*

De Lancre, *Tableau de l'Inconstance*, II, Discours i, says: "Les liures & les Inquisiteurs disét, que les sorciers composent & font ces onguens ou graisses, ou que le Diable les leur donne: Que la plus part se font auec de la graisse de petit enfant que Satan faict occire à des sorcieres. Mais ils tiennent que ces onguents ne peuuent seruir en ce cas à autre effect, que pour assoupir les sens des sorciers, afin que Satan iouisse mieux à son aise d'eux." Weyer, *De Lamiis*, III, 17, writes: "*De naturalibus pharmaci somniferis, quibus interdum illuduntur Lamiae, de earum item unguentis, & quibusdam plantis soporiferis, mentemque impense turbantibus.*" In his opinion the ointments of witches are toxic, producing excitement and delirium, or narcotic, awakening evil dreams. "Lamiarum quoque unguentum propemodum simile tradit Hieronymus Cardanus, post cuius inunctionem mirabilia uideri apparet."

Page 70. Memphite. "Albertus Magnus in Ægypto etiam nasci lapidem tradit, et Dioscorides, qui Memphites nuncupatur, a Memphi, magnitudine calculi, pinguis et uersicolor: quo contrito, et cum aqua uinoque epoto, stupor omnium sensuum inducatur, ut nullum omnino dolorem sentias."

Page 71. Smearing with a grease. Various outbreaks of the plague in Italy during the fifteenth and sixteenth centuries were said to be largely caused by sorcerers who at the instigation of the Devil smeared walls and doors with purulent matter, the poison of which fearfully increased the mortality. The Great Plague of Milan, 1629–30, is known as "La Peste degli Untori," and an old distich which had prophesied that in 1630 the Devil would endeavour to poison all Milan was widely quoted and believed. Hundreds of these *untori* were arrested and summarily put to death. See Ripamonte, *De Peste Mediolani*, and my *Geography of Witchcraft*, pp. 559–62.

Page 72. Aratus. The celebrated general of the Achaeans; 271–213 B.C. He wrote *Commentaries*, being a history of his own times down to 220 B.C., which are highly commended by Polybius, II, 40.

Page 72. Philip the Fair. Philip IV of France, died at Fontainebleau, 29 November, 1314. He was succeeded by his eldest son, Louis X, le Hutin, who died at Vincennes 5 June, 1316. Then followed his brother, the second son of Philip IV, Philip V, le Long. It was in this reign that the lepers were slain. He died at Longchamps, 3 January, 1322.

Page 72. Nicephorus. Callistus Xanthopulus Nicephorus was born in the latter part of the thirteenth century and died about 1350. His *Ecclesiastical History* has been edited by Duchène, 2 vols., folio, Paris, 1630.

Page 77. Circe. Vergil, *Eclogue* VIII, 70, has "Carminibus Circe socios mutauit Ulixi," but the touch with her wand is emphasized in the *Odyssey*, X, 237–40:

αὐτὰρ ἐπεὶ δῶκέν τε καὶ ἔκπιον, αὐτίκ' ἔπειτα
ῥάβδῳ πεπληγυῖα, κατὰ συφεοῖσιν ἐέργνυ.
οἱ δὲ συῶν μὲν ἔχον κεφαλάς, φωνήν τε τρίχας τε,
καὶ δέμας, αὐτὰρ νοῦς ἦν ἔμπεδος, ὡς τὸ πάρος περ.

Page 77. *Thessaly.* Thessaly was the legendary home of witchcraft, so that *Thessala*, a Thessalian woman, came almost to mean an enchantress.

Page 78. *Ovid.* The lines Boguet paraphrases are from the *Amores*, I, vii:

Num mea Thessalico languent deuota ueneno
  Corpora? num misero carmen et herba nocent? . . .
Carmine laesa Ceres sterilem uanescit in herbam:
  Deficiunt laesae carmine fontis aquae,
Ilicibus glandes, cantataque uitibus uua
  Decidit; et nullo poma mouente fluunt.
Quid uetat et neruos magicas torpere per artes?

Page 78. *Vergil.* *Eclogue* VIII, 70–71:

Carminibus Circe socios mutauit Ulixi;
Frigidus in pratis cantando rumpitur anguis.

Page 78. *Lucan.* *Pharsalia*, VI, 452–91.

Page 78. *Vergil.* *Eclogue* VIII, 77–78 :

Necte tribus nodis ternos, Amarylli, colores;
Necte, Amarylli, modo et "Ueneris" dic "uincula necto."

Page 79. *A staff.* See my *History of Witchcraft*, ch. iv, "The Sabbat," pp. 121–24.

Page 79. *El-phurkan.* Al Forkan is one of the names of the Koran, being derived from the verb *faraka*, to divide or distinguish, and chapter xxv of the Koran is also known as "Al Forkan."

Page 80. *Mirandola.* Giovanni Pico della Mirandola, 1463–94.

Eclogue III, 103: *Page* 80. *Vergil.*

Nescio quis teneros oculus mihi fascinat agnos.

"Suivant les anciens le Basilic était un reptile né d'un oeuf de coq (beaucoup de gens croient encore aux oeufs du coq). Son regard feudroyait à moins qu'on ne l'eut aperçu le premier."—Rion, Erreurs, *Prejugés populaires*, 1869. *Page* 81. *Basilisk.*

κατῶβλεψ or *κατῶβλεπων, i.e.* that looks down. "Apud Hesperios Æthiopas fons est Nigris, ut plerique existimauere Nili caput. . . . Iuxta hunc fera appellatur catoblepas, modica alioquin, ceterisque membris iners, caput tantum praegraue aegre ferens: id deiectum semper in terram: alias internecio humani generis, omnibus qui oculos eius uidere confestim exspirantibus. Eadem et basilisci serpentis est uis."—Pliny, *Historia Naturalis*, VIII, xxxii, xxxxiii. *Page* 81. *Catoblepas.*

Vergil, *Eclogue* IX, 53–54: *Page* 81 *Moeris.*

uox quoque Moerim
iam fugit ipsa; lupi Moerim uidere priores.

For an account of the baleful glances of sorcerers see *Malleus Maleficarum*, Part I; Q. 2, pp. 12–13 (translation), John Rodker, 1928.

To fashion mommets of wax and melt these at a fire or pierce them with pins in order to afflict the individual in whose likeness they are moulded is one of the oldest and most general of malign spells. See my *Geography of Witchcraft*, pp. 10, 11, 81–84, 104. *Page* 86. *Waxen images.*

Page 86. *Medea.* *Heroides*, VI, 91–2:

Deuouet absentes: simulacraque cerea figit,
Et miserum tenues in iecur urget acus.

And *Amores*, III, 7 (Boguet gives reference III, 6, as the elegy *Somnium* was restored as number 5 by Daniel Heinsius):

Sagaue Poenicea defixit nomina cera,
Et medium tenues in iecur egit acus?

Page 86. *Duffus.* At the end of the seventh century certain hags of Forres in Murray attempted to kill King Duffus by melting his image made of wax. See my *Geography of Witchcraft*, ch. i, pp. 12–13.

Page 86. *Charles IX.* "Et l'an M.D.LXXIIII au proces imprimé, qui fut fait à vn certain Gentil-homme, qui fut decapité à Paris, il fut trouué saisy d'vn image de cire ayant la teste & le coeur percé auec d'autres caracteres qui fut (peut estre) l'vne des principales causes de sa mort." Bodin, *Démonomanie*, II, 8. Charles IX died 30 May, 1574.

Page 87. *Plato.* "Mais Platon en l'vnziesme liure des loix, confirme ce discours des images de cire que font les sorcieres, & ne faut s'esbahir commēt celà fut sçeu." Bodin, *Démonomanie*, II, 8.

Page 87. *Medea.* In the tragedy of Euripides the Messenger cries to Medea:

πέπλοι δὲ λεπτοί, σῶν τέκνων δωρήματα
λεπτὴν ἔδαπτον σάρκα τῆς δυσδαίμονος.

Page 88. *Kill the children.* *Malleus Maleficarum*, Part II, Qn. 1, ch. 13. *How Witch Midwives commit most Horrid Crimes when they either Kill Children or Offer them to Devils in most Accursed Wise.*

Formicarius, c. III. *Malleus Maleficarum*, Part II, Qn. 1, ch. 6 (translation; John Rodker, 1928, p. 118). Stadlin buried a serpent under the threshold of the outer door of the house. *Page* 88. *Stadlin.*

See my *Geography of Witchcraft*, ch. v, pp. 389–96; also the Bibliography (p. 342), *History of Witchcraft*. *Page* 88. *Baron of Rays.*

Malleus Maleficarum, Part II, Qn. 1, ch. 7: *How, as it were, they Deprive Man of his Virile Member*. *Page* 90. *Virile member.*

Daemonolatreia, II, 4: "Perdifficiliter uitari posse quas ueneficae hominibus struunt insidias: quod de nocte in obseratas, clausasque domos, ignota specie ac forma illabantur: arctissimo somno decumbentes diris suis artibus obruant." *Page* 94. *Remy.*

Commentarius in titulum codicis Lib. IX de Maleficis et Mathematicis, Quaestio IV, discusses: "An malefici possint inducere pluuias, tempestates, grandines, et similia meteorologica, quibus fructibus aut seminibus noceant, ut d.L. significat?" The affirmative is demonstrated by authority, by philosophical reasoning, and by example. *Page* 97. *Binsfeld.*

Hoppo and Stadlin were two notorious witches of the school of one Staufer who lived at Berne, a sorcerer mentioned by Nider in his *Formicarius*. *Malleus Maleficarum* (translation, p. 148, Part II, Qn. 1, ch. 15). *Page* 97. *Sprenger.*

Page 97. *Caius Furius*

Pliny, *Historia Naturalis*, XVIII, 6, relates that Caius Furius Cresinus, whose lands were far richer in crops and fruit than those of any of his neighbours, was by them accused of witchcraft and the employment of spells, since, as they said, by these horrid arts his tilth was pregnant whilst their fields languished and were dry. Appearing on the appointed day before Spurius Albinus, who was to judge the cause, Furius displayed his mattocks and hoes, his sharp spades, his heavy ploughshares as well as the sleek oxen that drew them, together with his sturdy sons and Amazonian daughters. "These," cried he, "are my only spells, for I cannot show you my sleepless nights, my vigils, my early wakings, the sweat of my brow." So he was dismissed with much honour and praise.

Page 97. *Vergil.* *Eclogue* VIII, 98–99 :

> Moerim, saepe animas imis excire sepulcris
> atque satas alio uidi traducere messes.

Page 97. *Twelve tables.* Pliny, *Historia Naturalis,* XXVIII, 4: "Non et legum ipsarum in duodecim tabulis uerba sunt? 'Qui fruges excantasset.' Et alibi, 'Qui malum carmen incantasset.' "

Page 98. *Apollonius.* For his miracles see the *Life* by Philostratus, III, 39; for the staying of the plague at Ephesus, *idem,* VIII, 7.

Page 102. *Abracadabra.* This magical word is said to be formed from *Abrasax* or *Abraxas*, the name given by Gnostics to the Supreme Deity. Julius Africanus says that the word is efficacious in its pronunciation, and Serenus Sammonicus advises its use as a spell to cure asthma.

Gaspar fert myrrham, thus Balthazar, Melchior aurum. *Page 102 Gaspar.*

"Damnati sunt et qui remedia quartanis tertianisque collo annexa gestarent." Aelius Spartianus, *Antoninus Caracalla*, V. Salmasius glosses: "Plena sunt monumenta Graecorum et Latinorum huiusmodi remediis." S. John Chrysostom in his *Eighth Homily on the Epistle to the Colossians* very sternly reproves the wearing of such periapts and amulets. *Page 103 Caracalla.*

This is related in the life of Marcus Aurelius by Julius Capitolinus, xix. The soothsayers advised the Empress Faustina to bathe τὴν φύσιν in the blood of the gladiator of whom she was enamoured, "atque ita cum uiro concumberet. Quod quum esset factum, solutum quidem amorem, natum uero Commodum, gladiatorem esse non principem." *Page 103. Marcus Aurelius.*

See the *Life* by Philostratus, VIII, 7. The old man was supposed to be the genius of the pestilence who had assumed that form. *Page 103 Apollonius.*

De Praestigiis Daemonum, I, 7: "De humani sanguinis uictima, a diabolo inuenta, celebrataque in populo Dei, apud Graecos, et Romanos, et alios. Item de diuinatione ex mactatorum hominum uisceribus." *Page 104. Wier.*

The essay by John Addington Symonds, *Antinous*, collected in *Sketches and Studies in Italy and Greece*, Third Series (1898), should be consulted. See also my *Geography of Witchcraft*, ch. I, pp. 39–41. *Page 104. Antinous.*

Page 105. *Vitellius.* This is related by Suetonius, *Uitellius*, xiv, where he tells us that the Emperor received the prediction from a certain German seeress, "uaticinante Chatta muliere, cui uelut oraculo acquiescebat." Tacitus, *Germania*, viii, mentions one Veleda as being a noted prophetess among the Germans in the time of Vespasian, whilst a little before the sibyl Aurinia was much revered and regarded.

Page 107. *Wedding ring.* This remedy is referred to by many writers, and in Thomas Shadwell's *The Lancashire Witches* (acted in 1681; 4to, 1682), Act III, when Sir Jeffery complains of a certain frigidity, "last night, when I would have been kind to my Wife, she bewitcht me, I found it so," Tegue O'Divelly advises: "Maak shome waater through de Ring of a Wedding . . . and dou wilt be sound agen: gra."

Page 107. *Bodin.* *De la Démonomanie des Sorciers*, III, 2, has the rubric: "Si les Sorciers peuvent asseurer la santé des hommes alaigres & donner guerison aux malades."

Page 107. *Bellarmine.* Blessed Robert Bellarmine, S.J., 1542–1621, in his *De notis Ecclesiae*.

Page 107. *Vespasian.* The account of the poor man who was blind and another who was lame presenting themselves before the tribunal of Vespasian and imploring him to heal them, declaring that the god Serapis had appeared to them in a dream and admonished them to seek the Emperor, who would restore them to health, is to be found in Suetonius, *Uespasianus*, vii. The historian says that Vespasian hesitated, but at length made the essay and both the blind and lame were healed. Tacitus gives an even fuller account of the miracles of Vespasian, and particularly emphasizes these two cures, adding: "Utrumque, qui interfuere, nunc quoque memorant, postquam nullum mendacio pretium." *Historiarum*, Liber IV, 81. Hume in his *Essay on Miracles* selects this incident as an example of successful imposture, but he has been completely answered by Paley in his *Evidences of Christianity*. The commentators on Suetonius and Paley agree that the affair was a juggle between the Egyptian priests, the patients and, perhaps, the Emperor. If this were not the case it may well be, as Tertullian thought and Boguet well suggests, a diabolic counterfeit. Spartianus in his life of Hadrian relates how that Emperor also healed a blind man.

Page 111. *Deuteronomy*, *xviii*, 10, 11.

"Neither let there be found among you anyone that shall expiate his son or daughter, making them to pass through the fire: or that consulteth soothsayers, or observeth dreams and omens, neither let there be any wizard, Nor charmer, nor any one that consulteth pythonic spirits, or fortune tellers, or that seeketh truth from the dead." *Leviticus*, xx, 6: "The soul that shall go aside after magicians, and soothsayers, and shall commit fornication with them, I will set my face against that soul, and destroy it out of the midst of its people."

Page 111 *magic.*

White magic, as it is termed.

Page 111. *Romans*, *iii*, 8.

"And not rather (as we are slandered, and as some affirm that we say) let us do evil, that there may come good? whose damnation is just."

Page 111. *Ochozias.* *IV Kings, i* (*A.V.*). *II Kings, i.*

Page 112. *Heliogabalus.* Concerning whose death Aelius Lampridius writes: "Post hoc in eum impetus factus est, atque in latrina ad quam confugerat occisus. Tractus deinde per publicum, additaque iniuria cadaueri est, ut id in cloacam milites mitterent. . . . Occisa est cum eo et mater Semiamira probrosissima mulier et digna filio." Bodin, *Démonomanie*, II, 3, writes: "Aussi lisons nous en Dion & Xeipheilin que l'Empereur Heliogabale des plus detestables hommes du monde en vsoit souuent & fist comparoir pas Necromantie son pere & Commode l'Empereur ausquels il demanda conseil de son estat: mais il fut tué auec sa mere cruellement & trainé aux cloaques auec sa mere."

Page 114. *Martha.* Plutarch is his *Life of Marius* (translated North) says: "He ever carried a Syrian woman in a litter about with him called Martha, with great reverence, whom they said had the spirit of prophecy in her: and that he even did sacrifice unto the gods by her order, and at such time as she willed him to do it. . . . She was always at Marius' sacrifices, apparelled in a gown of purple in grain, clasped to her with clasps, and held a spear in her hand wound all about with nosegays, and garlands of flowers tied on with laces. This manner of gest made many doubt whether Marius showed this woman openly, believing indeed that she had the spirit of prophecy: or else that knowing the contrary he made as though he did believe it, to help her feigning."

Psalm XC, 1. "He who dwelleth . . ." *Page* 114. *He who is helped.*

"Spranger & Nider qui en ont faict brusler vne infinité, demeurent d'accord que les Sorciers ne peuuent nuire aucunement aux officiers de Iustice, fussent ils les plus mechans du monde." Bodin, *Démonomanie*, III, 4. King James in his *Daemonologie*, Edinburgh, 1597, uses similar arguments to show that the bond-slaves of Satan cannot harm accredited officers of justice who are to take them, and that the authorities who prosecute these wretches must not fear their craft any more than a captain in the field is alarmed at "the small clack of a Pistolet" or "the rummishing shot of a cannon." *Page* 116. *Officers.*

Malleus Maleficarum, II, Qn. 1, Ch. 11, *ad finem*. Translated by Montague Summers, John Rodker, 1928, p. 137. *Page* 116. *Sprenger.*

Odyssey, X, 302–306: *Page* 117. *Moly.*

Ὣς ἄρα φωνήσας πόρε φάρμακον Ἀργειφόντης,
ἐκ γαίης ἐρύσας, καί μοι φύσιν αὐτοῦ ἔδειξεν.
ῥίζῃ μὲν μέλαν ἔσκε, γάλακτι δὲ εἴκελον ἄνθος·
μῶλυ δέ μιν καλέουσι θεοί· χαλεπὸν δέ τ' ὀρύσσειν
ἀνδράσι γε θνητοῖσι· θεοὶ δέ τε πάντα δύνανται.

The author of the seventy-ninth Carmen of the *Priapeia* has a rationalistic explanation:

Hinc legitur radix de qua flos aureus exit:
  Quem cum moly uocat, mentula moly fuit.

A name given to various kinds of Orchis. The Latin "Satyrion," a plant exciting sexual appetite, is sometimes translated as "ragwort" *Page* 117. *Satyrion.*

(*Senecio Jacobæa*). Pliny makes mention of it, *Historia Naturalis*, LXII, 10; and Caelius Aurelianus, III, has: "*Satyriasis* est uehemens ueneris appetentia. Uocatur autem ab herbae uirtute quam *Satyrion* uocant." So Quartilla in Petronius has a drink prepared from this aphrodisiac. In Italy there was, and perhaps is, a famous aphrodisiac named *Satirione*. See Machiavelli, *La Clizia*, iv, 2.

Page 117. *Pederasty.* Of Ancient Mexico, Bernal Diaz del Castillo (*circa* 1498–1570), the Spanish historian whose *Verdadera Historia de la conquista de Nueua España* was written in 1568, says: "Erant quasi omnes sodomia commaculati, et adolescentes multi, muliebriter uestiti, ibant publice, cibum quaerentes ab isto diabolico et abominabili labore."

Page 121. *Tears.* Debrio, *Disquisitiones Magicae*, V, ix, says: "Hoc enim ipsum pro certissimo signo ex fide dignorum antiqua relatione, ac propria experientia docente, adeo compertum est, quod etiamsi ad lachrymandum coniuratoribus hortetur et compellatur, si malefica exstitit, hoc ipsum scilicet lachrymas emittere, non potest: dabit quidem flebiles uoces, et ex sputo genas et oculos linire ac si fleret, attentabit: super quo a circumstantibus caute aduertendum erit."

Page 122. *Bells.* There exist some rough but apt lines which are quoted in the gloss of the *Corpus Iuris* to describe the functions of bells:

Laudo Deum uerum, plebem uoco, congrego clerum,
defunctos ploro, nimbum fugo, festa decoro.

Or, in another form:

Funera plango, fulmina frango, sabbata pango,
Excito lentos, dissipo uentos, paco cruentos.

Page 122. *Eyes . . . bent upon the ground.*

Bodin, *Démonomanie*, IV, 4, marks as a presumption of guilt: "la contenance du Sorcier, qui baisse ordinairement la veue contre terre, & n'ose regarder en face."

Page 124. *Theocritus.*

Idyll VI, 39:

ὡς μὴ βασκανθῶ δέ, τρὶς εἰς ἐμὸν ἔπτυσα κόλπον.

The charm was broken by spitting thrice. Diogenianus, Prov. IV, 82, has a reference to this line: εἰς κόλπον πτύει. ἐπὶ τῶν βασκαινομένων. Θεόκριτος. One may compare Juvenal, VII, 111–12:

> Tunc immensa caui spirant mendacia folles
> Conspuiturque sinus.

Upon which the old Scholiast glosses: "Propter fascinum uerborum ter sibi in sinu spuunt, et uidentur fascinum arcere."

Page 125. *Shaved.*

See the *Malleus Maleficarum*, Part III, Qn. 15. It is there laid down: "The third precaution to be observed in this tenth action is that the hair should be shaved from every part of the body. The reason for this is the same as for stripping her of her clothes, which we have already mentioned; for in order to preserve their power of silence they are in the habit of hiding some superstitious object in their clothes or in their hair, or even in the most secret parts of their bodies which must not be named."

Witches were also shaved in order that the Devil's mark might be discovered upon their bodies. This mark or *Stigma*, as Delrio terms it, "is given to them, as is alledg'd, by a Nip in any part of the Body, and it is blew."

Page 125. *Mark.* Ludovico Maria Sinistrari in his *Demoniality* writes: "The Devil imprints on them some mark, especially on those whose constancy he suspects. That mark, moreover, is not always of the same shape or figure: sometimes it is the likeness of a hare, sometimes a toad's foot, sometimes a spider, a puppy, a dormouse It is imprinted on the most hidden parts of the body: with men, under the eyelids, or it may be under the armpits, or on the lips, on the shoulder, the fundament, or somewhere else: with women, it is usually on the breast or the privy parts. Now, the stamp which imprints those marks is none other but the Devil's claw."

Page 130. *Schedules.* Bodin, *Démonomanie*, III, 2: "Un certain Aduocat de Paris, que ie ne veux nommer, qui fut deferé l'an mil cinq cens septāte vn, & de faict il confessa qu'estant malade à l'extremité, il se donna au Diable pour guarir, & luy mesme escriuit & signa la sedule de son sang."

Page 130. *Satan often kills witches.* See the *Malleus Maleficarum*, Part III, Qn. 13, translated by Montague Summers (John Rodker, 1928): "And some also are distinguished by the fact that, after they have admitted their crimes, they try to commit suicide by strangling or hanging themselves. And they are induced to do this by the Enemy, lest they should obtain pardon from God through sacramental confession." See further the note on this passage.

Page 131. *Judge.*

The judge in question was "M. Adam Martin, Baillif de Bieures."

Page 132. *Ascletario.*

This is related by Suetonius, *T. Flauius Domitianus*, XV.

Page 138. *Wolves.*

See my *Geography of Witchcraft*, pp. 22–26. The whole question of lycanthropy is discussed in the *Malleus Maleficarum*, at length by De Lancre, Bodin, and most demonologists. Hertz, *Der Werwolf*, may be consulted, and I have a forthcoming volume, *The Werewolf*. S. Augustine, *De Ciuitate Dei*, XVIII, 18, does not allow that evil powers and black magic can actually transform a man, but demons directly or mediately through a witch can and do cast a glamour so that to himself and to all who behold him a man may seem to be a wolf and be informed with all the savagery and appetites of the wolf nature. Indeed it is recorded that some lycanthropists have coupled with female wolves and have declared that this coitus was to them more natural and more pleasurable than connexion with a woman. S. Augustine says: "Nor can the devils create anything (whatever shows of theirs produce these doubts), but only cast a changed shape over that which God has made, altering only in show. Nor do I think the devil can form any soul or body into bestial or brutal members, and essences: but they have an unspeakable way of transporting man's phantasy in a bodily shape, unto other senses . . ." Ludwig Elich, in his *Daemonomagia*, xii, says that the devil wraps the man into the form of a wolf composed of thickly condensed air, which seems a very possible explanation of the phenomenon. It may be noted that

Boguet closely follows Bodin, *Démonomanie*, II, 6: "De la lycanthropie & si les esprits peuuent changer les hommes en bestes."

Page 138. Antæus. The legend said that at the festival of the Wolf-god Zeus Lycaeus, which was held every nine years on the Wolf-mountain in Arcadia, a man chosen by lot was stripped naked, his clothes being hung on an oak, and that then he ate of the entrails of animals mingled with human bowels. After this he swam across a lake, and on the further side was transformed into a wolf. If for nine years he refrained from tasting human flesh he could at the end of that time recover his former shape. S. Augustine, *De Ciuitate Dei*, XVIII, 17, quotes from Varro. See also Pliny, *Historia Naturalis*, VIII, xxxiv, 22. There are references in Plato, *Republic*, VIII, DE.; Polybius, VII, 13; Pausanias, VI, viii, 2; VIII, ii, 3–6, and other authors.

Page 138. Sigebert. Sigebert of Gembloux, the famous Benedictine historian, born *circa* 1035; died 5 November, 1112. His most celebrated work, *Chronica siue Chronographia*, was immensely popular, and very numerous MSS. copies exist.

Page 138. Vergil. *Eclogue* VIII, 97–98, speaking of magic herbs:

His ego saepe lupum fieri et se condere siluis
Moerim . . . uidi.

Page 139. Ovid. *Metamorphoseon* I, 232–33, of Lycaon:

Territus ille fugit; nactusque silentia ruris
Exululat, frustraque loqui conatur.

Job Fincel, *Wunderzeichen, Warhafftige Beschreibung und gründlich verzeicnus schrecklicher Wunderzeichen und Geschichten die von . . . MDXVII bis auff . . . MDLVI geschechen und ergangen sind, noch der Jarzal . . . Jhena*, 1556, 8vo. Hence the account is quoted by Weyer, *De Maleficio Affectis*, IV, 23, and Burton, *Anatomy of Melancholy*, Part I, Sect. 1, Mem. 1, Subs. 4, makes reference to this passage: "Wierus tells a story of such a one at Padua, 1541, that would not believe to the contrary, but that he was a wolf." Simon Goulart also records the circumstance in his *Histoires admirables* . . ., 1606. The book was translated into English, 1607, by E. Grimeston, and here Webster found a hint for the complexion of Duke Ferdinand's madness in *The Dutchesse of Malfy*, V, 2, where the Doctor says: *Page 139. Fincel.*

two nights since
One met the duke, 'bout midnight in a lane
Behind St. Markes church, with the leg of a man
Upon his shoulder; and he howl'd fearefully:
Said he was a woolffe: onely the difference
Was, a woolffes skinne was hairy on the outside,
His on the in-side: bad them take their swords,
Rip up his flesh, and trie.

The sexual power of a wolf was popularly supposed to lie in his tail, and accordingly, when during the old harvest rituals the corn-spirit was imagined as a wolf, particular attention was paid to his tail. In East Prussia, if a wolf were seen running through a field, the peasants took particular note whether he carried his tail high or dragged it on the ground. In the latter case *Page 139. No tails.*

they covered him with blessings and would even set out food for him, since he was fertilizing their fields and promised a rich tilth. In the former case aridity was threatened and they would curse and even try to kill him. A wolf without a tail was sexually considered exceptionally unlucky and malign.

Page 140. *Jacobins.* Dominicans, so called from their convent hard by the church of St. Jacques at Paris.

Page 140. *Gilles Garnier.* For an account of this notorious werewolf of Lyons who, being convicted of the "abominable crimes of lycanthropy and witchcraft," was burned alive 18 January, 1573, see my *Geography of Witchcraft*, ch. I, pp. 23–24; and ch. v, pp. 399–400.

Page 142. *Vincent.* Vincent of Beauvais, the celebrated encyclopædist. The most generally accepted dates assigned for his birth and death are respectively 1190 and 1264. It is thought that he was a member of the Dominican Order. The title of Vincent's great work is *Speculum maius*, which contains 80 books and 9885 chapters.

Page 142. *Belon.* Bodin, *Démonomanie*, II, 6: "Belon en ses obseruations imprimees à Paris, escript qu'il a veu en Egypte aux faux-bourgs de la ville du Cayre vn basteleur qui auoit vn asne auec lequel il discouroit, & parloit du meilleur sens qu'il eust: Et l'asne par gestes & signes à sa voix faisoit cognoistre, qu'il entendoit fort bien ce qu'on disoit."

Page 142. *Bartolomeo de Spina.* *Quaestio de Strigibus*: xix: "Experientiae apparentis conuersionis strigum in catos."

Malleus Maleficarum, Part II, Qn. 1, chap. 9. *Page* 142 *The Inquisitors.*

In Somersetshire there was a belief, still persisting in certain parts, that a hare might be a witch under that form. To my own knowledge when a hare has been seen in a field a farmer and his men will turn out to hunt the animal away lest it should bring ill-luck to, or cast a spell upon, the stock and cattle. Julian Cox, an old witch who was tried at the Taunton Summer Assizes in 1663 and executed, was commonly said to have been seen in the shape of a hare, evidence which was admitted by the court. James Device, one of the Lancashire coven of 1613, confessed that the Devil had appeared to him as a hare. *Page* 143. *Hares.*

"Omnia subiecisti sub pedibus eius, oues et boues universas: insuper et pecora campi." *Page* 145. *Psalm VIII.*

Andreas Osiander, 1498–1552, was for many years a preacher and pastor at St. Lornzkirche, Nuremberg, in which town he published his *Harmony*. *Page* 147. *Osiander.*

Pharsalia, VI, 543–46, of Erichto: *Page* 152 *Lucan.*

laqueum, nodosque nocenteis
Ore suo rupit: pendentia corpora carpsit
Abrasitque cruces: percussaque uiscera nimbis
Uulsit et incoctas admisso sole medullas.

Ars Poetica 338–40: *Page* 152. *Horace*

ficta uoluptatis causa sint proxima ueris,
ne quodcumque uelit poscat sibi fabula credi,
neu pransae Lamiae uiuum puerum extrahat aluo.

Page 152. *Apuleius.* *Metamorphoses*, II, 21–30, the relation of Thelyphron.

Page 155. *L.* 1. *de Siccar.* Lex Cornelia (Sullae), de sicariis et ueneficis. See the *Institutes* of Justinian, IV, xviii, 5.

Page 155. *Psalm* 106. (Douay, 105). "Et immolauerunt filios suos et filias suas daemoniis."

Page 155. *IV. Kings*, *xxiii.* 10. (*A.V.*, II *Kings*, xxiii) Cf Josias: "And he defiled Topheth, which is in the valley of the son of Ennom: that no man should consecrate there his son or his daughter through fire to Moloch."

Page 156. *Manasses.* *II Paralipomenon*, xxiii, 6: "He made his sons to pass through the fire in the valley of Benennom: he observed dreams, followed divinations, gave himself up to magic arts, had with him magicians, and enchanters: and he wrought many evils before the Lord, to provoke him to anger."

Page 157. *Stadlin.* *Malleus Maleficarum*, Part II, Qn. 1, ch. vi. "Moreover, Nider [in his *Formicarius*] tells of a wizard named Stadlin, who was taken in the diocese of Lausanne, and confessed that in a certain house where a man and his wife were living he had by his witchcraft successively killed in the woman's womb seven children, so that for many years the woman always miscarried."

Page 157. *Maxentius.* M. Aurelius Valerius Maxentius, Roman Emperor, A.D. 306–312. See Zosimus, II, 9–18; and the *Annales*, xii, 33, and xiii, 1, of

Joannes Zonaras. All authorities agree in representing Maxentius as a monster of lust and cruelty. Zosimus especially notes that he was superstitious to the last degree and wholly given to magical crafts. Many emperors, Commodus, Caracalla, Julian the Apostate, and others, were much addicted to the offering of human sacrifices, and these victims were immolated for the sake of *extispicium*, the examination of human entrails in order thereby to divine the future. Of Maxentius Eusebius precisely says that he indulged the same horrid passion: *νεογνῶν σπλάγχνα βρέφων διερευνομένου*.

Page 157. *Mantuanus.*

Blessed Baptista Mantuanus (or Spagnoli), the famous Renaissance poet, was born at Mantua 17 April, 1447, where also he died 22 March, 1516. Whilst yet young he joined the Carmelite Order, of which he is one of the glories. He was beatified by Leo XIII in 1890 and his feast is kept in the Order on 23 March. His *Opera omnia* were collected at Bologna in 1502, and as he excelled in every form of Latin verse, representative selections may be found from his vast store in most of the *Delitiae* and other treasuries of the later Latinists.

Page 157. *Bodin.*

Démonomanie, IV, 4. "Des Presomptions contre les Sorciers." "Les autres indices sont, la contenance du Sorcier, qui baisse ordinairement la veüe contre terre, & n'ose regarder en face, les variations aux interrogatoires & sur tout si le sorcier est descendu de pere ou mere, sorciers. Car c'est un argumēt bien grand auec le bruit commun, d'autant que le plus aggreable sacrifice que le Diable desire de telles gens, est de vouer & dedier leurs enfans à son seruice, si tost qu'ils sont nez."

Page 162. Levites. Upon the occasion of the idolatrous worship of the golden calf, Moses said: "If any man be on the Lord's side let him join with me. And all the sons of Levi gathered themselves together unto him: And he said to them: Thus saith the Lord God of Israel: Put every man his sword upon his thigh: go, and return from gate to gate through the midst of the camp, and let every man kill his brother, and friend, and neighbour. And the sons of Levi did according to the words of Moses, and there were slain that day about three and twenty thousand men." *Exodus*, xxxii, 26–28.

Page 169. Remy. Remy, *Daemonolatreia,* III, 12, emphasizes the stubborn malice of witchcraft: "Inueteratum hoc malum est, & plerumque ab ipsa iam adolescentia admissum & contractum. . . . Diserta atque aperta Domini uox est: Uir siue mulier, in quibus Pythonicus, uel diuinationis fuerit spiritus, morte moriantur: (*Leuiticus*, xx); . . . Ecce ut nullo nec aetatis, nec sexus discrimine, ac delectu supplicium est in eos diuina lege cõstitutum; qui eiusmodi uetitas, illicitasque artes exercent."

Page 169. Bodin. *Démonomanie*, IV, 5: "Car si la loy condamne a mort l'enfant qui n'a pas atteint la puberté pour n'auoir pas crié quand on tuoit son maistre, & n'auoir pas declaré les meurtriers, comme en cas pareil fut pendu & estranglé vn ieune enfant aagé d'onze ans, qui auoit tué d'vn coup de pierre vne fille, & l'auoit cachee . . . à plus forte raison doit l'enfant Sorcier, qui a attaint la puberté estre mis à mort, s'il n'a declaré les assemblees auec les Diables, mesmement estãt preuenu, & qu'il soit conuaincu, ne voulant rien confesser."

Pharsalia, IX, 1087–88: *Page* 170. *Lucan.*

sed parcimus annis,
donamusque nefas.

The important trial of Jeanne Harvillier was the occasion of Bodin's writing his famous treatise. The Preface of the *Démonomanie* commences: "Le iugement qui a esté conclud contre vne Sorciere, auquel ie fus appellé le dernier iour d'Auril, mil cinq cens septante & huict, m'a donné occasion di mettre la main à la plume, pour esclairir le subiect des Sorciers qui semble à toutes personnes estrange à merueilles, & à plusiers incroyable. La Sorciere que i'ay dict s'appelloit Ieanne Haruillier, natifue de Verbery pres Compeigne, accusee d'auoir fait mourir plusieurs hommes & bestes, comme elle confessa sans question, ny torture, combien que de prime face elle eust denié opiniatrement, & varié plusieurs fois. Elle confessa aussi que sa mere dés l'aage de douze ans l'auoit presentee au Diable, en guise d'vn grand homme noir. . . . Et que dés lors elle renonça Dieu, & promit seruir au diable. Et qu'au mesme instant elle eut copulation charnellement auec le Diable, continuant depuis l'aage de douze ans, iusques à cinquante, ou enuiron qu'elle fut prise. . . . Il fut trouué que trente ans au parauãt, elle auoit eu le foüet pour le mesme *Page* 170. *Bodin.*

crime, & sa mere cōdamnee à estre bruslee viue, par arrest de la Cour de Parlement, confirmatif de la sentence du Iuge de Sélis. . . . Ceux qui assisterent au iugement, estoyēt bien d'aduis qu'elle auoit bien merité la mort: mais sur la forme & genre de mort, il y en eut quelqu'vn plus doux, & d'vn naturel plus pitoyable, qui estoit d'aduis qu'il suffisoit de la faire pendre. Les autres apres auoir examiné les crimes detestables & les peines establies par les loix Diuines & humaines, . . . furēt d'auis qu'elle deuoit estre cōdānee a estre bruslee viues: ce qui fut arresté, & la sentence, dont il n'y eut point d'appel, executee le dernier iour d'Auril à la poursuyte de Maistre Claude Dofay, Procureur du Roy à Ribemont."

Page 180. *St. Fortunatus.* Bishop of Todi; 14 October, 537. S. Gregory the Great speaks with admiration of the extraordinary powers of this Saint in delivering the possessed and expelling demons. *Dialogues*, I, x. Also *Acta Sanctorum* (Bollandists), October, Vol. VI, p. 520 *sqq*.

Page 180. *St. Hilarion.* A disciple of S. Antony the Great. He was a hermit of the most extreme sanctity and austerity. His feast is kept 21 October. The Breviary lection for that day tells us: "Innumerabiles daemones in multis orbis terrae partibus ex hominum corporibus eiecit."

Page 180. *St. Bernard.* S. Bernard of Menthon, founder of the St. Bernard Alpine hospice, was so famous for his exorcisms and victories over Satan that he is represented on a public seal with the demon bound (*Recueil . . . de sphragistique*, Vol. IV,

p. 85. Cf. Blavignac, *Histoire de l'architecture sacrée* . . . p. 294). In art he often appears with the demon tied by his stole. Feast Day, 15 June. He died in 1008. *Acta Sanctorum*, June, Vol. II, p. 1077.

Page 180. *St. Martin.*

Bishop of Tours, born *circa* 316; died at Candes, Touraine, 397. Feast Day 11 November. S. Martin is one of the most famous thaumaturges of the world, and his cult was very popular throughout the centuries. Numbers of the possessed were delivered from demons at his tomb, and his relics were constantly honoured by pilgrimages from all countries. France has ever held him one of her greatest Saints.

S. Martin of Vertou is also greatly honoured as a scourge of devils and liberator of the possessed. He exorcized the daughter of a King of Spain (one account says of an English nobleman), and the old prose records:

> Liberata
> Et saluata
> Principis est filia:
> Ursus cedit
> Et obedit
> Remota saeuitia.

Page 180. *S. Gall.*

An Irishman by birth, he was one of the twelve disciples who accompanied S. Columbanus to Gaul. When his master went on to Italy in 612, S. Gall remained as a hermit in Switzerland, where he died about 646. Immediately God revealed the sanctity of His servant by countless miracles, and a chapel was erected upon the spot which had been his retreat. In time this became the famous Abbey of S. Gall, for many centuries one of the noblest Benedictine houses in Europe. The Feast Day of S. Gall is 16 October. S. Gall delivered from the demon by which she was possessed Fridiburga, the daughter of Cunzo, and betrothed of Sigebert, King of the Franks.

Page 180. Other holy men. Vast numbers of names might be given, such as Pope S. Linus; S. Gregory the Wonder-worker; S. Zeno of Verona; S. Ubald of Gubbio; S. Geminianus of Modena; S. Allyre of Clermont; S. Parthenius; S. Silvin; S. John the Thaumaturge, Bishop of Polybota; S. Hidulphus of Treves; S. Dié; S. Exsuperius, first Bishop of Bayeux; S. Januarius; S. Hubert; S. Giles; S. Nicolas the Great; S. Nicolas of Tolentino; S. Ouen; S. Lanfranc; S. Elpidius of Atella; S. Melanius; S. Mathurin; S. Aubin of Angers; S. Paternian of Vannes; S. Hervé; S. Samson; S. Frobert; S. Cyriacus; S. Albert the Carmelite; S. Theodore the Solitary; S. Eleutherius; S. Antoninus of Sorrento; S. Eustasius the Abbot; S. Venant; S. Dêle; S. Theotonius, Canon Regular; S. Philip of Argiro; S. Hugh of Lincoln; S. Norbert; S. Francis of Assisi; S. Antony of Padua; S. John of the Cross; S. Ignatius Loyola; S. Francis Xavier; S. John Baptist Vianney; S. Hermann Joseph; S. Dominic; S. Antony the Great; S. Gerard Majella, C.SS.R.; S. Bertrand of Comminges; S. Mary Magdalene; S. Marina; S. Dympna; S. Catherine of Siena; S. Colomba of Rieti; *cum multis aliis.*

St. Gregory, Bishop of Langres, who ruled that see 509–39, is locally much venerated. It was he who transferred the relics of S. Benignus. *Page* 182. *Gregory.*

Saint Aubin (Albinus), Bishop of Angers from 529 to 549, was a native of Vannes. See Lobineau, *Vies des Saints de la Bretagne* (1836), I, p. 123. *Page* 182. *Albinus.*

Eremite, or the Great. In art, as in the famous picture by Salvator Rosa, he is often seen chasing away the nightmare demons with a Cross. *Page* 182. *St. Antony.*

Virgin and Martyr. She usually appears trampling the demoniac dragon under her feet and holding up the Cross in her hand, since when Satan appeared to her in a terrible bestial form she put him to flight by the power of the crucifix. She is so depicted in a Gothic sculpture, Henry VII's Chapel; and in a picture by Lucas van Leyden. *Page* 182. *St. Margaret.*

The history of S. Justina and S. Cyprian, the converted magician, is well known. Feast Day of the two Martyrs, 26 September. *Page* 182. *St. Justina.*

Malleus Maleficarum, Part II, Qn. 1, ch. 2: "The witches met together and, by their art, summoned a devil in the form of a man, to whom the novice was compelled to swear to deny the Christian religion, never to adore the Eucharist, and to tread the Cross underfoot whenever she could do so secretly." Guazzo in the *Compendium Maleficarum* tells us that at the reception into that horrid company witches are required to "cast upon the ground and *Page* 183. *The Cross.*

trample under their feet in the mire the Cross, Holy Medals, *Agnus Dei*, should they possess such or carry them on their persons." In the *La-Bas* of Huysmans it is said of "Le Chanoine Docre" a composite figure, "Sa rage du sacrilège est telle qu'il s'est fait tatouer sous la plante des pieds l'image de la Croix, afin de pouvoir toujours marcher sur le Sauveur" (IX).

Page 185. *Theodosius.* Born *circa* 346; Roman Emperor of the East, 378–95. Valentinian II, Roman Emperor, 375–92, was, although at that time only some four or five years old, proclaimed Augustus by the army upon the death of his father, Valentinian I. When Valentinian II was expelled from Italy by Maximus, Theodosius defeated this latter and restored the Emperor to his Western authority in 391. Valentinian was murdered 15 May, 392, by Arbogastes.

Page 187. *St. Athanasius.* The passage is from the *De humanitate Uerbi et corporalis euis praesentia.* Peter Thyraeus, *De Spirituum Apparitionibus*, I, xvi, 420, writes: "Ueniat, inquit Athanasius, qui istorum dictorum experimentum capere uelit, (uidelicet, solo signo crucis daemones fugari) et in ipsis praestigiis daemonum et imposturis uaticiniorum et in miraculis Magiae, utatur signo Crucis ab ipsis deriso nomenque Christi inuocet; et uidebit, quomodo eius rei metu daemones fugiant, uaticinia conquiescant, Magiae et ueneficia iaceant."

Page 189. *Perfumes.* Sinistrari. *Demoniality*, lxviii–lxxvi, has dealt at length with this point, which he treats in a very masterly and skilful way.

This is related in the "Legend," the biography of S. Catherine, which was completed in 1395 by Blessed Raimondo delle Vigne, of Capua, her confessor. An Italian translation of the "Legend" is included in the first volume of Gigli's *L'opere della serafica Santa Caterina da Siena*, Siena and Lucca, 1707–54. *Page* 193. *St. Catherine.*

Born in Galatia, 368; died probably before 431. The identity of the author of the *Historia Lausiaca* and of the Bishop of Helenopolis, once disputed, is now generally accepted. He passed nine years among the monks, some of whom were hermits, some living in communities, who inhabited the Nitrian desert. During this period he learned the traditions of their great founders, S. Antony, S. Paul, S. Pachomius, S. Pambo, and the rest. The *Historia Lausiaca* is a history of the monks of Egypt and Palestine in the form of short biographies and many anecdotes. The best modern edition is that by Abbot Butler in two volumes, Cambridge, 1898 and 1904. *Page* 193. *Palladius.*

Communion may be given to those possessed. Thyraeus, *De Daemoniacis*, II, 365, says: "An forte ab Altaris Sacramento arcendi sunt daemoniaci? Non sunt. Patrum pro ipsis est sententia. Eis, inquit Crassianus, teste Diuo Thoma, qui ab immundis uexantur Spiritibus, communionem sacrosanctam a senioribus nostris nunquam inuenimus interdictam." *Page* 199. *Eucharist.*

Robert Gaguin, Trinitarian, 1425–1502. He was employed on various important businesses during the reigns of Louis XI and Charles *Page* 199. *Gaguin.*

VIII, and among the works he has left his historical tractates are considered particularly valuable.

Page 199. *Louis of Luxembourg.* Count of St. Pol, was delivered up by Charles of Burgundy to Louis XI. Condemned as a traitor, he was executed at Paris, 19 December, 1475.

Page 200. *Pontanus.* *De Bello Neapolitano*, V. "Nefarium ad sacrum, Magicaque ad maleficia concursum est. Quod in summis miseriis, ultimaque aquarum penuria perditissimis a sacerdotibus commentum esset, dum impie agendo, Dei simul iras et aeris turbationem ac tempestates exciunt. Inuenti enim ex oppidanis atque obsessis sunt, qui nocturnis in tenebris, deceptis castrorum uigiliis per asperrimas rupes furtim profecti ad litus trahentes secum imaginem affixi ad crucem CHRISTI, maledictis illam prius ac diro persecuti carmine, post in mare execrabundi immerserint, coelo, mari, terrisque tempestatem imprecati. Quo etiam tempore sacerdotes quidam mortalium omnium scelestissimi, dum satisfacere profanis militum artibus student, ritum nefarium secuti, quo, ut dictum est, in huiusmodi necessitatibus elici hymbres putantur, asino pro aedis foribus constituto, tanquam agenti animam cecinere funestum carmen. Post diuina Eucharistia in illius os palatumque iniecta conclamatum asinum funereis cantibus uiuum tandem ibidem pro templi foribus humauere. Hic uero uix dum perfecto sacro obnubescere aer, ac mare agitari uentis cum coepisset, diesque medius offundi tenebris. . . ." A terrible storm with much rain followed. *Pon-*

tani Opera Omnia, Basileae, 1538, II, pp. 574–75.

Malleus Maleficarum, Part II, Qn. 1. ch. 5. See the translation by Montague Summers; John Rodker, 1928; pp. 116–17. *Page* 200. *Inquisitors.*

The reference is to Charles IX, born 1550; reigned 1560, died 30 May, 1574. He was greatly suspect of encouraging sorcerers and of consulting with necromancers and witches. *Page* 200. *King.*

Bodin, *Démonomanie*, IV, 5: "La superstition est bien plus grande de porter . . . l'hostie consacree en sa pochette. Comme faisoit le President Gentil, qui fut trouué saisi d'vne Hostie par le bourreau, qui le pendit à Montfaucon." *Page* 201. *Gentil.*

Bodin, *Démonomanie*, IV, 5, says: "I'ay monstré qu'il y a crime de leze Maiesté diuine, fouillant les Sacremens ou prieres sacrees de charmes diaboliques." This is one of the most frequent and most horrible crimes practised by witches, for as there can be nothing more agreeable to their master than the profanation of the Body of the Lord, these witches use all their cunning to devise ways and means to secure the Host in order that they may abuse and befoul It in every hideous sort. Innumerable examples might be cited from the trials throughout the centuries. Even at the present day Satanists will pay considerable sums of money to those who, feigning devoutly to go to Holy Communion, retain God's Body in their mouths and presently spitting It forth into *Page* 201. *Mockery and derision.*

some handkerchief or cloth bear It away to sell for their thirty pieces of silver. Tabernacles are also broken open and the Contents filched. These scandals occur even now. From time to time gangs of Host-stealers are detected and broken up, as in 1855, when a society of these sacrilegious miscreants which carried on its horrid operations at Paris was traced and stamped out mainly owing to the effects of the Archbishop of Paris, Marie-Dominique-Auguste Siborn, who it is significant to note was assassinated 3 January, 1857, by a renegade priest named Verger. In 1874 and 1878 similar organizations of professional Host-stealers were suppressed in Paris, but there is evidence that the same activities are even now being pursued in London, and in other English cities, as well as in France, Italy, America, and indeed many countries beside.

Page 206. *Deuteronomy, xiii,* 1–3, 5. "If there rise in the midst of thee a prophet or one that saith he hath dreamed a dream, and he foretell a sign and a wonder, And that come to pass which he spoke, and he say to thee: Let us go and follow strange gods, which thou knowest not, and let us serve them: Thou shalt not hear the words of that prophet or dreamer: for the Lord your God trieth you, that it may appear whether you love him with all your heart, and with all your soul, or not. . . . And that prophet or forger of dreams shall be slain."

Page 206. *Leviticus, xxiv,* 16. "He that blasphemeth the name of the Lord, dying let him die: all the multitude shall stone him, whether he be a native or a stranger. He that blasphemeth the name of the Lord, dying let him die."

"The Chaldeans that fight against this city shall come and set it on fire, and burn it, with the houses upon whose roof they offered sacrifices to Baal, and pound out drink offerings to strange gods, to provoke me to wrath." *Page* 207. *Jeremiah, xxxii*, 29.

"Thou shalt not have strange gods before me." *Page* 207. *Exodus, xx*, 3.

After the worship of the gold calf the sons of Levi were commanded to kill the idolaters, "and then were slain that day about three and twenty thousand men." *Page* 207. *Exodus, xxxii*, 28.

"And Israel was initiated to Beelphegor: upon which the Lord being angry . . . Moses said to the judges of Israel: Let every man kill his neighbours, that have been initiated to Beelphegor. . . . And there were slain four and twenty thousand men." *Page* 207. *Numbers, xxv*, 3, 5, 9.

The prophet sent from Juda to Bethel to denounce Jeroboam was bidden, "Thou shalt not eat bread nor drink water," . . . but being deceived by an old prophet of Bethel, "he ate bread and drank water in his house. . . . And when he was gone, a lion found him in the way and killed him." *Page* 207. *III Kings (A.V. I Kings), xiii.*

Where all society with the Chanaanites, and especially intermarriages, are strictly forbidden. *Page* 208. *Exodus, xxxiv.*

No league nor fellowship to be made with the Chanaanites. "Thou shalt make no league with them, nor show mercy to them: Neither shalt thou make marriages with them. Thou shalt not give thy daughter to his son, nor take his daughter for thy son." *Page* 208. *Deuteronomy, vii.*

Page 208. *Numbers*, *xxv*. The people fall into fornication and idolatry, being initiated to Beelphegor. Four-and-twenty thousand are slain. Zambri, a prince of the tribe of Simeon, boldly has connexion in the brothel house with Cozbi, the daughter of a prince among the Madianites, whereupon Phinees, the son of Eleazar, the son of Aaron, takes a dagger "and thrust both of them through together, to wit, the man and the woman, in the genital parts." Phinees is highly praised and blessed.

Page 208. *Leviticus*, *xx*, 15, 16. "He that shall copulate with any beast or cattle, dying let him die: the beast also shall ye kill. The woman that shall lie under any beast, shall be killed together with the same: their blood be upon them."

Page 208. *Deuteronomy*, *xxvii*, 21. "Cursed be he that lieth with any beast: and all the people shall say: Amen."

Page 211. *Procedure*. These Instructions, which do not appear in every edition of the *Discours des Sorciers*, were long held as supremely authoritative, and they were used as the official hand-book and directory in trials of this kind by many local Parliaments and other courts of justice. They should be compared in detail with the Third Part of the *Malleus Maleficarum:* "The Third Part relating to the Judicial Proceedings in both the Ecclesiastical and Civil Courts against Witches and indeed all Heretics; Containing xxxv Questions in which is Most Clearly Set Out the Formal Rules for Initiating a Process of Justice, How it should be conducted, and the Method of Pronouncing Sentence."